Houghton
Mifflin
Harcourt

D1487116

Algebra

ISBN 978-0-54426-182-2

1 2 3 4 5 6 7 8 9 10 XXXX 22 21 20 19 18 17 16 15 14 13

4500000000 B C D E F G

Core Skills Algebra

Table of Contents

iii

Mathematics Correlation Chart

Skills	Page Numbers
Algebraic Expressions	6, 7
Area	9, 119
Box Plots	194
Comparing Functions	126, 127
Data Analysis	189, 190, 191, 192, 193, 194, 195
Distance, Rate, and Time	12
Exponential Functions	126, 127, 128, 129, 130, 131, 132, 133, 134, 135, 136, 137, 138, 139
Exponents and Radicals	43, 44, 45, 46, 47, 117, 120, 121
Factoring	56, 153, 154, 156, 158, 160
Frequency Tables	195
Graphing Absolute Value Equations	140, 141, 142, 143, 144, 145, 146
Graphing Linear Equations	76, 77, 78, 80, 81
Graphing Linear Inequalitites	113, 114
Graphing Quadratic Equations	84, 85, 86, 87, 88, 90
Histograms	193
Intercepts	67
Inverse Functions	71
Linear Applications	68, 70, 79, 183
Linear Equations	65, 66
Literal Equations	39, 40, 41, 99
Operations with Linear Equations	74
Piecewise Functions	148, 149
Polynomial Expressions - Adding	48
Polynomial Expressions - Dividing	52, 55, 58, 59
Polynomial Expressions - Monomials	14, 15, 16
Polynomial Expressions - Multiplying	20, 51, 53, 54, 57, 59, 151, 152, 155, 157, 159
Polynomial Expressions - Simplifying	17, 18, 19, 50
Polynomial Expressions - Subtracting	49
Proportions	122, 123
Real Numbers	5, 8
Relations and Functions	62, 63, 64
Scatter Plots and Regression	184, 185, 186, 187, 188

Skills	Page Numbers
Sequences	72, 73
Simple Interest	11
Solving Absolute Value Equations	147
Solving One-Variable Equations	22, 23, 24, 25, 26, 27, 28, 29, 30, 31, 32, 33, 34, 35, 36, 37, 38
Solving One-Variable Inequalities	109, 110, 111, 112, 115
Solving Quadratic Equations by Completing the Square	173, 174, 175
Solving Quadratic Equations by Factoring	164, 165, 166, 167, 168, 169, 170, 171, 172
Solving Quadratic Equations by Graphing	162
Solving Quadratic Equations Using Square Roots	118, 119, 163
Solving Quadratic Equations Using the Quadratic Formula	176, 177, 178, 179, 180
Systems of Inequalities	116
Systems of Linear and Quadratic Equations	106, 107
Systems of Linear Equations by Elimination	93, 94, 95, 96, 97, 98
Systems of Linear Equations by Graphing	92
Systems of Linear Equations by Substitution	99, 100, 101
Systems of Linear Equations Practice and Applications	102, 103, 104, 105
Transformations - Absolute Value	141, 143, 144, 145, 146
Transformations - Linear	82, 83
Transformations - Quadratic	85, 87, 88
Volume	10
Writing Linear Equations	69
Writing Quadratic Equations	89

Formula Chart

Area of a Rectangle: $A = lw$

Volume of a Rectangular Prism: $V = lwh$

Slope: $m = \frac{y_2 - y_1}{x_2 - x_1}$

Slope-Intercept Form: $y = mx + b$

Distance: $d = \sqrt{(x_2 - x_1)^2 + (y_2 - y_1)^2}$

Simple Interest: $I = prt$

Quadratic Formula: $\frac{-b \pm \sqrt{b^2 - 1ac}}{2a}$

Perfect Square Trinomials: $(x + y)^2 = x^2 + 2xy + y^2$ and $(x - y)^2 = x^2 - 2xy + y^2$

Difference of Two Squares: $x^2 - y^2 = (x - y)(x + y)$

Preview

Evaluate each expression if $a = 8$, $b = 4$, and $c = 2$.

1. $ac + b =$ _____

2. $\dfrac{a + b}{c} =$ _____

3. $3b - 2c =$ _____

4. $a + b - c =$ _____

5. In the formula $I = prt$, find p when I is $300, r is 4%, and t is 1 year.

_____

6. In the formula $F = \left(C \times \dfrac{9}{5}\right) + 32$, find F when C is $45°$.

_____

Simplify.

7. $-3x + x + (-7x) =$ _____

8. $3t(1.5r) =$ _____

9. $\dfrac{9z}{3} =$ _____

10. $\dfrac{1}{4}(8a - a) =$ _____

Solve.

11. $8a - 5 = 3a + 15$

12. $2b + 6 = b - 4$

_____   _____

13. $3x - 2 = 2(x + 3)$

14. $\dfrac{a}{2} + 3 = \dfrac{2a}{8}$

_____   _____

15. Three times a number increased by 15 is equal to 30. What is the number?

_____

16. The length of a rectangle is 3 times the width. The area is 48 square inches. Find the length and width.

_____

Simplify.

17. $(-3)^2(2)^3 =$ _____

18. $2ab^2(3c) =$ _____

19. $(2x^2y)(-3xy^3) =$ _____

20. $(ab^2)^3 =$ _____

21. $\dfrac{2x^3}{x^2} =$ _____

22. $\dfrac{-8a^3b}{4ab^3} =$ _____

23. $(3a - 3b) + (-a + 5b) =$ _____

24. $(4a + 2b) - (a + 3b) =$ _____

25. $4a^2 - 5b^3 + 3a^2 =$ _____

26. $\dfrac{x}{3y} \cdot \dfrac{3y}{x} =$ _____

27. $\dfrac{a}{b^2} \div \dfrac{a}{b} =$ _____

28. $\dfrac{8ab + 10a^2b}{2ab} =$ _____

Multiply.

29. $3(2x - y) =$ _____

30. $(r + s)(2r + s) =$ _____

31. $2a(a^2 - 3b) =$ _____

32. $2x^2(x^2 + 3x + 7) =$ _____

33. $(x + y)^2 =$ _____

34. $(x + y)(2x - 3y) =$ _____

35. Create a table of solutions for 3 values of x and graph the equation of $2x + 3y = 6$.

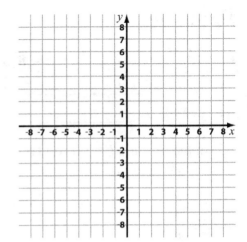

Solve each system of equations.

36. $x + y = 6$ and $x - y = 4$ _____

37. $3x + 2y = 26$ and $3x - 2y = 10$ _____

38. $2x + 3y = 9$ and $x - 2y = 1$ _____

39. $5x - 2y = 3$ and $2x + 5y = 7$ _____

40. $a + 4b = 12$ and $2a - b = 6$ _____

41. $\frac{1}{2}x + y = 6$ and $\frac{1}{2}x - y = 2$ _____

Simplify.

42. $\sqrt{16x^2y^4}$

_____

43. $\sqrt{25x^2y^4z^8}$

_____

44. $\sqrt{40x^4y^6z^{10}}$

_____

Factor each polynomial.

45. $x^2 + 2xy + y^2 =$

_____

46. $9x^2 + 12xy + 4y^2 =$

_____

47. $2x^2 + 7x - 4 =$

_____

Solve.

48. $x^2 - 7x + 6 = 0$

_____

49. $2x^2 + 5x + 2 = 0$

_____

50. $x^2 + 16 = -8x$

_____

51. The length of a rectangle is 4 inches more than the width. The area of the rectangle is 45 square inches. Find the length and width.

_____

52. The product of two consecutive whole numbers is 600. What are the numbers?

_____

Simplify each expression and identify the units.

53. You burn calories at a rate of 15 calories per minute when running and 6 calories per minute when walking. Suppose you exercise for 60 minutes by running for r minutes and walking for the remaining time. The expression $15r + 6(60 - r)$ represents the calories burned. _____

Solve.

54. $5(x + 3) \geq -10$ _____

55. $-x + 4 < 2x + 13$ _____

Preview
Core Skills Algebra

Tell whether each pairing of numbers describes a function. Explain.

56. D: {0, 1, 2, 3, 4}, R: {0, 1, 4, 9, 16}

_____

57. D: {0, 1, 2, 2, 3, 4}, R: {0, 1, 4, 6, 9, 16}

_____

58.

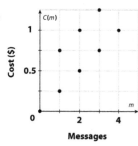

_____

59. What is the inverse function of
$f(n) = 4n + 16$?

_____

60. Write the first four terms of the sequence with
$f(1) = 3$ and $f(n) = f(n - 1) + 3$ for $n \geq 1$ with
the domain equal to the set of integers ≥ 2.

_____

For each graph, tell what change will transform the black line onto the gray line.

61.

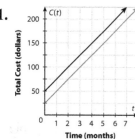

_____

62.

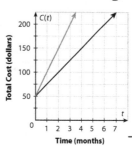

_____

63. Write the equation for the graph shown.

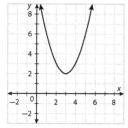

_____

64. Graph the solution to the system of
linear equations: $-x + y = 3$ and $2x + y = 6$.

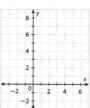

65. Using a graphing calculator, sketch the
solution to the system of equations:
$f(x) = -4.9x^2 + 50x + 25$
$g(x) = 30x$

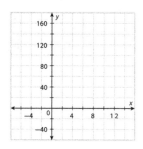

66. Graph the system of linear inequalities:
$x + 2y > 2$ and $-x + y \leq 4$.

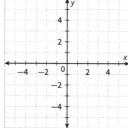

3

Simplify.

67. $\sqrt[3]{(xy)^6}$

_____

68. $\sqrt{x} \cdot \sqrt[3]{x}$

_____

69. $\dfrac{\sqrt{x}}{\sqrt[4]{x}}$

_____

70. $(27x^9)^{\frac{2}{3}}$

_____

Write an equation for each function shown on the graphs.

71.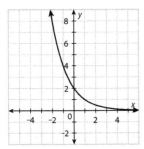

_____

72.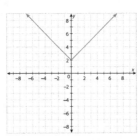

_____

73. What is the solution to the absolute value equation shown in the graph?

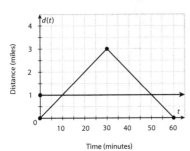

_____

Antonio surveyed 60 of his classmates about their participation in school activities as well as whether they have a part-time job. The results are shown in the two-way relative frequency table below. Use the table to complete the exercises.

Activity / Job	Clubs Only	Sports Only	Both	Neither	Total
Yes	$\frac{12}{60} = 0.2$	$\frac{13}{60} \approx 0.217$	$\frac{16}{60} \approx 0.267$	$\frac{4}{60} \approx 0.067$	$\frac{45}{60} = 0.75$
No	$\frac{3}{60} = 0.05$	$\frac{5}{60} \approx 0.083$	$\frac{5}{60} \approx 0.083$	$\frac{2}{60} \approx 0.033$	$\frac{15}{60} = 0.25$
Total	$\frac{15}{60} = 0.25$	$\frac{18}{60} = 0.3$	$\frac{21}{60} = 0.35$	$\frac{6}{60} = 0.1$	$\frac{60}{60} = 1$

74. What is the joint relative frequency of students surveyed who participate in school clubs only and have part-time jobs?

_____

75. What is the marginal relative frequency of students surveyed who do not have a part-time job?

_____

76. What is the conditional relative frequency that a student surveyed participates in both school clubs and sports, given that the student has a part-time job?

_____

4

Real Numbers

Every number belongs to a **set** of numbers. Some numbers belong to more than one set.

Natural Numbers   {1, 2, 3, 4, ...}

Whole Numbers   {0, 1, 2, 3, 4, ...}

Integers   {..., –3, –2, –1, 0, 1, 2, 3, ...}

Rational Numbers   {all numbers that can be written in the form $\frac{a}{b}$, where a and b are integers and $b \neq 0$}

The **absolute value** of a number is its distance from 0 on a number line.
Look at 3 and –3. They are both 3 units away from 0.

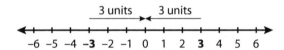

Name all the sets to which each of the following numbers belong.
Write *natural numbers, whole numbers, integers,* or *rational numbers.*

1. 13

_____

_____

2. –5

_____

_____

3. $\frac{1}{5}$

_____

_____

4. 0

_____

_____

Find the absolute value of each number.

5. |–7| = _____   **6.** |0| = _____   **7.** |–17| = _____   **8.** |22| = _____

9. |–12| = _____   **10.** |–19| = _____   **11.** |–11| = _____   **12.** |26| = _____

Name the two numbers that have the given absolute value.

13. 23   **14.** 14   **15.** 32   **16.** 29

_____   _____   _____   _____

5

Simplifying Expressions

Identify the property being illustrated.

1. $a(9 - 7) = (9 - 7)a$

_____

2. $6(5x + 2) = 30x + 12$

_____

3. $9 + (3b + 8) = (3b + 8) + 9$

_____

4. $8m + (9m + 2) = (8m + 9m) + 2$

_____

Simplify the expression.

5. $12x + 4y + 3x + y$

_____

6. $6(n - 8) - 4n$

_____

7. $-2(2x - 5) + 5x + 6$

_____

8. $8b + 3(2b + c) - 3$

_____

For Exercises 8 and 9, simplify each expression and identify the units.

9. You purchase n cans of tennis balls at $4.50 per can from an online retailer. There is a tax of 8% on your order. There are also shipping costs of $7 per order. The expression $4.5n + 0.08(4.5n) + 7$ can be used to represent the total cost.

_____

10. You are making n loaves of bread for a bake sale and the recipe calls for 3.25 cups of flour per loaf. You are also making $n + 1$ pies for the bake sale, and the pie recipe calls for 2 cups of flour per pie. The expression $3.25n + 2(n + 1)$ can be used to represent the total amount of flour required for the bread and the pies.

_____

11. A student says that the perimeter of a rectangle with side lengths $(2x - 1)$ inches and $3x$ inches can be written as $(10x - 1)$ inches, because $2(2x - 1) + 2(3x) = 10x - 1$. Explain why this statement is incorrect.

_____

_____

Writing Expressions

An **algebraic expression** consists of one or more numbers and variables, along with arithmetic operations. Here are some examples of algebraic expressions.

$$c - rs \qquad 8 \cdot 3x \qquad 9a(5b) \qquad \frac{a}{f} - 5$$

Remember, $a \times b$, ab, $a \cdot b$, and $a(b)$ all mean to multiply a times b. The fraction $\frac{a}{b}$ means $a \div b$.

Use these examples to help you write algebraic expressions.

Verbal Expression	Operation	Algebraic Expression
the product of 7 and y	multiplication	$7y$
9 more than a	addition	$a + 9$
a number decreased by y	subtraction	$n - y$
a number separated into 5 equal parts	division	$\frac{n}{5}$

Write an algebraic expression for each verbal expression. Use the variable n when no variable is indicated.

1. y multiplied by z _____

2. the difference between e and f _____

3. the sum of p and q _____

4. the quotient of b and 7   _____

5. 2 more than r _____

6. a decreased by 6   _____

7. 12 divided by a number   _____

8. the product of 3 and a number   _____

9. 8 less than a number   _____

10. a number increased by 1   _____

11. a number times 100   _____

12. a number subtracted from 20   _____

13. 32 decreased by t _____

14. 7 multiplied by a number   _____

15. 28 separated into g equal parts _____

16. the difference between 25 and a number _____

Real Numbers

1. Given that the set of integers is closed under multiplication, prove that the set of rational numbers is closed under multiplication.

   _____

   _____

   _____

2. Given that the set of rational numbers is closed under multiplication, how can you prove that the set of rational numbers is closed under division?

   _____

   _____

   _____

3. Given that the set of rational numbers is closed under multiplication, prove that the product of a nonzero rational number and an irrational number is an irrational number.

   _____

   _____

   _____

   _____

   _____

4. Given that 3 is a rational number and $\sqrt{3}$ is an irrational number, classify each number below as either rational or irrational. Explain your reasoning.

   a. $3 + \sqrt{3}$

   _____

   b. $3 - \sqrt{3}$

   _____

   c. $(3 + \sqrt{3})(3 - \sqrt{3})$
   Hint: Use the distributive property to carry out the multiplication.

   _____

8

Missing Factors in the Area Formula

You can use the formula for the area of a rectangle to find the length or width if you know the area and the other dimension. Substitute the known values and solve for the unknown value.

Find the length when the area is 4,200 square feet and the width is 60 feet.

$$A = lw$$

$$4,200 = 60l$$

$$\frac{4,200}{60} = \frac{60l}{60}$$

$$70 = l$$

The length is 70 feet.

Solve. Use the formula for area of a rectangle.

1. Find the length when the area is 1,000 square feet and the width is 20 feet.

2. Find the length when the area is 750 square meters and the width is 25 meters.

3. Find the length when the area is 1,800 square centimeters and the width is 30 centimeters.

_____

4. Find the length when the area is 7,500 square yards and the width is 75 yards.

5. Find the width when the area is 1,200 square feet and the length is 40 feet.

6. Find the width when the area is 300 square feet and the length is 15 feet.

_____

7. Find the width when the area is 720 square inches and the length is 60 inches.

8. Find the width when the area is 17.5 square meters and the length is 5 meters.

9. Find the width when the area is 18 square miles and the length is 4.5 miles.

_____

9

Missing Factors in the Volume Formula

If you know the volume of a rectangular prism and two of the dimensions, you can use the formula $V = lwh$ to solve for the other dimension. Substitute the known values and solve for the unknown value.

Find the width when the volume is 1,800 cubic centimeters, the height is 6 centimeters, and the length is 30 centimeters.

$$V = lwh$$
$$1,800 = 30 \cdot w \cdot 6$$
$$1,800 = 180w$$
$$\frac{1,800}{180} = \frac{180w}{180}$$
$$w = 10$$

The width is 10 centimeters.

Solve. Use the formula for volume of a rectangular prism.

1. Find the height when the volume is 2,100 cubic meters, the length is 20 meters, and the width is 7 meters.

   _____

2. Find the height when the volume is 960 cubic feet, the length is 20 feet, and the width is 8 feet.

   _____

3. Find the height when the volume is 1,500 cubic yards, the length is 25 yards, and the width is 10 yards.

   _____

4. Find the length when the volume is 252 cubic meters, the width is 7 meters, and the height is 4 meters.

   _____

5. Find the length when the volume is 480 cubic feet, the width is 4 feet, and the height is 12 feet.

   _____

6. Find the length when the volume is 900 cubic inches, the width is 25 inches, and the height is 6 inches.

   _____

7. Find the width when the volume is 480 cubic feet, the length is 20 feet, and the height is 6 feet.

   _____

8. Find the width when the volume is 1,080 cubic meters, the length is 18 meters, and the height is 6 meters.

   _____

9. Find the width when the volume is 800 cubic yards, the length is 40 yards, and the height is 4 yards.

   _____

Missing Factors in the Simple Interest Formula

If you know the value for three of the variables in the formula $I = prt$, you can solve for the unknown value. Find the missing factor.

Remember, when using the formula, write r as a decimal.

When $p = \$500$, $I = \$25$, and $t = 1$ year, find r.

$I = prt$

$25 = (500)(r)(1)$

$25 = 500r$

$\frac{25}{500} = \frac{500r}{500}$

$\frac{25}{500} = r$

$0.05 = 5\% = r$

The interest rate is 5%.

Solve. Use the formula for simple interest.

1. Find the principal when the interest is $432, the rate is $6\frac{1}{4}\%$, and the time is 3 years.

   _____

2. Find the principal when the interest for one year amounts to $20 at 5%.

   _____

3. Find the principal when the rate is 5%, the time is 2 years, and the interest is $120.

   _____

4. Find the rate when the interest is $300, the time is 3 years, and the principal is $2,000.

   _____

5. Find the rate when the principal is $420, the time is 6 months, and the interest is $12.60. (Hint: $t = \frac{1}{2}$)

   _____

6. Find the rate when the interest is $24, the time is 2 years, and the principal is $200.

   _____

7. Find the time when the principal is $250, the rate is 6%, and the interest is $45.

   _____

8. Find the time when the principal is $50, the rate is 7%, and the interest is $17.50.

   _____

9. Find the time when the principal is $250, the rate is 4%, and the interest is $20.

   _____

Name _____ Date _____

Missing Factors in the Distance Formula

If you know the distance and either the rate or the time, you can solve for the unknown value. Use the formula $D = rt$ and substitute the known values. Then find the missing factor.

Find r when $D = 50$ miles and $t = 2$ hours.

$D = rt$

$50 = r(2)$

$\frac{50}{2} = \frac{2r}{2}$

$25 = r$

The rate is 25 miles per hour.

Solve. Use the distance formula.

1. A plane was sighted over two different observation posts that were 650 miles apart. The plane passed over the first post at 4:00 A.M. and over the second post at 6:30 A.M. At what speed was the plane traveling?

   _____

2. If it took a plane 6 hours to fly from Tampa to Los Angeles, a distance of 2,496 miles, at what rate of speed was the flight made?

   _____

3. Find r when $D = 1,400$ miles and $t = \frac{1}{2}$ hour.

   _____

4. Find r when $D = 1,500$ miles and $t = 3$ hours.

   _____

5. Find t when $D = 1,750$ kilometers and $r = 350$ kilometers per hour.

   _____

6. Find t when $D = 180$ kilometers and $r = 45$ kilometers per hour.

   _____

7. Find t when $D = 420$ meters and $r = 70$ meters per second.

   _____

8. Find t when $D = 113.5$ feet and $r = 45.4$ feet per second.

   _____

9. Find r when $D = 2,150$ miles and $t = 5$ hours.

   _____

10. Find r when $D = 247.5$ miles and $t = 4.5$ hours.

   _____

12

© Houghton Mifflin Harcourt Publishing Company

Unit 1
Core Skills Algebra

Unit 1 Review

Simplify each expression.

1. $a - 4 + 7z + 11$

2. $4(x + y) - 5x - y$

3. $x - 5(y + 2) + (3x + 1)$

_____

_____

_____

Evaluate each expression for $a = 6$, $b = 10$, $c = 3$.

4. $a + b$

5. ab

_____

_____

6. $(c + 2)b$

7. $7c - \frac{1}{2}b$

_____

_____

Identify the property being illustrated.

8. $8m + (9m + 2) = (8m + 9m) + 2$

9. $k + 5k + 8 = (1 + 5)k + 8$

_____

_____

Solve.

10. $(11)9 = w$

11. $a = \frac{1}{2}(15 + 3)$

12. $f = 4(4) + 3(10)$

13. $\frac{15 + 13}{12 - 5} = b$

_____

_____

_____

_____

14. $8k = 40$

15. $x + 23 = 79$

16. $19 + m = 100$

17. $4x = 10$

_____

_____

_____

_____

18. Using the formula $A = lw$, find l when A is 48 square feet and w is 8 feet.

19. Using the formula $I = prt$, find p when $I = \$45$, r is $4\frac{1}{2}\%$, and t is 2 years.

20. Use the formula $C = (F - 32) \times \frac{5}{9}$ to find C when F is 113°.

_____

_____

_____

21. You and two friends all have the same meal for lunch. Each meal costs c dollars plus a tax of 6% of the cost and a tip of 20% of the cost. You use a 10-dollar gift certificate. You can represent the total cost with the expression $3c + (0.06 + 0.20)(3c) - 10$. Simplify the expression and identify the unit.

22. Lizzie has already volunteered 20 hours at her school library. From now on, she plans to volunteer five hours per week at the library. Write an algebraic expression to represent the total number of hours she will volunteer.

_____

_____

Terms, Coefficients, and Monomials

An algebraic expression has different parts.

A **term** is a number, a variable, or a product or quotient of numbers and variables.

An **expression** consists of one or more terms and one or more operations.

Constants are terms that do not contain variables.

The **coefficient** of a term is the numerical factor. When there is no number in front of a variable, the coefficient 1 is understood. Coefficients may be integers, fractions, or decimals.

A **monomial** is a number, a variable, or a product of numbers and variables. So, the term $\frac{s}{t}$ is not a monomial because division is indicated by the variable in the denominator.

Examples of Terms				
$\frac{a}{b}$	$-6x^2$	5	a	$8mn$

Examples of Expressions			
$4 + b$	$ab - c$	$x + \frac{b}{t}$	$2a + 7ab - 1$

Examples of Constants				
-7	2	$\frac{3}{4}$	0.8	π

Examples of Coefficients				
Term:	$-7y$	m	$-x$	$\frac{3}{4}x$ or $\frac{3x}{4}$
Coefficient:	-7	1	-1	$\frac{3}{4}$ or 0.75

Examples of Monomials			
$9xy$	0.5	$-7k$	$\frac{4}{5}b$

Circle the constants.

1. -7 $4m$ 9 $\frac{1}{10}$

    $-m$ 14 $x + y$ $2x$

Circle the monomials.

2. $5x$ a $a + b$ $2xy$

    $x - 2y$ $\frac{1}{3}a$ $a - 2b$ $\frac{12}{z}$

Circle the coefficient of each term.

3. $5a$ **4.** $4s$ **5.** πd **6.** $-42b$

7. $1{,}250r$ **8.** $1.5n$ **9.** $-9m$ **10.** $\frac{2}{3}x$

Write the coefficient of each term.

11. $\frac{x}{2}$ **12.** $\frac{-3y}{4}$ **13.** z **14.** $\frac{3a}{2}$

_____   _____   _____   _____

15. $0.4r$ **16.** $\frac{m}{4}$ **17.** $-a$ **18.** $\frac{3b}{5}$

_____   _____   _____   _____

Multiplying Monomials

Recall that a monomial is a number, a variable, or a product of numbers and variables. To multiply two or more monomials, multiply the coefficients and variables separately.

Remember:

- The product of two numbers with the same sign is positive.
- The product of two numbers with different signs is negative.
- When there is no number in front of a variable, the coefficient 1 is understood.
- $ab = ba$
- In simplest form, the variables are in alphabetical order.

Multiply: $(4b)(8a)$
$= (4 \cdot 8)ab$
$= 32ab$

Multiply: $-7(-4pq)$
$= -7(-4)pq$
$= 28pq$

Multiply: $3t(-7m)(-a)$
$= 3(-7)(-1)amt$
$= 21amt$

Multiply.

1. $4(5a) =$

2. $5(6b) =$

3. $9m(6) =$

4. $3(7a) =$

5. $3(7xy) =$

6. $(9mn)(4) =$

7. $2(6rs) =$

8. $(8ab)(8) =$

9. $(-4)(-5x) =$

10. $(7a)(-4) =$

11. $(3b)(-9) =$

12. $-2(-25c) =$

13. $(4a)(3b) =$

14. $5t(10s) =$

15. $(-4x)(-9z) =$

16. $2mn(-7p) =$

17. $\frac{1}{2}y(6) =$

18. $4(\frac{1}{2}x) =$

19. $20t(\frac{1}{4}a) =$

20. $25(\frac{1}{2}m) =$

21. $3s(0.4r) =$

22. $5c(0.6b) =$

23. $5v(0.8t) =$

24. $6(0.7z) =$

25. $6(3b)(2c) =$

26. $7(5t)(3r) =$

27. $(4x)(3y)(9z) =$

28. $(-3)(4m)(10n) =$

29. $(-19rs)(-5t)(-3) =$

30. $(-4f)(16e)(12) =$

31. $-35y(-4x)(5z) =$

32. $t(32s)(4r) =$

15

Multiplying and Dividing Monomials

Remember, to multiply monomials, multiply their coefficients and variables separately.

To divide a monomial by an integer, divide the coefficient by the integer and write the variable or variables.

Multiply or divide.

1. $8(8n) =$

2. $\frac{36y}{-9} =$

3. $3a(-5b) =$

4. $\frac{-56n}{-8} =$

5. $\frac{24ab}{8} =$

6. $36m(-\frac{1}{4}n) =$

7. $\frac{72r}{3} =$

8. $\frac{-64p}{16} =$

9. $4(-2t)(-5s) =$

10. $\frac{150x}{-15} =$

11. $(-9j)(0.2k) =$

12. $(-12x)(-6) =$

13. $\frac{-4.5w}{-5} =$

14. $(-7ab)(-6c)(-2) =$

15. $-16(\frac{1}{2}x) =$

16. $9pq(-r) =$

17. $5(0.13k) =$

18. $\frac{-84fg}{-12} =$

19. $\frac{2}{3}b(18) =$

20. $\frac{63cd}{-7} =$

21. $\frac{33rs}{-6} =$

22. $-4m(7h) =$

23. $\frac{-49g}{-7} =$

24. $4(-12hy) =$

25. $\frac{-3}{6}i(42j) =$

26. $\frac{1.6f}{4}g =$

27. $\frac{-78z}{-13} =$

28. $\frac{-2.8r}{-7} =$

29. $\frac{-160t}{8} =$

30. $(-15w)(\frac{-ev}{3}) =$

31. $(-4v)(-14d) =$

32. $(-18k)(-mj) =$

33. $(-3b)(-2r)(-3p) =$

34. $21(\frac{-1}{3}t) =$

35. $-16dj(-5q) =$

36. $-15ng(\frac{-1}{5}d) =$

37. $\frac{70s}{-14} =$

38. $\frac{1}{4}m(-16) =$

39. $\frac{69n}{-3} =$

40. $\frac{3}{11}gt(22) =$

16

The Distributive Property

To **distribute** means to give something to each member of a group. The **Distributive Property** multiplies a factor by each term within parentheses. A negative sign in front of parentheses indicates multiplication by -1.

Remember:

- The product of two numbers with the same sign is positive.
- The product of two numbers with different signs is negative.

Simplify: $7(x + 2)$

$= 7(x) + 7(2)$

$= 7x + 14$

Simplify: $-(2y + 3)$

$= -1(2y) + (-1)(3)$

$= -2y - 3$

Simplify: $y(5x - 4)$

$= 5x(y) - 4(y)$

$= 5xy - 4y$

Simplify.

1. $6(y - 1) =$

_____

2. $r(3 - t) =$

_____

3. $5(7 + n) =$

_____

4. $x(2 - a) =$

_____

5. $-9(r - 4) =$

_____

6. $4(c + 2) =$

_____

7. $-7(1 + t) =$

_____

8. $g(4s + 6) =$

_____

9. $p(7 - 2g) =$

_____

10. $7(5y - 8) =$

_____

11. $-2(6 - 5a) =$

_____

12. $-8(1 + 2d) =$

_____

13. $k(-10 - 7r) =$

_____

14. $-14(a + b) =$

_____

15. $s(-4 - 8t) =$

_____

16. $-8(3p - 2q) =$

_____

17. $-m(x + 3) =$

_____

18. $9(2x + y) =$

_____

19. $c(-3e + 9g) =$

_____

20. $-(9 - m) =$

_____

21. $3(2b - 5c + d) =$

_____

22. $-3x(9 - 2y) =$

_____

23. $n(3j - 8k) =$

_____

24. $t(3x + 2) =$

_____

25. $5a(2b - 1) =$

_____

26. $-9b(1 + 3a) =$

_____

27. $4(m - 5n) =$

_____

28. $2r(-6s + t) =$

_____

29. $-5(9s - 2t + v) =$

_____

30. $-(p + 2q - r) =$

_____

31. $2x(3y - 4z) =$

_____

32. $2k(m + 3n - 7) =$

_____

Simplifying Expressions with Parentheses

A more complex expression involving the Distributive Property might include additional operations or additional expressions within parentheses. Follow the order of operations, the Distributive Property rule, and the rules of combining like terms to simplify the expression. Remember, a negative sign in front of parentheses indicates multiplication by -1.

Simplify:

$-3(8a + 5b) + 3b$

$= -3(8a) + (-3)(5b) + 3b$

$= -24a + (-15b) + 3b$

$= -24a + (-15 + 3)b$

$= -24a - 12b$

Simplify:

$4 - (r + 7)$

$= 4 + (-1)(r + 7)$

$= 4 + (-1)(r) + (-1)(7)$

$= 4 - r - 7$

$= -r - 3$

Simplify:

$4(r + s) + 3(r + 2s)$

$= 4r + 4s + 3r + 6s$

$= (4 + 3)r + (4 + 6)s$

$= 7r + 10s$

Simplify:

1. $4(-7x + 3y - 2z) =$

2. $-2(4m + 9n) + 3mn =$

3. $8(7 - 5ab) - 2ab =$

4. $-(4p + 3q) + 7p =$

5. $-(6x + y - z) =$

6. $-(-2r + 7s) + 2(r + s) =$

7. $8y - (3 - 6y) =$

8. $-7 + (9x - 8) =$

9. $2x + 3y - (x + 5y) =$

10. $2a + 3b + 2(a - 2b) =$

11. $3x - 5y + 4(x - 3y) =$

12. $5m + 4n + 3(2m - 5n) =$

13. $5t - 4s - 3(2t - 3s) =$

14. $4m + 3n - 2(m + 3n) =$

15. $7x - 4y - 5(2y - x) =$

16. $2(3b + 4) - (b - 5) =$

17. $3(5x - 2y) - (4x + 3y) =$

18. $3(m + 2n) - 4(2m + n) =$

Simplifying Fractional Expressions

Expressions with negative or positive fractions are simplified using the same rules as for integers. First, separate each fractional coefficient by multiplying the term by the **reciprocal** of the divisor. For example, $\frac{x}{2} = \frac{1}{2}x$ because the reciprocal of 2 is $\frac{1}{2}$. This step allows you to collect like terms or to use the Distributive Property in order to simplify an equation. Dividing by an integer is the same as multiplying by its reciprocal.

Simplify: $a + \frac{a}{4}$

$= a + \frac{1}{4}a$ Separate the fractional coefficient.

$= (1 + \frac{1}{4})a$ Add like terms.

$= 1\frac{1}{4}a$

Simplify: $\frac{-8m + 6n}{2}$

$= \frac{1}{2}(-8m + 6n)$ Separate the fractional coefficients.

$= \frac{1}{2}(-8m) + \frac{1}{2}(6n)$ Use the Distributive Property.

$= -4m + 3n$

Simplify.

1. $\frac{k}{3} - \frac{4k}{3} =$

2. $\frac{-x}{7} + \frac{4x}{7} =$

3. $\frac{-5n}{6} + \frac{5n}{6} =$

4. $\frac{-r}{4} + s - \frac{3r}{4} =$

5. $\frac{y}{3} + r - \frac{5y}{3} =$

6. $c + x + \frac{3x}{4} =$

7. $\frac{r}{2} - \frac{3r}{2} =$

8. $\frac{-3a}{5} + x + \frac{3a}{5} =$

9. $\frac{2y}{3} - c - y =$

10. $\frac{1}{2}(-16p + 8) =$

11. $\frac{-1}{3}(6y + 1) =$

12. $\frac{2}{5}(10a - 5) =$

13. $\frac{7x + 21y}{7} =$

14. $\frac{24a + 2b}{4} =$

15. $\frac{a + 4a}{-5} =$

Multiplying Fractional Expressions

To multiply fractional expressions, multiply numerators and then multiply denominators. Write as a fraction and simplify if possible.

Remember:
- If the signs of two factors are the same, the product is positive.
- If the signs are different, the product is negative.

Simplify: $\frac{-y}{4} \cdot \frac{x}{5}$

$= (-y)(x) = -xy$ Multiply the numerators.

$= (4)(5) = 20$ Multiply the denominators.

$= \frac{-xy}{20}$

Simplify.

1. $\frac{-b}{3} \cdot \frac{a}{5} =$

2. $\frac{-t}{4} \times \frac{-r}{8} =$

3. $\frac{q}{7} \cdot \frac{-p}{8} =$

_____

4. $\frac{x}{2} \times \frac{n}{-2} =$

5. $\frac{h}{5} \cdot \frac{3k}{7} =$

6. $\frac{x}{8} \times \frac{-4}{7} =$

_____

7. $\frac{-3y}{4} \cdot \frac{-z}{2} =$

8. $\frac{9}{10} \times \frac{p}{3} =$

9. $\frac{-5n}{8} \cdot \frac{2}{-3} =$

_____

10. $\frac{-8a}{9} \times \frac{3b}{10} =$

11. $\frac{2z}{3} \cdot \frac{9x}{3} =$

12. $\frac{3e}{-2} \times \frac{-4f}{9} =$

_____

13. $\frac{3v}{4} \cdot \frac{-5}{9w} =$

14. $\frac{3y}{-10} \times \frac{5x}{9} =$

15. $\frac{-a}{5} \cdot \frac{3b}{-4} =$

_____

Unit 2 Review

Write the coefficient of each term.

1. $\frac{5x}{3}$

2. $-a$

3. $\frac{n}{7}$

4. $3.5q$

_____

5. $\frac{7b}{3}$

6. w

7. $\frac{-5z}{2}$

8. $\frac{y}{5}$

_____

Simplify.

9. $-3(17q) =$

10. $-7(-26st) =$

11. $(-8x)(9y) =$

12. $(-5k)(2.4y) =$

_____

13. $\frac{15x}{5} =$

14. $\frac{-25rs}{-5} =$

15. $\frac{54y}{-6} =$

16. $\frac{105mn}{-3} =$

_____

17. $9(r - 3) =$

18. $w(4 + 6m) =$

19. $-4(16p + 8) =$

20. $a(-32c - 6d) =$

_____

21. $\frac{21x}{4} \cdot \frac{2y}{3} =$

22. $\frac{-30rs}{-6} \cdot \frac{p}{5} =$

23. $\frac{4y}{-6} \cdot \frac{s}{4} =$

24. $\frac{10m}{-3} \cdot \frac{n}{2} =$

_____

Simplify the following expressions.

25. $k + 7 - (2k + 5) =$

26. $r + 2 - 3(5 - 2r) =$

27. $2(3a + 5b) + 3(5a - 3b) =$

_____

28. $\frac{a}{2} + b + \frac{a}{2} =$

29. $\frac{3}{4}(-12x + 20) =$

30. $\frac{42b + 70}{7} =$

_____

Exploring Equations

Tell whether each value of the variable is a solution of the equation $1.06p = 53$. Show your reasoning.

1. $p = 40$

_____

2. $p = 45$

_____

3. $p = 50$

_____

4. $p = 55$

_____

5. Mark buys 5 movie tickets online for $60. The online fee for each ticket is $1.50.

　　a. Write a verbal model for the situation.

_____

_____

　　b. Write an equation from the verbal model. Simplify, if possible.

_____

　　c. Solve the equation using a guess-and-check strategy. Show your work.

_____

_____

6. Ellie received a 15% discount for renewing a magazine subscription. She paid $26.35. Write an equation to find the price before the discount. Solve the equation using a guess-and-check strategy. Show your work.

_____

_____

_____

Missing Addends and Missing Factors

To solve an equation with a missing **addend** or **factor**, use the **inverse operation** to isolate the variable on one side of the equal sign. That is, solve for a missing addend by subtracting the known number from both sides of the equation, as in the first example. Solve for a missing factor by dividing, as in the second example. Check the solution by substituting the value of the variable in the original equation.

Solve: $r + 9 = 21$	Solve: $9n = 99$
$r + 9 - 9 = 21 - 9$	$\frac{9}{9}n = \frac{99}{9}$
$r = 12$	$n = 11$
The solution is 12. Check: $12 + 9 = 21$	The solution is 11. Check: $9(11) = 99$

Solve. Check.

1. $b + 9 = 17$

2. $10 + a = 40$

3. $8y = 40$

4. $12n = 48$

_____

_____

_____

_____

5. $2a = 8$

6. $5b = 35$

7. $z + 14 = 30$

8. $4x = 100$

_____

_____

_____

_____

9. $p + 33 = 333$

10. $7r = 77$

11. $b \cdot 6 = 90$

12. $17 + m = 83$

_____

_____

_____

_____

13. $d \cdot 20 = 180$

14. $19 + n = 9$

15. $4y = 4$

16. $f + 12 = 24$

_____

_____

_____

_____

17. $7x = 1$

18. $0 + k = 44$

19. $5z = 400$

20. $s + 40 = 555$

_____

_____

_____

_____

21. $6r = 3$

22. $7 + a = 8\frac{1}{2}$

23. $c + \frac{2}{3} = 5$

24. $2x = 6$

_____

_____

_____

_____

23

Solving Addition Equations

To solve the equation $4 + x = 10$, find the value of x that makes the equation true. Since x is a missing addend, the solution is $10 - 4$, or 6. It is important to check the solution by substituting 6 for x in the original equation. Since $4 + 6$ is 10, the solution is correct.

When an addition equation involves integers, a slightly different process is used to find the solution. You can add the same number to both sides of an equation without changing its solution. The goal is to isolate the variable on one side of the equation, with the constants on the other side, so the solution will be obvious. In the first example, the number 4 is added to both sides because 4 is the opposite of -4. The left side of the equation becomes $x + 0$, or simply x.

Solve: $x + (-4) = 9$

$x + (-4) + 4 = 9 + 4$

$\qquad x = 13$

The solution is 13.

Check: $13 + (-4) = 9$

Solve: $5 + n = -2$

$5 + n - 5 = -2 - 5$

$\qquad n = -7$

The solution is -7.

Check: $5 + (-7) = -2$

Solve: $a + 9 = 7$

$a + 9 + (-9) = 7 + (-9)$

$\qquad a = -2$

The solution is -2.

Check: $-2 + 9 = 7$

Solve. Check.

1. $x + 2 = 5$

2. $x + (-15) = 3$

3. $x + 4 = 8$

4. $x + (-2) = 29$

_____

5. $x + 23 = 23$

6. $a + 4 = -1$

7. $n + (-5) = 1$

8. $t + (-33) = 30$

_____

9. $r + 15 = 2$

10. $h + (-9) = -9$

11. $y + 12 = 0$

12. $d + 7 = 9$

_____

13. $k + (-10) = 1$

14. $c + 17 = 27$

15. $x + 54 = 36$

16. $m + (-9) = 72$

_____

17. $f + 19 = 0$

18. $m + (-5) = 19$

19. $z + 9 = -10$

20. $x + (-3) = 3$

_____

Solving Subtraction Equations

To isolate the variable in a subtraction equation, you can add the same number to both sides. Or, you can rewrite the equation as addition and then solve.

Solve: $x - 6 = 4$

$x - 6 + 6 = 4 + 6$

$x = 10$

The solution is 10.

Check: $10 - 6 = 4$

Solve: $n - (-4) = 8$

$n + 4 = 8$

$n + 4 + (-4) = 8 + (-4)$

$n = 4$

The solution is 4.

Check: $4 - (-4) = 8$

Solve: $z - 9 = 0$

$z - 9 + 9 = 0 + 9$

$z = 9$

The solution is 9.

Check: $9 - 9 = 0$

Solve. Check.

1. $x - 13 = 15$

2. $z - 7 = 4$

3. $y - (-12) = -10$

4. $r - 66 = 100$

_____

5. $y - 3 = 3$

6. $m - 9 = -7$

7. $z - 48 = 84$

8. $x - (-25) = 10$

_____

9. $x - (-3) = -3$

10. $p - 6 = -4$

11. $y - 82 = 70$

12. $h - 16 = 15$

_____

13. $r - (-12) = 5$

14. $t - 61 = -21$

15. $a - (-1) = 0$

16. $b - (-2) = -1$

_____

25

Solving Multiplication Equations

One way to solve a multiplication equation such as $7n = 28$ is to think of the missing factor. The solution to $7n = 28$ is $28 \div 7$, or 4.

Remember that another way to solve an equation is to isolate the variable so the solution is obvious. You can multiply or divide both sides of an equation by any number (except zero) without changing its solution. For $7n = 28$, divide both sides by 7. The equation becomes $\frac{7n}{7} = \frac{28}{7}$, or $1n = \frac{28}{7}$. So, $n = 4$.

Solve: $4x = -32$

$$\frac{4x}{4} = \frac{-32}{4}$$

$$x = -8$$

The solution is -8.

Check: $4(-8) = -32$

Solve: $-m = 5$

$$(-1)(-m) = (-1)(5)$$

$$m = -5$$

The solution is -5.

Check: $-(-5) = 5$

Solve: $-3y = -3$

$$\frac{-3y}{-3} = \frac{-3}{-3}$$

$$y = 1$$

The solution is 1.

Check: $-3(1) = -3$

Solve. Check.

1. $6x = 36$

_____

2. $-8y = 48$

_____

3. $-n = 9$

_____

4. $3m = -10$

_____

5. $-2x = 16$

_____

6. $23y = 92$

_____

7. $3x = 18$

_____

8. $2a = -24$

_____

9. $25k = 50$

_____

10. $-3x = -9$

_____

11. $6r = 24$

_____

12. $-14y = 56$

_____

13. $-7x = -14$

_____

14. $-m = -2$

_____

15. $3n = -18$

_____

16. $5x = 25$

_____

26

Solving Division Equations

To isolate the variable in a division equation, you can multiply both sides by the same number.

Solve: $\frac{x}{2} = 6$

$(2)\frac{x}{2} = (2)6$

$x = 12$

Check: $\frac{12}{2} = 6$

Solve: $\frac{-b}{3} = 9$

$(-3)\left(\frac{-b}{3}\right) = (-3)9$

$b = -27$

Check: $-\left(\frac{-27}{3}\right) = 9$

Solve: $\frac{y}{5} = 0$

$(5)\frac{y}{5} = (5)0$

$y = 0$

Check: $\frac{0}{5} = 0$

Solve. Check.

1. $\frac{x}{4} = 8$

2. $\frac{x}{3} = -2$

3. $\frac{w}{5} = 2$

4. $\frac{z}{9} = 10$

_____ _____ _____ _____

5. $\frac{-f}{8} = -8$

6. $\frac{p}{9} = -9$

7. $\frac{t}{6} = 3$

8. $\frac{h}{7} = 0$

_____ _____ _____ _____

9. $\frac{a}{10} = 7$

10. $\frac{b}{2} = -20$

11. $\frac{-m}{1} = 6$

12. $\frac{z}{1} = 1$

_____ _____ _____ _____

13. $\frac{-y}{15} = 1$

14. $\frac{-w}{4} = 20$

15. $\frac{d}{25} = 4$

16. $\frac{-r}{36} = -2$

_____ _____ _____ _____

Mixed Practice Solving Equations

Remember that when isolating the variable in an equation, you can add, subtract, multiply, or divide both sides by the same number. Always check your solution in the original equation.

Solve. Check.

1. $a + (\text{-}5) = 8$

2. $r - 9 = 13$

3. $\frac{y}{2} = 5$

4. $3m = 9$

5. $t + 2 = 1$

6. $b - (\text{-}4) = 0$

7. $\frac{n}{3} = \text{-}2$

8. $7k = 7$

9. $s + 6 = 0$

10. $z - 6 = \text{-}3$

11. $\frac{\text{-}d}{3} = \text{-}9$

12. $\text{-}x = 4$

13. $\frac{k}{3} = 5$

14. $r + 7 = \text{-}1$

15. $\text{-}2c = 4$

16. $y - 5 = 7$

17. $w - 18 = 27$

18. $9m = 12$

19. $\frac{s}{4} = 5$

20. $b + 12 = 11$

21. $\frac{\text{-}h}{3} = 8$

22. $t - 9 = \text{-}4$

23. $f + 7 = \text{-}11$

24. $7y = \text{-}35$

25. $g + 5 = 4$

26. $\text{-}z = 12$

27. $\frac{a}{3} = 0$

28. $m - 5 = 7$

29. $5b = \text{-}8$

30. $l + 24 = \text{-}2$

31. $z - 3 = \text{-}15$

32. $\frac{n}{12} = 9$

33. $x + 73 = 27$

34. $7r = \text{-}49$

35. $\frac{\text{-}a}{13} = \text{-}1$

36. $h - 81 = 9$

37. $c + 15 = \text{-}93$

38. $t - 1 = \text{-}60$

39. $16x = \text{-}4$

40. $\frac{\text{-}a}{1} = 8$

The Fractional Equation

One method for solving an equation such as $\frac{3x}{4} = 15$ is to multiply both sides by 4 and then divide both sides by 3.

A simpler method to solve the same equation is to think of $\frac{3x}{4}$ as $\frac{3}{4}x$. This is a multiplication equation with a fractional coefficient. It can be solved by multiplying both sides by the reciprocal of $\frac{3}{4}$, which is $\frac{4}{3}$.

Solve: $\frac{3x}{4} = 15$

$\left(\frac{4}{3}\right)\frac{3x}{4} = \left(\frac{4}{3}\right)15$

$x = 20$

Check: $\frac{3(20)}{4} = 15$

Solve: $\frac{2n}{3} = -4$

$\left(\frac{3}{2}\right)\frac{2n}{3} = \left(\frac{3}{2}\right)(-4)$

$n = -6$

Check: $\frac{2(-6)}{3} = -4$

Solve. Check.

1. $\frac{2n}{3} = 14$

2. $\frac{7r}{3} = 7$

3. $\frac{n}{4} = -6$

4. $\frac{2a}{5} = 8$

_____

5. $\frac{3x}{5} = -12$

6. $\frac{2y}{5} = 24$

7. $\frac{2r}{7} = 12$

8. $\frac{3y}{7} = 6$

_____

9. $\frac{3a}{4} = 15$

10. $\frac{3z}{10} = 9$

11. $\frac{5x}{8} = -10$

12. $\frac{4z}{5} = 24$

_____

13. $\frac{5a}{8} = 25$

14. $\frac{-7m}{10} = 21$

15. $\frac{3x}{10} = 3$

16. $\frac{-2r}{5} = 48$

_____

29

Solving Equations with Like Terms

Some equations contain the same variable in more than one term. Combine the like terms on each side of the equation. Then solve and check.

Solve: $5a + 4a = 45$

$9a = 45$

$\dfrac{9a}{9} = \dfrac{45}{9}$

$a = 5$

Check: $5(5) + 4(5) = 45$

$25 + 20 = 45$

Solve: $3b - 5b = 4$

$-2b = 4$

$\dfrac{(-2b)}{-2} = \dfrac{4}{-2}$

$b = -2$

Check: $3(-2) - 5(-2) = 4$

$-6 - {-10} = 4$

Solve: $4r + r = -5$

$5r = -5$

$\dfrac{5r}{5} = \dfrac{(-5)}{5}$

$r = -1$

Check: $4(-1) + (-1) = -5$

$-4 + {-1} = -5$

Solve. Check.

1. $-15c + 10c = 100$

2. $m + 7m = 48$

3. $2x + 3x = 25$

4. $5z + 2z = 41 - 6$

_____

_____

_____

_____

5. $8a - 5a = 60$

6. $15a - 3a = 60$

7. $-8x + 6x = 38$

8. $-8z - 3z = 24 - 2$

_____

_____

_____

_____

9. $14b - 6b = 48$

10. $-6b + 5b = 55$

11. $3x - x = 46$

12. $3r + 2r = 31 - 6$

_____

_____

_____

_____

13. $5x - 2x = 120$

14. $14b - 9b = 65$

15. $7x - 3x = 12$

16. $x - 3x = 18 + 6$

_____

_____

_____

_____

30

Writing Equations to Solve Problems

A problem may include information about the relationship between a number and an unknown quantity. To solve such a problem, first define a variable to represent the unknown quantity. Then write and solve an equation to find the value for the unknown.

Three fifths of a certain number is 18. What is the number?

Define a variable.	Write an equation.	Solve the equation.	Check:
Let n = the number.	Three fifths of n is 18.	$\left(\frac{5}{3}\right)\frac{3}{5}n = \left(\frac{5}{3}\right)18$	$\frac{3}{5}(30) = 18$
	$\frac{3}{5}n = 18$	$n = 30$	The number is 30.

Write an equation. Solve. Check.

1. Three fourths of a number is 36. What is the number?

2. One fifth of what number is 14?

3. One third of a certain number is equal to 15. What is the number?

4. Five times a certain number is equal to 35. What is the number?

5. A certain number when divided by 3 is equal to 20. What is the number?

6. Two times a certain number plus three times the number is 30. What is the number?

Equations with More Than One Unknown

A problem may contain more than one unknown quantity. Sometimes the unknown quantities are related in a way that you can use the same variable to express both quantities. Use the following steps to solve such a problem.

1. Define a variable to represent one unknown quantity. Then use the same variable to write an expression for the other unknown.
2. Write and solve an equation.
3. State the answer to the question that is asked. Sometimes the answer must include both unknowns.

Jeffrey's father is three times as old as Jeffrey. The sum of their ages is 60 years. How old is each?

Define a variable.	Write an equation.	Solve the equation.
Let a = Jeffrey's age.	The sum of a and $3a$ is 60.	$a + 3a = 60$
$3a$ = his father's age	$a + 3a = 60$	$4a = 60$
		$a = 15$, so $3a = 45$

Jeffrey is 15 years old. His father is 45 years old.

Write an equation. Solve. Check.

1. Quanisha's father is four times as old as Quanisha, and the sum of their ages is 50 years. How old is each?

   _____

2. Leroy and Aaron have $7.20. Aaron has five times as much as Leroy. How much does each boy have?

   _____

3. Together, Thomas and Tyrone have $24.00. Thomas has three times as much as Tyrone. How much does each have?

   _____

4. Ling is twice as old as her sister. The sum of their ages is 42 years. How old is each?

   _____

5. Deidra and Shelby inherited an estate of $3,000. Deidra is to receive two times as much as Shelby. How much does each receive?

   _____

6. From Kansas City to Denver is twice as far as from Kansas City to St. Louis. The two distances together total 900 miles. What are the two distances?

   _____

Solving Two-Step Equations

Some equations require two steps in order to find the solution. First, add or subtract from both sides to isolate the constants on one side. Then multiply both sides by the reciprocal of the coefficient (or divide by the coefficient) in order to isolate the variable. Check the solution against the original equation.

Solve: $2x - 5 = 71$

Step 1: $2x = 71 + 5$

$2x = 76$

Step 2: $x = \frac{76}{2}$

$x = 38$

Check: $2(38) - 5 = 71$

$71 = 71$

Solve: $4a + 7 = -49$

Step 1: $4a = -49 - 7$

$4a = -56$

Step 2: $a = \frac{-56}{4}$

$a = -14$

Check: $4(-14) + 7 = -49$

$-49 = -49$

Solve: $-3y - 4 = 11$

Step 1: $-3y = 11 + 4$

$-3y = 15$

Step 2: $y = \frac{15}{-3}$

$y = -5$

Check: $-3(-5) - 4 = 11$

$11 = 11$

Solve. Check.

1. $3x - 5 = 16$

2. $-14r - 7 = 49$

3. $25a - 4 = 96$

4. $60y - 7 = 173$

_____

5. $7x + 3 = -4$

6. $23y + 6 = 75$

7. $17a + 9 = 77$

8. $-2m + 9 = 7$

_____

9. $8a - 7 = 65$

10. $19b - 4 = 72$

11. $52x + 4 = -100$

12. $-6z + 15 = 3$

_____

13. $2r + 45 = 15$

14. $33b - 3 = 96$

15. $-75x + 5 = 230$

16. $35z + 12 = 82$

_____

33

Variables on Both Sides of Equations

Sometimes you need to rewrite an equation so that a variable is on only one side of the equation. To accomplish this, add or subtract the smallest variable term to or from both sides of the equation. Then add, subtract, multiply, or divide in order to isolate the variable.

Solve: $4x - 5 = 3x + 1$

$4x - 5 + (-3x) = 3x + 1 + (-3x)$

$x - 5 = 1$

$x - 5 + 5 = 1 + 5$

$x = 6$

Check: $4(6) - 5 = 3(6) + 1$

$19 = 19$

Solve: $3x + 5 = x + 13$

$3x + 5 - x = x + 13 - x$

$2x + 5 = 13$

$2x + 5 - 5 = 13 - 5$

$2x = 8$

$x = 4$

Check: $3(4) + 5 = 4 + 13$

$17 = 17$

Solve: $7x - 1 = 15 + 3x$

$7x - 1 - 3x = 15 + 3x - 3x$

$4x - 1 = 15$

$4x - 1 + 1 = 15 + 1$

$4x = 16$

$x = 4$

Check: $7(4) - 1 = 15 + 3(4)$

$27 = 27$

Solve. Check.

1. $8x + 4 = 5x - 11$ **2.** $2x - 1 = 4x + 3$ **3.** $3x - 5 = x - 7$ **4.** $4x + 3 = 8 - x$

_____   _____   _____   _____

5. $7x - 16 = x + 8$ **6.** $6x + 3 = 5x + 3$ **7.** $15x + 5 = 10x - 15$ **8.** $2x + 3 = x + 10$

_____   _____   _____   _____

9. $8x - 9 = 19 + x$ **10.** $3x + 6 = 8 + x$ **11.** $9x + 20 = 4x - 25$ **12.** $5x - 6 = 12 + 2x$

_____   _____   _____   _____

13. $x - 2 = 2x - 4$ **14.** $4x - 12 = 2x + 2$ **15.** $5x + 1 = 10 + 2x$ **16.** $2x - 4 = x + 8$

_____   _____   _____   _____

w

Solving Linear Equations

Find the solution for each equation. Use the properties of equality and other properties to justify each solution.

1. $2x - 3 = 9 - x$

2. $4x - 7 = x + 5$

_____

_____

3. $25 + 10(12 - x) = 5(2x - 7)$

4. $\frac{1}{2}(6x + 4) = x + 3(x + 1)$

_____

_____

5. Given the function $f(x) = 5x - 9$, find the set of values of x such that $f(x) = 6$. Justify your solution by using the properties of equality.

6. Given the functions $f(x) = -12x + 7$ and $g(x) = 4x - 9$, find the set of values of x such that $f(x) = g(x)$. Justify your solution by using the properties of equality.

_____

_____

35

Clearing Fractions

When an equation contains fractions on both sides, it is helpful to multiply both sides by a **common denominator** of the fractions. This process of eliminating fractions is called **clearing fractions.**

Solve: $\frac{x}{2} + 5 = \frac{x}{3} + 8$

$(6)\left(\frac{x}{2} + 5\right) = (6)\left(\frac{x}{3} + 8\right)$

$3x + 30 = 2x + 48$

$3x - 2x = 48 - 30$

$x = 18$

Check: $\frac{18}{2} + 5 = \frac{18}{3} + 8$

$9 + 5 = 6 + 8$

$14 = 14$

Solve: $\frac{3x}{2} + 2 = \frac{x}{2} + 4$

$(2)\left(\frac{3x}{2} + 2\right) = (2)\left(\frac{x}{2} + 4\right)$

$3x + 4 = x + 8$

$3x - x = 8 - 4$

$2x = 4$

$x = 2$

Check: $\frac{3(2)}{2} + 2 = \frac{2}{2} + 4$

$5 = 5$

Solve: $\frac{2x}{3} - 6 = \frac{x}{9} + 4$

$(9)\left(\frac{2x}{3} - 6\right) = (9)\left(\frac{x}{9} + 4\right)$

$6x - 54 = x + 36$

$6x - x = 36 + 54$

$5x = 90$

$x = 18$

Check: $\frac{2(18)}{3} - 6 = \frac{18}{9} + 4$

$6 = 6$

Solve. Check.

1. $\frac{5x}{4} + 2 = \frac{x}{4} + 7$

2. $\frac{x}{2} - 3 = \frac{x}{7} + 2$

3. $\frac{x}{5} + 7 = \frac{x}{10} + 8$

_____

_____

_____

4. $\frac{x}{3} + 5 = \frac{x}{6} - 6$

5. $\frac{x}{2} + 4 = \frac{x}{4} - 1$

6. $\frac{x}{4} + 5 = \frac{x}{8} + 6$

_____

_____

_____

7. $\frac{x}{3} - 6 = \frac{x}{9}$

8. $\frac{x}{7} + 8 = 4 + \frac{3x}{7}$

9. $\frac{2x}{3} + 12 = \frac{5x}{2} - 10$

_____

_____

_____

Equations with Parentheses

When an equation contains parentheses, simplify each side before solving the equation. When you remove parentheses, remember to multiply each term within the parentheses by the factor in front of the parentheses. If the factor is negative, the sign of each term within the parentheses must be changed when the parentheses are removed.

Solve: $5(x + 4) = 4(x + 6)$
$$5x + 20 = 4x + 24$$
$$5x - 4x = 24 - 20$$
$$x = 4$$
Check: $5(4 + 4) = 4(4 + 6)$
$$40 = 40$$

Solve: $5b - 3(4 - b) = 2(b + 21)$
$$5b - 12 + 3b = 2b + 42$$
$$5b + 3b - 2b = 42 + 12$$
$$6b = 54$$
$$b = 9$$
Check: $5(9) - 3(4 - 9) = 2(9 + 21)$
$$60 = 60$$

Solve. Check.

1. $3(x + 2) = 2(x + 5)$

2. $3x - (2x - 7) = 15$

3. $2b - 7(3 + b) = b + 3$

_____

_____

_____

4. $4(x - 3) = 2(x - 1)$

5. $7x - (x - 1) = 25$

6. $9a - 3(2a - 4) = 15$

_____

_____

_____

7. $4(x - 1) = 2(x + 4)$

8. $7 - 12(3 + b) = 31$

9. $5x - 2(4 - x) = 20$

_____

_____

_____

10. $5x + 3 = 4(x + 2)$

11. $5x - (x + 6) = 10$

12. $4(2x - 5) - 3(x + 10) = -15$

_____

_____

_____

13. $3(x - 1) = 2x + 3$

14. $3x - 1 = 2(x + 3)$

15. $3(x - 1) = 2(x + 3)$

_____

_____

_____

Writing Equations to Solve Problems

Solve.

1. The length of a building is three times the width. The perimeter is 560 feet. Find the length and width. (Hint: $2l + 2w = P$)

2. The sum of two consecutive numbers is 85. Find the numbers.

_____

3. The perimeter of a rectangular-shaped parking lot is 420 meters. The length is twice the width. Find both dimensions.

4. Three numbers added together total 180. The second number is twice the first, and the third is three times the first. Find each number.

_____

5. The length of a rectangular-shaped garden is four times the width. The perimeter is 100 feet. Find both dimensions.

6. Three numbers added together total 500. The second number is four times the first, and the third is five times the second. Find each number.

_____

7. The width of a rectangle is one-fifth as much as the length. The perimeter is 120 centimeters. Find the length and width.

8. The sum of three consecutive numbers is 42. What are the numbers?

_____

Literal Equations

1. Show and justify the steps for solving $x + a = b$ for x. Then use the literal equation's solution to obtain the solution of $x + 2 = -4$.

2. Show and justify the steps for solving $ax = b$ for x, where $a \neq 0$. Then use the literal equation's solution to obtain the solution of $3x = -15$.

3. Show and justify the steps for solving $ax = bx + c$ for x, where $a \neq b$. Then use the literal equation's solution to obtain the solution of $4x = 2x + 14$.

More Literal Equations

Solve each formula for the given variable.

1. Formula for distance traveled:
$d = rt$, for t

2. Formula for the flow of a current in an electric circuit: $V = IR$, for I

_____

3. Formula for density:
$D = \frac{m}{V}$, for V

4. Formula for the lateral surface area of a cylinder: $SA = 2\pi rh$, for r

_____

5. Formula for the surface area of a rectangular prism: $SA = 2(lw + hw + hl)$, for w

6. Formula for the area of a trapezoid:
$A = \frac{1}{2}(a + b)h$, for b

_____

40

Writing Formulas

1. An electrician sent Bonnie an invoice in the amount of a dollars for 6 hours of work that was done on Saturday. The electrician charges a weekend fee, f, in addition to an hourly rate, r. Bonnie knows what the weekend fee is. Write a formula Bonnie can use to find r, the rate the electrician charges per hour.

_____

2. The swimming pool shown is made up of a square and two semicircles. Write a formula for the perimeter P in terms of x, and then solve for x to find a formula for the side length of the square in terms of P.

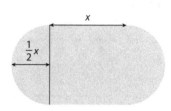

_____

3. Kai purchased a plot of land shaped like the figure shown. Write a formula he can use to find the length of the side labeled x if he knows the area, A, of his lot and n?

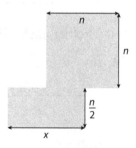

_____

Unit 3 Review

Solve. Check.

1. $a + (-25) = 75$

_____

2. $x - 37 = 94$

_____

3. $r + (-12) = 3$

_____

4. $5x = 45$

_____

5. $-15y = 105$

_____

6. $25x = 10$

_____

7. $\frac{2a}{3} = 4$

_____

8. $\frac{x}{2} = 6$

_____

9. $5x - 2x = 9$

_____

10. $5x + 6x = 1$

_____

11. $4r - 3 = 3$

_____

12. $5x + 7 = 2x + 8$

_____

13. $3m + 1 = 6m - 5$

_____

14. $\frac{3x}{4} = 7 + \frac{x}{6}$

_____

15. $\frac{5x}{2} - 10 = \frac{x}{4} - 1$

_____

16. $\frac{3x}{10} = \frac{9}{5}$

_____

17. $5y - 2(y + 2) = 5$

_____

18. $6y - 4 = 2(2y + 1)$

_____

Solve.

19. Together, Leslie and Lakita have $15.25. Lakita has $0.25 more than Leslie. How much does each have?

_____

20. Marcos is 7 years older than his sister, Rosa. The sum of their ages is 1 less than 3 times Rosa's age. How old is each?

_____

Tell whether each value of the variable is a solution of the equation $1.06p = 41.34$. Show your reasoning.

21. $p = 36$

_____

_____

22. $p = 39$

_____

_____

23. Solve for x.

$\frac{3x}{2} + 7x - 7 = 3(2x + 1)$

24. Solve the formula.

$E = \frac{1}{2}kx^2$ for k.

_____

_____

Multiplying Monomials with the Same Base

To multiply monomials that have the same base, add their exponents. For example, $(2^3)(2^2) = 2^{3+2} = 2^5$, because $(2^3)(2^2) = (2 \cdot 2 \cdot 2)(2 \cdot 2) = 2^5$. Therefore, $(a^6)(a^3) = a^{6+3} = a^9$.

When the monomials have coefficients other than 1, multiply the coefficients first.

Simplify: $s \cdot s$

$s^1 \cdot s^1 = s^{1+1}$

$= s^2$

Simplify: $(3m^4)(3m^3)$

$(3m^4)(3m^3) = (3 \cdot 3)m^{4+3}$

$= 9m^7$

Simplify: $(d^3ef)(de^4)$

$(d^3ef)(de^4) = (d^{3+1})(e^{1+4})(f^1)$

$= d^4e^5f$

Simplify.

1. $(a^3)(a^5) =$

2. $(b^3)(b^4) =$

3. $(c^5)(c^6) =$

4. $(d^3)(d^7) =$

5. $5^2 \cdot (5^3 \cdot 5^1) =$

6. $(a^3b)(ab^2) =$

7. $(m^5n)(m^2n) =$

8. $(x^6y)(xy^3) =$

9. $(abc)(a) =$

10. $(xyz)(x^2) =$

11. $(rst)(s^2) =$

12. $(def)(e^5) =$

13. $(a^3xy)(ay^2) =$

14. $(a^4bc)(ab^2) =$

15. $2(y^3 \cdot y^2) =$

16. $(b^3df^3)(b^5d) =$

17. $(7m^2n^2)(m^6n^2) =$

18. $(6a^5b^6)(3ab) =$

19. $(8b^3cd)(2b) =$

20. $(5x^2y^3)(5x^2y^3) =$

21. $(9ay)(-8y) =$

22. $(-6ab^2)(-9bc) =$

23. $(2xy^3)(6x^4) =$

24. $2mr(-6mr^6) =$

25. $(4z^5)(12yz) =$

26. $3^2(q^1 \cdot q^2) =$

27. $(-16z^3)(9yz) =$

28. $(-15r^6)(-5r^3s) =$

29. $(15x^3y^2)(2axy) =$

30. $(-10bc^3d)(-5bcd) =$

31. $(6x^3y)(-6axy) =$

32. $(8c^2d)(6abd^2) =$

43

Powers of Powers

When a base with an exponent is raised to another exponent, such as $(2^2)^3$, simplify by multiplying the two exponents. You can check the multiplication by showing the factors and adding the exponents.

Remember to multiply the exponents of *all* the factors in each expression, including coefficients. If no exponent is used, the exponent 1 is understood.

Simplify: $(2^2)^3$

$(2^2)^3 = 2^{2 \cdot 3} = 2^6 = 64$

Check:

$(2^2)^3 = (2^2 \cdot 2^2 \cdot 2^2)$

$\quad = 2^{2 + 2 + 2} = 2^6 = 64$

Simplify: $(3x^3)^3$

$(3x^3)^3 = (3^{1 \cdot 3})(x^{3 \cdot 3})$

$\quad = 3^3 x^9 = 27x^9$

Check:

$(3x^3)^3 = (3 \cdot 3 \cdot 3)(x^3 \cdot x^3 \cdot x^3)$

$\quad = 27x^{3 + 3 + 3} = 27x^9$

Simplify: $(2ab^2)^2(a^2)^3$

$(2ab^2)^2(a^2)^3 = (2^2a^2b^4)(a^6)$

$\quad = 2^2 a^{2 + 6} b^4$

$\quad = 4a^8b^4$

Simplify.

1. $(3^2)^3 =$

2. $(4^2)^2 =$

3. $(5^2)^3 =$

4. $(6^3)^2 =$

5. $(2a^4)^2 =$

6. $(3h^3)^4 =$

7. $(2n^5)^4 =$

8. $(5k^7)^3 =$

9. $(a^4b)^4 =$

10. $(st)^6 =$

11. $(xy^3z)^5 =$

12. $(m^2np)^8 =$

13. $(a^4b)^2 =$

14. $(y^2z)^2 =$

15. $(mn^4)^3 =$

16. $(p^6q)^3 =$

17. $(m^2n^4)^2 =$

18. $(p^5q^2)^2 =$

19. $(r^2s^4)^3 =$

20. $(x^4y^2)^4 =$

21. $(2c^2de^3)^2 =$

22. $(4x^3y^2z)^2 =$

23. $(2mn^5p^3)^4 =$

24. $(5r^4s^2t^3)^3 =$

Simplify.

25. $(ab^4)(a^2b)^2 =$

26. $(m^2n)(m^6n)^2 =$

27. $(j^2k^3)(j^2k^2)^3 =$

28. $(xy)^2(x^3y^2)^3 =$

29. $(mn^2)^3(m^2n^3)^4 =$

30. $(g^4h)^3(g^4h^2)^3 =$

31. $(-3y^2)^2(x^2y^2)^3 =$

32. $(7pq^3)^2(p^4q^6)^3 =$

33. $(3x)^3(xy^4)^2 =$

Dividing Monomials with the Same Base

Division is the inverse of multiplication. When monomials are multiplied, exponents of like bases are added. When monomials are divided, exponents of like bases are subtracted. Study the examples. When monomials have coefficients other than 1, remember to divide the coefficients.

Recall that expressions such as $\frac{5}{5}$ and $\frac{a}{a}$ equal 1. If you use the rule for dividing monomials, you will see why $a^0 = 1$.

$\frac{a}{a} = a^{1-1} = a^0 = 1.$

Simplify: $\frac{a^7}{a^4}$

$\frac{a^7}{a^4} = a^{7-4} = a^3$

Check:

$\frac{a^7}{a^4} = \dfrac{\overset{1}{\cancel{a}} \cdot \overset{1}{\cancel{a}} \cdot \overset{1}{\cancel{a}} \cdot \overset{1}{\cancel{a}} \cdot a \cdot a \cdot a}{\underset{1}{\cancel{a}} \cdot \underset{1}{\cancel{a}} \cdot \underset{1}{\cancel{a}} \cdot \underset{1}{\cancel{a}}}$

$= a^3$

Simplify: $\frac{b^3}{b}$

$\frac{b^3}{b} = \frac{b^3}{b^1} = b^{3-1} = b^2$

Check:

$\frac{b^3}{b} = \dfrac{\overset{1}{\cancel{b}} \cdot b \cdot b}{\underset{1}{\cancel{b}}} = b^2$

Simplify: $\frac{3c^2}{c^2}$

$\frac{3c^2}{c^2} = 3c^{2-2} = 3c^0 = 3(1) = 3$

Check:

$\frac{3c^2}{c^2} = \frac{3}{1} \cdot \dfrac{\overset{1}{\cancel{c}} \cdot \overset{1}{\cancel{c}}}{\underset{1}{\cancel{c}} \cdot \underset{1}{\cancel{c}}} = 3$

Simplify.

1. $\frac{a^4}{a^4} =$

2. $\frac{d^6}{d^3} =$

3. $\frac{b^8}{b^4} =$

4. $\frac{m^8}{m^3} =$

5. $\frac{c^9}{c^5} =$

_____ _____ _____ _____ _____

6. $\frac{x^5}{x^3} =$

7. $\frac{y^5}{y^3} =$

8. $\frac{a^6}{a^4} =$

9. $\frac{m^7}{m^2} =$

10. $\frac{s^5}{s^2} =$

_____ _____ _____ _____ _____

11. $\frac{x^2}{x} =$

12. $\frac{a^5}{a^4} =$

13. $\frac{c^7}{c^4} =$

14. $\frac{c^9}{c^3} =$

15. $\frac{m^2}{m^2} =$

_____ _____ _____ _____ _____

16. $\frac{4z}{2z} =$

17. $\frac{3a^5}{a^3} =$

18. $\frac{5e^5}{e} =$

19. $\frac{9t}{t} =$

20. $\frac{6d^4}{3d} =$

_____ _____ _____ _____ _____

21. $\frac{2x^3}{x^2} =$

22. $\frac{10a^2}{a^2} =$

23. $\frac{20b^3}{4b^2} =$

24. $\frac{2d^6}{d^4} =$

25. $\frac{3b^5}{b^4} =$

_____ _____ _____ _____ _____

26. $\frac{4a}{2} =$

27. $\frac{2y^3}{y} =$

28. $\frac{5e^6}{5e} =$

29. $\frac{6d^6}{6} =$

30. $\frac{8f^8}{2f^2} =$

_____ _____ _____ _____ _____

45

Fractions and Negative Exponents

When subtracting exponents, you may get a negative exponent. A negative exponent means that the variable will remain in the denominator.

Simplify: $\frac{x^2}{x^3}$

$\frac{x^2}{x^3} = x^{2-3} = x^{-1} = \frac{1}{x}$

Check:

$\frac{x^2}{x^3} = \frac{\overset{1}{\cancel{x}} \cdot \overset{1}{\cancel{x}}}{\underset{1}{x} \cdot \underset{1}{\cancel{x}} \cdot \cancel{x}} = \frac{1}{x}$

Simplify: $\frac{18y^2}{9y^4}$

$\frac{18y^2}{9y^4} = \frac{18}{9}(y^{2-4})$

$= 2 \cdot y^{-2} = 2 \cdot \frac{1}{y^2} = \frac{2}{y^2}$

Check:

$\frac{18y^2}{9y^4} = \frac{18}{9} \cdot \frac{\overset{1}{\cancel{y}} \cdot \overset{1}{\cancel{y}}}{y \cdot y \cdot \underset{1}{\cancel{y}} \cdot \underset{1}{\cancel{y}}}$

$= 2 \cdot \frac{1}{y \cdot y} = \frac{2}{y^2}$

Simplify: $\frac{-30x}{15x^3}$

$\frac{-30x}{15x^3} = \frac{-30}{15} \cdot x^{1-3}$

$= -2 \cdot x^{-2} = \frac{-2}{x^2}$

Check:

$\frac{30x}{15x^3} = \frac{-30}{15} \cdot \frac{\overset{1}{\cancel{x}}}{\underset{1}{\cancel{x}} \cdot x \cdot x}$

$= -2 \cdot \frac{1}{x \cdot x} = \frac{-2}{x^2}$

Simplify.

1. $\frac{x^3}{x^8} =$

2. $\frac{y^2}{y^3} =$

3. $\frac{a^2}{a^5} =$

4. $\frac{b}{b^2} =$

5. $\frac{s^2}{s^4} =$

_____ _____ _____ _____ _____

6. $\frac{x^4}{x^6} =$

7. $\frac{a^3}{a^4} =$

8. $\frac{y^2}{y^7} =$

9. $\frac{b^9}{b^{10}} =$

10. $\frac{d^{12}}{d^{14}} =$

_____ _____ _____ _____ _____

11. $\frac{-y}{y^2} =$

12. $\frac{-x^2}{x^6} =$

13. $\frac{-z}{z^3} =$

14. $\frac{-r^3}{r^5} =$

15. $\frac{-d}{d^4} =$

_____ _____ _____ _____ _____

16. $\frac{15c}{5c^2} =$

17. $\frac{21x}{7x^3} =$

18. $\frac{27b}{3b^4} =$

19. $\frac{-18r^2}{8r^3} =$

20. $\frac{12e^2}{2e^4} =$

_____ _____ _____ _____ _____

21. $\frac{12x^4}{6x^5} =$

22. $\frac{15y}{5y^2} =$

23. $\frac{6a^4}{a^8} =$

24. $\frac{10b^2}{2b^6} =$

25. $\frac{27z^2}{9z^5} =$

_____ _____ _____ _____ _____

Simplify using a negative exponent.

26. $\frac{-12a^2}{4a^3} =$

27. $\frac{16b^4}{-4b^6} =$

28. $\frac{-18x^3}{2x^9} =$

29. $\frac{-90r^2}{10r^4} =$

30. $\frac{-14z^3}{-7z^4} =$

_____ _____ _____ _____ _____

Reducing Algebraic Fractions to Lowest Terms

Algebraic fractions can be reduced to lowest terms. First, reduce the fraction formed by the coefficients to lowest terms. Then divide the like bases.

Remember, when dividing, subtract the exponents.

Reduce: $\dfrac{20x^3y}{5x^2y^2}$

$\dfrac{20x^3y}{5x^2y^2} = \dfrac{20}{5} \cdot x^{3-2} \cdot y^{1-2}$

$= 4x^1 \cdot y^{-1} = 4x \cdot \dfrac{1}{y} = \dfrac{4x}{y}$

Reduce: $\dfrac{a^2b^3c}{a^3b^5}$

$\dfrac{a^2b^3c}{a^3b^5} = a^{2-3} \cdot b^{3-5} \cdot c$

$= a^{-1} \cdot b^{-2} \cdot c^1 = \dfrac{1}{a} \cdot \dfrac{1}{b^2} \cdot c$

$= \dfrac{c}{ab^2}$

Reduce: $\dfrac{8rst^3}{16st^2}$

$\dfrac{8rst^3}{16st^2} = \dfrac{8}{16} \cdot r^1 \cdot s^{1-1} \cdot t^{3-2}$

$= \dfrac{1}{2} \cdot r^1 \cdot s^0 \cdot t^1 = \dfrac{rt}{2}$

Remember, $s^0 = 1$.

Simplify.

1. $\dfrac{x^3y^2}{x^2y^2} =$

2. $\dfrac{a^2b^2}{a^3b} =$

3. $\dfrac{a^4b^2}{a^2b^4} =$

4. $\dfrac{x^6y^3z}{x^4yz^2} =$

5. $\dfrac{xy^3z^6}{x^2y^2z^4} =$

6. $\dfrac{6x^2y^4}{2x^3y^2} =$

7. $\dfrac{12x^3y^5}{3x^4y^2} =$

8. $\dfrac{8ab^2c^3}{16a^2b^2c^3} =$

9. $\dfrac{25a^3b^2c^3}{5ab^2c^3} =$

10. $\dfrac{6a^4b^2c}{24a^2b^3c^4} =$

11. $\dfrac{15x^3y}{-5x^3y^2} =$

12. $\dfrac{-5x^2y}{10xy^2} =$

13. $\dfrac{16x^4y}{-4x^3y^2} =$

14. $\dfrac{10x^3y^2}{-5x^4y} =$

15. $\dfrac{-8xy^5}{24x^2y^3} =$

16. $\dfrac{4ab^2}{-20a^3b} =$

17. $\dfrac{-15x^2y^3}{5x^3y^2} =$

18. $\dfrac{-24x^2y^4}{6x^4y^2} =$

19. $\dfrac{7a^3b^2}{-35a^2b^3} =$

20. $\dfrac{-48xy^2z^3}{8x^3y^2z} =$

21. $\dfrac{-15xy}{-5x^2y^2} =$

22. $\dfrac{-6xy^3z^5}{-36x^2y^2z^4} =$

23. $\dfrac{-7x^4y^3}{-14x^2y^4} =$

24. $\dfrac{-16a^3b^4}{-8a^4b^3} =$

25. $\dfrac{-35ab^3}{-7a^2b} =$

26. $\dfrac{8a^2y}{12ay^2} =$

27. $\dfrac{16xy^2}{10x^3y} =$

28. $\dfrac{12ab^2c}{18a^2bc} =$

29. $\dfrac{10ab^2c^3}{15a^3b^2c} =$

30. $\dfrac{14a^4b^2c}{12a^3b^3c^3} =$

Name _____ Date _____

Adding Binomials

A **binomial** is the sum or difference of two monomials. An example of a binomial is $5a + bc$ or $4x^2 - 2y$. To add two binomials together, group the like terms and add their coefficients.

Add: $(a + b) + (a - b)$

$= (a + a) + (b - b)$

$= 2a + 0$

$= 2a$

Add: $(5a + 3b) + (3a - b)$

$= (5a + 3a) + (3b - b)$

$= 8a + 2b$

Add: $(8xy - 2y) + (-5y)$

$= 8xy + (-2y + -5y)$

$= 8xy + (-7y)$

$= 8xy - 7y$

Add.

1. $(4a - 2b) + (4a + 2b) =$

2. $(3x - y) + (3x + y) =$

3. $(6m - 7n) + (4m - 7n) =$

4. $(5y + 4z) + (3y - 3z) =$

5. $(6x - 3y) + (x + 4y) =$

6. $(2ab - a) + (-2ab + a) =$

7. $(-7a + b) + (-3a - b) =$

8. $(9r - s) + (4r - s) =$

9. $(6m - n) + (-3m + 3n) =$

10. $(r + 5st) + (r + st) =$

11. $(4b - 3cd) + (-3b - cd) =$

12. $(-6xy - 8z) + (-8z - 6xy) =$

13. $(7x + 2y) + (-3y + x) =$

14. $(cd + d) + (cd + d) =$

15. $(7ab - 6yz) + (-9yz + 3ab) =$

16. $(5m - 6n) + (-2m - n) =$

17. $(xy - x) + (x - xy) =$

18. $(18p - 19q) + (10p - 14q) =$

19. $(xyz + z) + (xyz - z) =$

20. $(-rst + t) + (6rst + 6t) =$

21. $(6ab - abc) + (ab + 6abc) =$

22. $(7y - yz) + (7y - yz) =$

23. $(10xy - z) + (xy - 10z) =$

24. $(5ab - abc) + (5ab - abc) =$

Unit 4
Core Skills Algebra

Subtracting Binomials

Recall that subtracting is the same as adding the opposite. To subtract a binomial, add its opposite. Do this by first changing the sign of each term of the binomial being subtracted. Then group the like terms and add.

Subtract: $(x + y) - (2x + y)$

$= (x + y) + (-2x - y)$

$= (x - 2x) + (y - y)$

$= -x + 0$

$= -x$

Subtract: $(x + y) - (-3x + y)$

$= (x + y) + (3x - y)$

$= (x + 3x) + (y - y)$

$= 4x + 0$

$= 4x$

Subtract: $(-7rs - 5t) - (5rs + t)$

$= (-7rs - 5t) + (-5rs - t)$

$= (-7rs - 5rs) + (-5t - t)$

$= -12rs + (-6t)$

$= -12rs - 6t$

Subtract.

1. $(x + y) - (x - y) =$

2. $(2a + 4b) - (3a - b) =$

3. $(8m + 6n) - (7m - 5n) =$

4. $(x - y) - (x + y) =$

5. $(3a - b) - (6a + 2b) =$

6. $(10m - n) - (6m + 2n) =$

7. $(x - y) - (-x + y) =$

8. $(b - 4c) - (-3b - c) =$

9. $(-6r - 2s) - (-r - 3s) =$

10. $(3a - 2cd) - (2b + 3cd) =$

11. $(6m + 2np) - (3m - 5np) =$

12. $(8rs - t) - (6t + 5rs) =$

13. $(-2x + yz) - (x - 5yz) =$

14. $(6pq - 4rs) - (6pq - 4rs) =$

15. $(-7rs - 5t) - (5t + rs) =$

16. $(8x - 5yz) - (-x - 4yz) =$

17. $(7x + 5wy) - (-2x + 3wy) =$

18. $(-8mn + 6p) - (-5mn + 6p) =$

19. $(-4 + xyz) - (5 + xyz) =$

20. $(4p - 5qt) - (-5qt + 4p) =$

21. $(-t + rs) - (t - rs) =$

22. $(10z + xyz) - (10xyz + z) =$

23. $(3abc - c) - (2abc + c) =$

24. $(rst - 2rs) - (3rst - 4rs) =$

Simplifying Polynomials with Exponents

A **polynomial** is an expression that can be written as a sum of monomials. A binomial is one kind of polynomial. Simplifying polynomials with exponents is done by adding and subtracting like terms. Like terms must have the same variables raised to the same exponents.

Remember, to subtract terms in parentheses, add the opposite. Be sure to change the sign of each term within the parentheses. Then group like terms and add.

Simplify:

$3x^2 + 5y + 2x^2 + y$

$= (3x^2 + 2x^2) + (5y + y)$

$= 5x^2 + 6y$

Simplify:

$8x^3 - 5y^2 - (3x^3 + 2y^2 + y)$

$= 8x^3 - 5y^2 + (-3x^3 - 2y^2 - y)$

$= (8x^3 - 3x^3) + (-5y^2 - 2y^2) - y$

$= 5x^3 - 7y^2 - y$

Simplify:

$2x^4 + 3x^3 - (-6x^4) + 2$

$= (2x^4 + 6x^4) + 3x^3 + 2$

$= 8x^4 + 3x^3 + 2$

Simplify.

1. $4x^3 + 3y^2 + 3x^3 + 4y^2 =$

_____

2. $5a^2 + 4b^2 + 3a^2 + 5b^2 =$

_____

3. $b^2 + 9c^2 + 4b^2 + 3c^2 =$

_____

4. $9m^2 + n - (m^2 + 6n^2) =$

_____

5. $5x^2 + 3y - (3x^2 + 5y) =$

_____

6. $9a^2 + 4b - (6a^2 + 7b) =$

_____

7. $5b^2 - 7b - (3b^2 - 9b) =$

_____

8. $7m^2 - 3n^4 - (4m^2 - 7n^4) =$

_____

9. $4x^2 - 5y - (3x^2 - 2y) =$

_____

10. $9x^3 - 4y^2 - (-x^3 - 3y^2) =$

_____

11. $5a^3 - 4b^2 - (-3a^3 - 5b^2) =$

_____

12. $8b^3 - 7b^2 - (-b^3 - b^2) =$

_____

13. $-4m^2 - 3m - (-4m^2 - 2m) =$

_____

14. $-5x^2 + 4y^3 - (3x^2 + 2y^3) =$

_____

15. $-6x + 9y^2 - (-6x - 2y^2) =$

_____

16. $-(8a^3 + 7a^2 + a) + 3a^2 =$

_____

17. $-(4b^3 - 5b^2) + b^3 - b^2 + b =$

_____

18. $-(9m + 9m^2) + 3m^2 + 3m =$

_____

19. $-(3 + 2x^2 + 4x^4) - (4x^4) =$

_____

20. $-(c^2 - b^2) + c^2 + b^2 + 1 =$

_____

21. $-(-4 - x^2) - (-2 + 4x^2 + x) =$

_____

22. $-3x^4 + 3x^2 - (3x^4 + x^3) =$

_____

23. $-(15m - 6m^2) + (-5m + 4m) =$

_____

24. $-(7a^4 - 7a^4) + 3a^4 + 9a^4 =$

_____

50

Multiplying Algebraic Fractions

Algebraic fractions are multiplied in exactly the same way as fractions with integers. Simplify whenever possible. Then multiply the numerators and multiply the denominators. When negative numbers are multiplied, remember the following rule.

Rule: The product of two factors with the same sign is positive. The product of two factors with different signs is negative.

Solve: $\dfrac{x}{a} \cdot \dfrac{a}{b}$

$$\dfrac{x}{\cancel{a}} \cdot \dfrac{\cancel{a}^{1}}{b} = \dfrac{x}{b}$$

Solve: $\dfrac{-x^2}{a^2} \cdot \dfrac{a}{b}$

$$\dfrac{-x^2}{a^2} \cdot \dfrac{a}{b} = \dfrac{-x^2}{a \cdot \cancel{a}} \times \dfrac{\cancel{a}^{1}}{b}$$
$$= \dfrac{-x^2}{ab}$$

Solve: $\dfrac{-2xy}{a^2} \cdot \dfrac{-a^4}{x^2}$

$$= \dfrac{-2\cancel{x}y}{\cancel{a} \cdot \cancel{a}} \cdot \dfrac{-(\cancel{a} \cdot \cancel{a} \cdot a \cdot a)}{x \cdot \cancel{x}}$$
$$= \dfrac{(-2y)}{1} \cdot \dfrac{(-a^2)}{x} = \dfrac{2a^2y}{x}$$

Simplify.

1. $\dfrac{p}{q} \cdot \dfrac{q}{p} =$

_____

2. $\dfrac{x}{2a} \times \dfrac{2a}{9y} =$

_____

3. $\dfrac{3x^2}{4b} \cdot \dfrac{40y}{x^2} =$

_____

4. $\dfrac{x^2}{4} \times \dfrac{4a}{2x} =$

_____

5. $\dfrac{a^2}{x^3} \cdot \dfrac{1}{a} =$

_____

6. $\dfrac{6a^2}{x^3} \times \dfrac{12x^3}{b} =$

_____

7. $\dfrac{-4b^2}{x} \cdot \dfrac{2x^5}{b} =$

_____

8. $\dfrac{-9a^2}{y} \times \dfrac{6y}{15a} =$

_____

9. $\dfrac{-15c}{6b^2} \cdot \dfrac{12b^3}{5c} =$

_____

10. $\dfrac{-5x^2}{12a} \times \dfrac{-6x}{10a} =$

_____

11. $\dfrac{-9a^3}{4x^2} \cdot \dfrac{-8x^4}{3a} =$

_____

12. $\dfrac{5a}{-6x^2} \times \dfrac{3x^3}{-10a^2} =$

_____

13. $\dfrac{4ab}{c} \cdot \dfrac{c}{2a} =$

_____

14. $\dfrac{3y^2z}{4x} \times \dfrac{2xz}{9y^2} =$

_____

15. $\dfrac{p}{pq^2} \cdot \dfrac{pq^2}{p^2} =$

_____

16. $\dfrac{a+b}{c} \times \dfrac{c}{a+b} =$

_____

17. $\dfrac{3(x+y)}{x-y^2} \cdot \dfrac{2(x-y^2)}{3} =$

_____

18. $\dfrac{5}{a^2+b^2} \times \dfrac{-(a^2+b^2)}{10x} =$

_____

Unit 4
Core Skills Algebra

Dividing Algebraic Fractions

To divide fractions with integers, multiply by the reciprocal of the second fraction. Use this same method for algebraic fractions. Remember to simplify when possible.

Solve: $\dfrac{3a^2}{x} \div \dfrac{3a}{x^2}$

$= \dfrac{\overset{a}{\cancel{3a^2}}}{\cancel{x}} \cdot \dfrac{\overset{x}{\cancel{x^2}}}{\underset{1}{\cancel{3a}}} = ax$

Solve: $\dfrac{2x^2y}{3} \div 4a$

$= \dfrac{\overset{1}{\cancel{2x^2y}}}{3} \cdot \dfrac{1}{\underset{2}{\cancel{4a}}} = \dfrac{x^2y}{6a}$

Solve: $\dfrac{a+b}{2} \div \dfrac{a+b}{4}$

$= \dfrac{\overset{1}{\cancel{(a+b)}}}{\underset{1}{\cancel{2}}} \cdot \dfrac{\overset{2}{\cancel{4}}}{\underset{1}{\cancel{(a+b)}}} = 2$

Simplify.

1. $\dfrac{x^2}{a} \div \dfrac{x^4}{a^2} =$

_____

2. $\dfrac{m}{n^3} \div \dfrac{m^3}{n} =$

_____

3. $\dfrac{z^4}{b^2} \div \dfrac{z}{b^3} =$

_____

4. $\dfrac{2x^2y}{3} \div \dfrac{4xy^2}{15} =$

_____

5. $\dfrac{6ab}{7xy} \div \dfrac{18a^2b^2}{28x^2y^2} =$

_____

6. $\dfrac{15x^2y}{9ab} \div \dfrac{5xy^2}{3ab} =$

_____

7. $\dfrac{2xy}{9} \div 4 =$

_____

8. $\dfrac{5ab}{6x} \div 10 =$

_____

9. $\dfrac{9x^2y^2}{ab} \div 3 =$

_____

10. $\dfrac{10x^2y}{3} \div 5xy =$

_____

11. $\dfrac{9a^2b^2}{6} \div 3ab =$

_____

12. $\dfrac{3ab^3}{2} \div 6b^2 =$

_____

13. $\dfrac{-12a^3}{5} \div 4 =$

_____

14. $\dfrac{-15x^2y}{2} \div 5xy =$

_____

15. $\dfrac{-16xy^2}{3} \div 4xy =$

_____

16. $\dfrac{18a^2}{5} \div \dfrac{1}{10} =$

_____

17. $\dfrac{15x^2y}{4} \div \dfrac{1}{2} =$

_____

18. $\dfrac{21a^3b^2}{5} \div \dfrac{3}{20} =$

_____

19. $\dfrac{a+b}{2} \div \dfrac{2(a+b)}{4a} =$

_____

20. $\dfrac{a-b}{4a} \div \dfrac{a-b}{8} =$

_____

21. $\dfrac{a^2+b^2}{6} \div \dfrac{a^2+b^2}{12x} =$

_____

52

Multiplying Polynomials by Monomials

To multiply a polynomial by a monomial, multiply each term of the polynomial by the monomial.

Remember:

- When like bases are multiplied, add the exponents.
- Use the rules for products of negative and positive numbers.

Simplify: $a(a + b)$

$= (a \cdot a) + (a \cdot b)$

$= a^2 + ab$

Simplify: $2a^2(a + b + 2c)$

$= (2a^2 \cdot a) + (2a^2 \cdot b) + (2a^2 \cdot 2c)$

$= 2a^3 + 2a^2b + 4a^2c$

Simplify: $-2xy(5x^2 + 2y)$

$= (-2xy \cdot 5x^2) + (-2xy \cdot 2y)$

$= -10x^3y - 4xy^2$

Simplify.

1. $x(x + y) =$

2. $y(2x + y) =$

3. $x^3(x + 2y) =$

4. $2x(x + y) =$

5. $3x(2x + 3y) =$

6. $6a^3(2a - b) =$

7. $-2b(2a + b) =$

8. $-2b(3a + b) =$

9. $-3b^3(-4a + 3b) =$

10. $4x(x^2 + y) =$

11. $2b(2b^2 - a^2) =$

12. $-5c^2(-3c^3 - 4) =$

13. $2x(3x - 5y - 2z) =$

14. $-2y(-2x + 3y - 4z) =$

15. $3b^2(5a + 4b - 2c) =$

16. $4b(4a^2 - 5b^2 - 3c^2) =$

17. $-2b(7a - 3b^4 - 1) =$

18. $-3c^2(-4c^2 - 3c + 2) =$

19. $2xy(5x - 2y + 3z) =$

20. $xz(x + y - z) =$

21. $-2ab^2(-4a - 4b - 4) =$

22. $-xyz(5x - 3y + 4z) =$

23. $2abc(a^2 + b^2 + c^2) =$

24. $-4xy^2z(xy + yz) =$

53

Multiplying Binomials

When multiplying two binomials, each term in the second binomial must be multiplied by each term in the first binomial. Then add the products.

Find the product: $(x + 3)(x - 2)$

$x(x - 2) + 3(x - 2)$

$x^2 - 2x + 3x - 6$

$x^2 + x - 6$

Classify each expression as a *monomial, binomial, trinomial,* or *polynomial*. Use the most descriptive term.

1. $3x^2$

2. $3x^2 - 4$

3. $18x^3 + 5x^2 - 2x + 29$

4. $x - 12$

5. $4x + x^2 + 1$

6. $y^2 + 17$

Find each product.

7. $(x + 2)(x + 3)$

8. $(x + 7)(x + 11)$

9. $(x + 4)^2$

10. $(x - 1)(x + 1)$

11. $(2x + 13)(x - 6)$

12. $(2x - 5)(3x + 1)$

13. $(3x - 8)^2$

14. $(9x - 7)(9x + 7)$

Dividing Polynomials by Monomials

When dividing a polynomial by a monomial, divide each term of the polynomial by the monomial. Divide each term separately.

Remember, when dividing, subtract exponents of like bases.

Simplify: $\dfrac{x^2 + xy}{x}$

$= \dfrac{x^2}{x} + \dfrac{xy}{x}$

$= x^{2-1} + (x^{1-1}y)$

$= x + y$

Simplify:

$\dfrac{-6a^3 + 12a^2 - 9a}{3a}$

$= \dfrac{-6a^3}{3a} + \dfrac{12a^2}{3a} - \dfrac{9a}{3a}$

$= -2a^2 + 4a - 3$

Simplify:

$\dfrac{-9a^3y + 12a^2y^2 - 6ay^3}{-3ay}$

$= \dfrac{-9a^3y}{-3ay} + \dfrac{12a^2y^2}{-3ay} + \dfrac{-6ay^3}{-3ay}$

$= 3a^2 - 4ay + 2y^2$

Divide.

1. $\dfrac{a^2 + a}{a} =$

2. $\dfrac{6xy - 4z}{2} =$

3. $\dfrac{8xy + 6xy}{2x} =$

4. $\dfrac{10ab + 15ac + 20ad}{5a} =$

5. $\dfrac{18x^2 + 24xy + 16xz}{2x} =$

6. $\dfrac{6a^2y + 12ay^2 + 18ay^3}{6a} =$

7. $\dfrac{-4a^2 + 10a + 2}{2} =$

8. $\dfrac{12x^4 - 16x^3 - 24x^2}{4x^2} =$

9. $\dfrac{-25x^3 - 20x^2 + 15x}{5x} =$

10. $\dfrac{9x^4 + 15x^3 + 21x^2}{-3x^2} =$

11. $\dfrac{18a^3y + 24a^2y^2 + 30ay^3}{-6ay} =$

12. $\dfrac{10x^2y + 15xy^2 + 20y^2}{-5y} =$

13. $\dfrac{-12x^3 - 9x^2 - 15x}{-3x} =$

14. $\dfrac{-16a^4 - 24a^3 - 16a^2}{-8a} =$

15. $\dfrac{-24x^3y - 12x^2y^2 - 18xy^3}{-6xy} =$

16. $\dfrac{4x^2y + 12xy - 8xy^2}{2xy} =$

17. $\dfrac{-15x^3y + 12x^2y^2 - 18xy^3}{-3xy} =$

18. $\dfrac{-18c^2d - 24c^2d^2 + 12cd^3}{-6cd} =$

Identifying Common Monomial Factors

If one factor of a number is known, division can be used to find another factor. For example, since 3 is a factor of 24, divide 24 by 3 to find another factor, 8. Similarly, if one factor of a polynomial is known, divide to find another factor.

The **common monomial factor** of a polynomial is a monomial that is a factor of all the terms in the polynomial. In the example below, the common factors are 3 and a, since 3 and a are factors of each term. The common monomial factor of the entire polynomial is $3a$. To find the other factor, divide the polynomial by $3a$.

Find the common monomial factor of $12ab - 6ac + 3ad$. Since 3 and a are factors of each term, the common monomial factor is $3a$. Divide by $3a$.

$$\frac{12ab - 6ac + 3ad}{3a} = 4b - 2c + d \qquad \text{The two factors are } 3a \text{ and } 4b - 2c + d.$$

Write the polynomial as the product of the monomial and a polynomial.

$$12ab - 6ac + 3ad = 3a(4b - 2c + d)$$

Find the common monomial factor. Divide to find another factor. Then write the polynomial as the product of the monomial and a polynomial.

1. $7mn - 14mp - 21mq =$

2. $5x^3 - 10x^2 + 15x =$

3. $4ax + 8ay - 12az =$

4. $6a^3b - 12a^2b^2 + 18ab^3 =$

5. $10x^3 + 8x^2 - 2x =$

6. $9a^2b^2 + 6ab + 15 =$

7. $8x^2y + 4xy - 12xy^2 =$

8. $10x^3 - 12x^2 - 6x =$

9. $20a^3b - 15a^2b^2 + 10ab^3 =$

10. $16xy^3 - 12x^2y^2 + 20x^2y^3 =$

11. $3a^2 - 15a^3y + 18a^4y^2 =$

12. $20ab^3 - 15a^2b^2 - 25a^3b =$

Multiplying Polynomials by Binomials

Multiplying binomials by binomials may be thought of as multiplying a binomial by two monomials. Parentheses are often used to show multiplication of binomials. Multiply each term of the first binomial by each term of the second binomial. Combine like terms. Two polynomials are multiplied in the same way as two binomials.

Remember, when multiplying different variables, put them in the product in alphabetical order. This will make it easier to find like terms.

Multiply:
$(4a + 3b)(2a + b)$

$= 4a(2a + b) + 3b(2a + b)$

$= 8a^2 + 4ab + 6ab + 3b^2$

$= 8a^2 + 10ab + 3b^2$

Multiply:
$(x - y^2)(x - y^2)$

$= x(x - y^2) - y^2(x - y^2)$

$= x^2 - xy^2 - xy^2 + y^4$

$= x^2 - 2xy^2 + y^4$

Multiply:
$(a + c)(a + b + c)$

$= a(a + b + c) + c(a + b + c)$

$= a^2 + ab + ac + ac + bc + c^2$

$= a^2 + ab + 2ac + bc + c^2$

Multiply.

1. $(a + b)(a + b) =$

2. $(-ab + c)(-ab - c) =$

3. $(2x + y)(2x + y) =$

4. $(3a - 2b)(3a - 2b) =$

5. $(x^2y - z)(xy + z) =$

6. $(-2c + d)(c + 2d) =$

7. $(x - 4y)(-3x - 2y) =$

8. $(-a + 2b)(a - 2b) =$

9. $(-2abc + d)(3a - 4) =$

10. $(-y - 2z)(y - 2z) =$

11. $(3a - 4b)(a + 3b) =$

12. $(-6x + 2y)(6x - y) =$

13. $(xy + z)(xy + z) =$

14. $(2ab - c)(4ab - 3c) =$

15. $(3xy^4 + y^3)(4x^3y - x) =$

16. $(ac + b - d)(a^2 - c) =$

17. $(2x - y)(x - y + z) =$

18. $(gk - 2k - m)(g - 2k) =$

19. $(x + y)(2x^2 - x + 1) =$

20. $(2d^2 + h - 2w)(3h + d) =$

21. $(4x^2 - 2xy - y^2)(x - y) =$

Dividing Polynomials by Binomials

Polynomials are divided by binomials in much the same way that numbers are divided. Look at the first example. Divide the first term of the dividend (a^2) by the first term of the divisor (a). The result is a. Place the a in the quotient, multiply both terms of the divisor by a, and subtract. Bring down the next term and continue dividing until the remainder is zero.

Divide.

$$
\begin{array}{r}
a + b \\
a + b \overline{\smash{)}a^2 + 2ab + b^2} \\
\underline{a^2 + ab} \downarrow \\
ab + b^2 \\
\underline{ab + b^2} \\
0
\end{array}
$$

Divide.

$$
\begin{array}{r}
a - b \\
a - b \overline{\smash{)}a^2 - 2ab + b^2} \\
\underline{a^2 - ab} \downarrow \\
-ab + b^2 \\
\underline{-ab + b^2} \\
0
\end{array}
$$

Divide.

$$
\begin{array}{r}
x + 3 \\
2x + 7 \overline{\smash{)}2x^2 + 13x + 21} \\
\underline{2x^2 + 7x} \downarrow \\
6x + 21 \\
\underline{6x + 21} \\
0
\end{array}
$$

Divide.

1. $a - 2b \overline{\smash{)}a^2 - 4ab + 4b^2}$

2. $x - y \overline{\smash{)}x^2 - 2xy + y^2}$

3. $a + 2b \overline{\smash{)}a^2 + 4ab + 4b^2}$

4. $x - 5 \overline{\smash{)}x^2 - 4x - 5}$

5. $3x - 2y \overline{\smash{)}9x^2 - 12xy + 4y^2}$

6. $5a + 2b \overline{\smash{)}25a^2 + 20ab + 4b^2}$

7. $5 + x \overline{\smash{)}25 + 10x + x^2}$

8. $4 + 2x \overline{\smash{)}16 + 16x + 4x^2}$

9. $2x + 3y \overline{\smash{)}4x^2 + 12xy + 9y^2}$

Multiplying and Dividing Polynomials

Multiply.

1. $2b(3b^2 - 4b + 6) =$

2. $3xy(4x^2 - 2xy - 3y^2) =$

3. $4x^2(10 + 3y^2) =$

_____

4. $(x + 2)(x^2 - 3x + 5) =$

5. $(2a + 3b)(2a^2 - 3ab + b^2) =$

6. $(2x - 1)(3x^3 - 2x^2 - x) =$

_____

7. $3x - 2(2x^2 - 5x) =$

8. $3x(2x^2 - 5x + 4) - 2 =$

9. $2(6 + 2a - 3a^2) - 12 =$

_____

10. $3(x - y + z)(x + y + z) =$

11. $(6x^2 - x)(2y + 3)3y =$

12. $7b(-4b^2) + 3b(b^2 + 2b) =$

_____

Divide:

13. $\dfrac{x^2 + 4x}{x} =$

14. $\dfrac{6x^2 + 3x}{3x} =$

15. $\dfrac{2y^2 - 4y}{2y} =$

_____

16. $\dfrac{2x(x + 2x)}{2x^2} =$

17. $\dfrac{6y(3y^2 - xy + x^2y)}{y^2} =$

18. $\dfrac{xy(12 + 9x - 6x^2)}{3x} =$

_____

19. $x + 1\overline{)x^2 + 3x + 2} =$

20. $6x - 6\overline{)6x^2 - 24x + 18} =$

21. $3 - 2x\overline{)6 + 5x - 6x^2} =$

_____

59

Unit 4 Review

Simplify.

1. $(cd^3)(c^2) =$

_____

2. $(-5xy^3)(5x^5y) =$

_____

3. $(xy^3z^4)^3 =$

_____

4. $\dfrac{m^9}{m^3} =$

_____

5. $\dfrac{-8a^3b^2c}{12ab^2c^3} =$

_____

6. $(xy - x) + (5xy + 3x) =$

_____

7. $(-b - 4) - (b + 2) =$

_____

8. $-(15m^2 + 6m^3) - (-5m) =$

_____

9. $\dfrac{4ab}{6a} \cdot \dfrac{3b}{2ab} =$

_____

10. $\dfrac{3x^2y}{z} \cdot \dfrac{z^2}{3} =$

_____

11. $\dfrac{-12x^3}{5} \div 4x =$

_____

12. $\dfrac{x^2 - x}{x} =$

_____

13. $\dfrac{10xy + 4z}{2} =$

_____

14. $\dfrac{16a^4 - 12a^2 - 4a}{4a} =$

_____

15. $x(x - y) =$

_____

16. $-2y(-2x^2 + y + 3) =$

_____

17. $(3a + 4b)(a - 6b) =$

_____

18. $(a^2 + b^2 + 3)(ab - b) =$

_____

19. $(2x + 1)(x + 3) =$

_____

20. $(7x - 1)(3x - 5) =$

_____

21. $(12x - 5)(3x + 6) =$

_____

Divide.

22. $x + 1 \overline{)x^2 - x - 2}$

_____

23. $x + 2y \overline{)x^2 + 4xy + 4y^2}$

_____

24. $2x - 3y \overline{)4x^2 - 12xy + 9y^2}$

_____

Find the common monomial factor. Divide to find another factor. Then write the polynomial as the product of the monomial and a polynomial.

25. $12az - 8bz + 16cz =$

26. $9fy + 15gy - 27y =$

_____

_____

Cumulative Review

Solve.

1. $5(a + 3) = 25$

2. $5x = 135$

3. $\frac{2s}{3} = 16$

_____

_____

_____

4. $3(a + 3b) - (a + 2b) =$

5. $-3y^2 + 2y^3 - (5x^2 + 7y^2) =$

6. $(4a^2x)^2 =$

_____

_____

_____

Simplify.

7. $3a(2b^3 + c^2) =$

8. $\frac{-125rs^5}{-25s^3} =$

9. $\frac{a}{4} + \frac{3a}{4} - \frac{1}{2} =$

_____

_____

_____

10. $\frac{-15a^4b^{10}c^6}{-3ab^2c^3} =$

11. $\frac{3a}{4} \div \frac{9a^4}{16} =$

12. $\frac{4ab^2}{3} \div \frac{12a^2b^2}{a} =$

_____

_____

_____

13. $\frac{10x^3}{(a + b)} \cdot \frac{6(a + b)}{20x^2} =$

14. $(4a + 2b)(3a - b + b^2) =$

15. $\frac{-9a^3}{x^4} \cdot \frac{3x^4}{a} =$

_____

_____

_____

16. $\frac{-24x^2y - 20y^4z^6 + 10y}{-2y} =$

17. $5x - 6\overline{)5x^2 + 9x - 18} =$

18. $(5q - 7)(3q + 5) =$

_____

_____

_____

Solve.

19. The sum of three consecutive numbers is 279. Find the numbers.

20. Find the length of a rectangular prism with a height of 2 feet, width of 3 feet, and volume of 30 cubic feet.

_____

_____

21. Write an algebraic expression for the following phrase: The price of a meal plus a 15% tip for the meal. Simplify if possible.

22. Write and simplify an equation or inequality for this situation: Jacob can afford to spend at most $50 for a birthday dinner at a restaurant, including a 20% tip.

_____

_____

Functions and Relations

A pair of numbers such as (*x*, *y*) is called an **ordered pair.** In an ordered pair, the *x*-value is always given first. A **relation** is a set of ordered pairs. The *x*-values in a relation make up the **domain,** and the *y*-values make up the **range.** A **function** is a relation in which each *x*-value has only one *y*-value.

Identify the domain and range of the relation {(3, 4), (−1, 2), (−2, 4)}.

The domain is {−1, −2, 3}.
The range is {2, 4}.

Is this relation a function?
{(7, 8), (−1, 5), (2, 6), (−1, 3)}

No, because the *x*-value −1 has more than one *y*-value.

Identify the domain and range for each relation.

1. {(0, −3), (2, 5), (−4, 2)}

Domain: _____

Range: _____

2. {(−9, 1), (3, 1), (0, 3)}

Domain: _____

Range: _____

3. {(9, −5), (−1, −2), (−3, −5), (1, −2)}

Domain: _____

Range: _____

4. {(4, −1), (−8, −1), (−4, −1), (8, −1)}

Domain: _____

Range: _____

5. {(6, 2), (0, −4), (1, −3), (4, 0)}

Domain: _____

Range: _____

6. {(1, 3), (−1, 1), (−4, −2), (3, 5)}

Domain: _____

Range: _____

Determine whether each of the following relations is a function.

7. {(0, 23), (2, 5), (24, 2)} _____

8. {(0, 28), (0, 22), (25, 1)} _____

9. {(1, 26), (3, 4), (21, 26), (6, 7)} _____

10. {(4, 21), (5, 21), (4, 6), (7, 8)} _____

Relations

1. Make a two-column table. List the numbers of Set A from least to greatest in the first column. List the numbers of Set B from least to greatest in the second column.

Set A
3 0 5
4 1 2

Set B
4 6 2
3 5 7

2. If *n* represents any number in Set A, what expression represents the number that it is related to in Set B?

_____

Use the relation {(-2, -6), (-1, -3), (0, 0), (1, 3), (2, 6), (3, 9)} for Exercises 3 and 4.

3. What is the domain of the relation? What is the range of the relation?

_____

_____

4. Draw a mapping diagram to show the relation.

Graph points to represent each relation.

5. **Domain   Range**

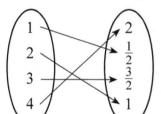

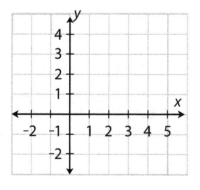

6. $\{(1, -\frac{1}{2}), (2, -1), (3, -\frac{3}{2}), (4, -2)\}$

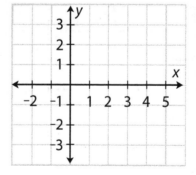

Unit 5
Core Skills Algebra

Representing Functions

Tell whether each pairing of numbers describes a function. If so, identify the domain and the range. If not, explain why not.

1. Each whole number from 0 to 9 is paired with its opposite.

   _____

2. Each odd number from 3 to 9 is paired with the next greater whole number.

   _____

3. The whole numbers from 10 to 12 are paired with their factors.

   _____

4. Each even number from 2 to 10 is paired with half the number.

   _____

5. {(36, 6), (49, 7), (64, 8), (81, 9), (36, –6), (49, –7), (64, –8), (81, –9)}

   _____

6. {(–64, –4), (–27, –3), (–8, –2), (–1, –1), (0, 0), (1, 1), (8, 2), (27, 3), (64, 4)}

   _____

7. Whitley has a $5 gift card for music downloads. Each song costs $1 to download. The amount of money left on the card can be represented by the function $M(d) = 5 - d$, where d is the number of songs she has downloaded.

   a. Make a table and graph the function.

d	$M(d)$	$(d, M(d))$

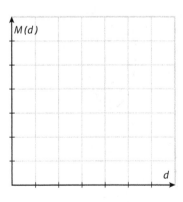

   b. Identify the domain and range of the function and the units of the independent and dependent variables.

   _____

   _____

Equations with Two Variables

The equation $x + 2y = 15$ has two variables and many solutions. To find a solution, choose a value to substitute for one of the variables, then solve the equation for the other variable. Each solution may be written as an ordered pair in the form (x, y).

Solve: $x + 2y = 15$ when $x = 7$

$$7 + 2y = 15$$
$$2y = 15 - 7$$
$$2y = 8$$
$$\frac{2y}{2} = \frac{8}{2}$$
$$y = 4$$

The equation $x + 2y = 15$ is true when x is 7 and y is 4, so (7, 4) is a solution.

Solve: $x + 2y = 15$ when $y = 9$

$$x + 2(9) = 15$$
$$x + 18 = 15$$
$$x = 15 - 18$$
$$x = -3$$

The equation $x + 2y = 15$ is true when x is -3 and y is 9, so (-3, 9) is a solution.

Solve each equation using the given value of x or y. Write the ordered pair which makes the equation true.

1. $x + 2y = 10$ when $x = 0$

2. $x + 2y = 10$ when $y = 3$

3. $x + 2y = 10$ when $x = 2$

_____

_____

_____

4. $2x + 2y = 4$ when $y = 0$

5. $2x + 2y = 4$ when $y = 2$

6. $2x + 2y = 4$ when $x = 4$

_____

_____

_____

7. $x + y = -1$ when $x = 3$

8. $x + y = -1$ when $x = -1$

9. $x + y = -1$ when $y = 4$

_____

_____

_____

65

Unit 5
Core Skills Algebra

Discrete Linear Functions

Andrea receives a $40 gift card to use at a town pool. It costs her $8 per visit to swim. A function relating the value of the gift card, *v*, to the number of visits, *n*, is $v(n) = 40 - 8n$.

1. Graph the function. Label axes and scales.

2. What is the initial value of the gift card?

   _____

3. What is the constant difference in the value of the card before and after she uses it to swim?

   _____

4. Identify the domain and the range of the function.

   _____

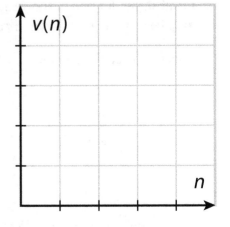

5. Is the function a discrete linear function? Are its outputs an arithmetic sequence? Why or why not?

   _____

   _____

   _____

Myrta earns $2 per chore. A function relating the money she earns, *m*, to the number of chores, *n*, is $m(n) = 2n$.

6. Graph the function for $n = 1$ through $n = 5$.

7. Identify the range of the function using set notation.

   _____

   _____

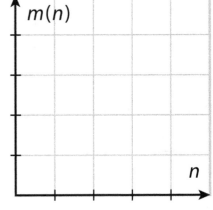

8. Is the function a discrete linear function? Are its outputs an arithmetic sequence? Why or why not?

   _____

   _____

   _____

Finding Intercepts

The **y-intercept** of a line is the point $(0, y)$, where the line crosses the y-axis. To find the y-intercept, substitute 0 for x in the linear equation and solve for y. Likewise, the **x-intercept** is the point $(x, 0)$, where the line crosses the x-axis. To find the x-intercept, substitute 0 for y and solve for x.

Find the y-intercept of
$y = 4x - 7$.

Let $x = 0$.

$y = 4(0) - 7$

$y = -7$

The y-intercept is -7.
The ordered pair is $(0, -7)$.

Find the x-intercept of
$y = 3x + 6$.

Let $y = 0$.

$0 = 3x + 6$

$-6 = 3x$

$-2 = x$

The x-intercept is -2.
The ordered pair is $(-2, 0)$.

At what points does the line
$y = 2x - 8$ cross the x- and
y-axes?

Let $x = 0$.   Let $y = 0$.

$y = 2(0) - 8$ $0 = 2x - 8$

$y = -8$ $8 = 2x$

                        $4 = x$

The y-intercept is -8.
The x-intercept is 4.

The graph crosses the x-axis at $(4, 0)$ and the y-axis at $(0, -8)$.

Find the x- and y-intercepts.

1. $y = x + 1$

2. $y = 2x - 4$

3. $y = -2x + 6$

_____   _____   _____

At what points does each line cross the x- and y-axes?

4. $y = x - 3$

5. $y = 4x - 3$

6. $y = ^-x + 5$

_____   _____   _____

Continuous Linear Functions

1. The functions $f(x)$ and $g(x)$ are defined by the table and graph below.

x	$f(x)$
0	-2
1	1
2	4
3	7
4	10
5	13

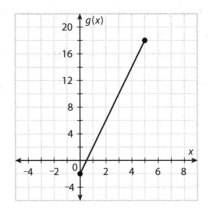

a. Compare the domains, initial values, and ranges of the functions.

_____

_____

_____

b. Explain why the functions are linear. Tell whether each function is *discrete* or *continuous*.

_____

_____

_____

2. Grace works between 10 and 20 hours per week while attending college. She earns $9.00 per hour. Her hours are rounded to the nearest quarter hour. Her roommate Frances also has a job. Her pay for t hours is given by the function $f(t) = 10t$, where $5 \leq t \leq 15$. Her hours are not rounded.

a. Find the domain and range of each function.

_____

_____

_____

b. Compare their hourly wages and the amount they each earn per week.

_____

_____

_____

Writing Linear Functions

Write each linear function, *f(x)*, using the given information.

1. The graph of the function has a slope of 4 and a *y*-intercept of 1.

   _____

2. The graph of the function has a slope of 0 and a *y*-intercept of 6.

   _____

3. The graph of the function has a slope of $-\frac{2}{3}$ and a *y*-intercept of 5.

   _____

4. The graph of the function has a slope of $\frac{7}{4}$ and a *y*-intercept of 0.

   _____

5.

x	f(x)
-3	8
0	5
3	2

   _____

6.

x	f(x)
0	-3
2	0
4	3

   _____

7.

x	f(x)
1	-1
2	5
3	11

   _____

8.

x	f(x)
5	-2
10	-6
15	-10

   _____

9.

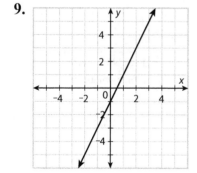

   _____

10.

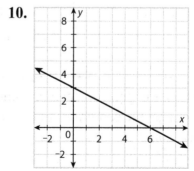

   _____

Interpreting Linear Graphs

1. The graph shows the amount of gas remaining in the gas tank of Mrs. Liu's car as she drives at a steady speed for 2 hours. How long can she drive before her car runs out of gas?

   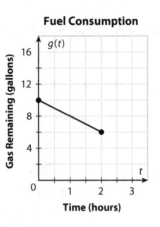

   Fuel Consumption

   a. Interpret the question by describing what aspect of the graph would answer the question.

   _____

   _____

   b. Write a linear function whose graph includes the segment shown.

   _____

   _____

   c. Describe how to use the function to answer the question, and then answer the question.

   _____

2. Jamal and Nathan exercise by running one circuit of a basically circular route that is 5 miles long and takes them past each other's home. The two boys run in the same direction, and Jamal passes Nathan's home 12 minutes into his run. Jamal runs at a rate of 7.5 miles per hour while Nathan runs at a rate of 6 miles per hour. If the two boys start running at the same time, when, if ever, will Jamal catch up with Nathan before completing his run?

   a. Identify the independent and dependent variables, how they are measured, and how you will represent them.

   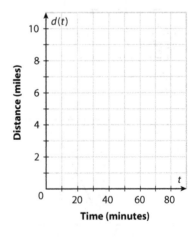

   _____

   _____

   _____

   b. Write distance-run functions for Jamal and Nathan.

   _____

   c. Graph the functions, find the intersection point, and check the point against the conditions of the problem to answer the question.

   _____

70

Linear Functions and Their Inverses

Find the inverse, $g(x)$, of each function.

1. $f(x) = x - 1$

_____

2. $f(x) = \text{-}x + 4$

_____

3. $f(x) = 2x - 3$

_____

4. $f(x) = \frac{2}{3}x + 6$

_____

5. $f(x) = 3x - \frac{3}{4}$

_____

6. $f(x) = -\frac{5}{2}x - \frac{15}{2}$

_____

7. The formula to convert a temperature F measured in degrees Fahrenheit to a temperature C measured in degrees Celsius is $C = \frac{9}{5}(F - 32)$. You can think of this formula as function $C(F)$. Find the inverse function $F(C)$ and describe what it does.

_____

8. A cylindrical candle 10 inches tall burns at rate of 0.5 inch per hour.

a. Write a rule for the function $h(t)$, the height (in inches) of the candle at time t (in hours since the candle was lit). State the domain and range of the function.

_____

b. Find the inverse function $t(h)$. State the domain and range of the function.

_____

c. Explain how the inverse function is useful.

_____

_____

9. Prove that the inverse of a non-constant linear function is another non-constant linear function by starting with the general linear function $f(x) = mx + b$ where $m \neq 0$ and showing that the inverse function $g(x)$ is also linear. Identify the slope and y-intercept of the graph of $g(x)$.

_____

10. Can a constant function have an inverse function? Why or why not?

_____

_____

71

Sequences

Write the first four terms of each sequence. Assume that the domain of the function is the set of consecutive integers starting with 1.

1. $f(n) = (n - 1)^2$

_____

2. $f(n) = n + \frac{1}{n} + 3$

_____

3. $f(n) = 4(0.5)^n$

_____

4. $f(n) = \sqrt{n - 1}$

_____

5. $f(1) = 2$ and $f(n) = f(n - 1) + 10$ for $n \geq 2$ _____

6. $f(1) = 16$ and $f(n) = \frac{1}{2}f(n - 1)$ for $n \geq 2$ _____

7. $f(1) = 1$ and $f(n) = 2f(n - 1) + 1$ for $n \geq 2$ _____

8. $f(1) = f(2) = 1$ and $f(n) = f(n - 2) - f(n - 1)$ for $n \geq 3$ _____

9. Each year for the past 4 years, Donna has gotten a raise equal to 5% of the previous year's salary. Her starting salary was $40,000.

    a. Complete the table to show Donna's salary over time.

    b. Write a recursive rule for the sequence in the table. Assume that the domain of the function is the set of consecutive integers starting with 0, so the first term of the sequence is $f(0)$.

Year (position number)	Salary ($) (term of sequence)
0	$40,000
1	
2	
3	
4	

_____

_____

    c. What is $f(7)$, rounded to the nearest whole number? What does $f(7)$ represent in this situation?

_____

_____

Write the 12th term of each sequence. Assume that the domain of the function is the set of consecutive integers starting with 1.

10. $f(n) = 3n - 2$

_____

11. $f(n) = 2n(n + 1)$

_____

More Sequences

1. The diagram shows the first four figures in a pattern of dots.

Figure (position number)	Number of dots (term of sequence)
1	1
2	
3	
4	
5	

   a. Draw the next figure in the pattern.

   b. Use the pattern to complete the table.

   c. Write an explicit rule for the sequence in the table. Assume that the domain of the function is the set of consecutive integers starting with 1.

   _____

   d. How many dots will be in the 10th figure of the pattern?

   _____

Write an explicit rule for each sequence. Assume that the domain of the function is the set of consecutive integers starting with 1.

2.

n	f(n)
1	6
2	7
3	8
4	9
5	10

3.

n	f(n)
1	3
2	6
3	9
4	12
5	15

4.

n	f(n)
1	1
2	$\frac{1}{2}$
3	$\frac{1}{3}$
4	$\frac{1}{4}$
5	$\frac{1}{5}$

_____   _____   _____

Write a recursive rule for each sequence. Assume that the domain of the function is the set of consecutive integers starting with 1.

5.

n	f(n)
1	8
2	9
3	10
4	11
5	12

6.

n	f(n)
1	2
2	4
3	8
4	16
5	32

7.

n	f(n)
1	27
2	24
3	21
4	18
5	15

_____   _____   _____

Operations with Linear Functions

1. Given $f(x) = -2x$ and $g(x) = 4x - 8$, find $h(x) = f(x) + g(x)$.

   _____

2. Given $f(x) = 3x - 5$ and $g(x) = -2x + 1$, find $h(x) = f(x) - g(x)$.

   _____

3. Given $f(x) = -2$ and $g(x) = 5x - 6$, find $h(x) = f(x) \cdot g(x)$.

   _____

4. Given $f(x) = 4$, $g(x) = x + 1$, and $h(x) = x$, find $j(x) = f(x) \cdot [g(x) + h(x)]$.

   _____

5. To raise funds, a club is publishing and selling a calendar. The club has sold $500 in advertising and will sell copies of the calendar for $20 each. The cost of printing each calendar is $6. Let c be the number of calendars to be printed and sold.

   a. Write a rule for the function $R(c)$, which gives the revenue generated by the sale of the calendars.

   _____

   b. Write a rule for the function $E(c)$, which gives the expense of printing the calendars.

   _____

   c. Describe how the function $P(c)$, which gives the club's profit from the sale of the calendars, is related to $R(c)$ and $E(c)$. Then write a rule for $P(c)$.

   _____

6. The five winners of a radio station contest will spend a day at an amusement park with all expenses paid. The per-person admission cost is $10, and each person can spend $20 on food. The radio station will pay for all rides, which cost $2 each. Assume that each person takes the same number r of rides.

   a. Write a rule for the function $C(r)$, which gives the cost per person.

   _____

   b. Write a rule for the function $P(r)$, which gives the number of people.

   _____

   c. Describe how the function $T(r)$, which gives the radio station's total cost, is related to $C(r)$ and $P(r)$. Then write a rule for $T(r)$.

   _____

Name _____ Date _____

Unit 5 Review

Identify the domain and the range for each relation. Then tell whether the relation is a function.

1. $\{(-6, 4), (0, 6), (2, 0)\}$

Domain: _____

Range: _____

Function? _____

2. $\{(4, -1), (-1, 3), (-4, 1), (-4, 5)\}$

Domain: _____

Range: _____

Function? _____

Solve each equation using the given value of x or y. Write the ordered pair which makes the equation true.

3. $2x + y = 4$ when $x = 3$

_____

4. $5x - 2y = 2$ when $x = 2$

_____

5. $x + y = -2$ when $y = 3$

_____

6. The cost of sending m text messages at $0.25 per message can be represented by the function $C(m) = 0.25m$. Graph the function by graphing the ordered pairs. Use the scale 1–5 on the horizontal axis and the scale 0, 0.25, 0.5, 0.75, and 1 on the vertical axis.

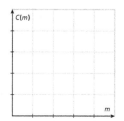

7. Avocados cost $1.50 each. Green beans cost $1.50 per pound. The total cost of a avocados is $C(a) = 1.5a$ and the total cost of g pounds of green beans is $C(g) = 1.5g$. Complete tables to find a few values for each function. Then graph each function.

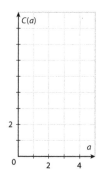 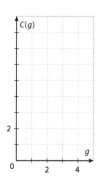

Write a linear function for each description.

8.

x	$f(x)$
-1	5
3	-3
7	-11

_____

9. The slope of the line is 3 and the y-intercept is -1.

_____

Write the inverse function for each function.

10. $f(x) = \frac{1}{2}x - 1$ _____

11. $f(x) = 2x + 1$ _____

12. Write the first four terms of the sequence with $f(1) = 3$ and $f(n) = f(n - 1) + 2$ for $n \geq 2$.

_____

75

Graphing Solutions

You can graph solutions to equations with two variables.

Graph the solutions to $2x - y = 6$, when $x = 0, 1, 3,$ and 4.

Substitute each value for x into the equation and then solve for y. Write each solution in a table. Plot each coordinate pair solution on the coordinate graph.

Find y when $x = 0$.

$$2(0) - y = 6$$
$$0 - y = 6$$
$$y = -6$$

Find y when $x = 1$.

$$2(1) - y = 6$$
$$2 - y = 6$$
$$y = -4$$

Find y when $x = 3$.

$$2(3) - y = 6$$
$$6 - y = 6$$
$$y = 0$$

Find y when $x = 4$.

$$2(4) - y = 6$$
$$8 - y = 6$$
$$y = 2$$

x	y
0	-6
1	-4
3	0
4	2

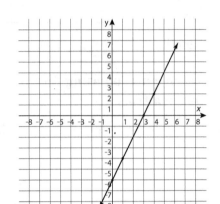

Complete each table of solutions to the given equation. Graph each solution.

1. $3x + 4y = 12$

x	y
-4	___
0	___
4	___
8	___

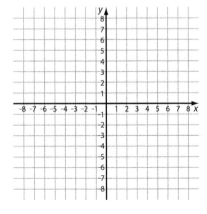

2. $3x - 3y = 15$

x	y
-2	___
0	___
5	___
2	___

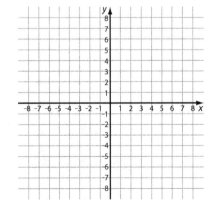

3. $y = 4 - 2x$

x	y
0	___
___	0
1	___
___	-2

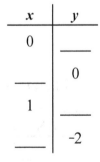
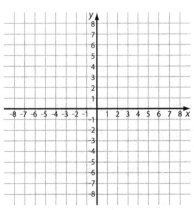

76

Linear Equations in Two Variables

Tell whether each ordered pair is a solution to the equation.

1. $-5x + 2y = 4$; $(4, 8)$ _____

2. $2x - 7y = 1$; $(11, 3)$ _____

Complete each table and graph each equation.

3. $-2x + y = 3$

x	y

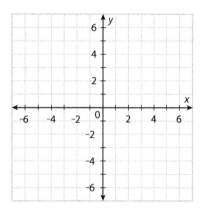

4. $3x = -6$

x	y

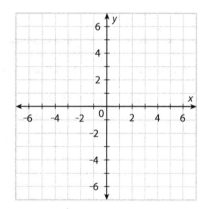

5. $4x + 5y = 0$

x	y
0	
	-4
-5	

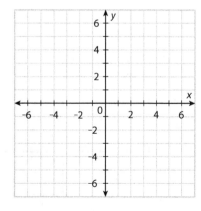

Graphing Linear Equations

For the 2-variable equations that we have studied, the graphs of all the solutions lie on a line. For this reason, equations of this type are called **linear equations.** To graph a linear equation, begin by choosing a value to substitute for either x or y. Then solve for the other variable. Repeat this process to find three or more ordered-pair solutions. Finally, graph the solutions and draw the line through those points.

Draw a graph of the solutions to the equation $x - 2y = 6$.

Select values of x and find the corresponding values of y. Try starting with $x = 0$. Make a table like the one below.

x	y
0	-3
2	-2
6	0

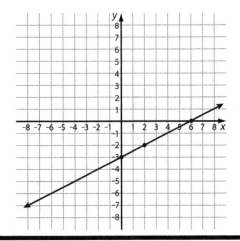

Plot the points and draw a straight line through them to show the graph of the solutions.

Make a table of 3 solutions. Graph each solution. Draw a straight line through the points.

1. $4x - y = 4$

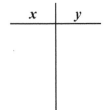

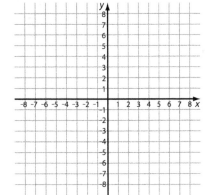

2. $2x + 3y = 6$

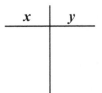

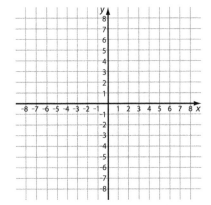

3. $x + y = -8$

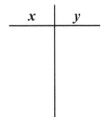

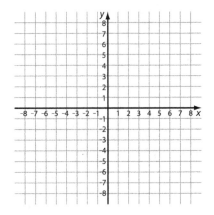

78

Name _____ Date _____

Using Slope

1. Calculate the rate of change of the function in the table. _____

Tickets for rides	10	12	14	16
Total cost of carnival ($)	12.50	14.00	15.50	17.00

Estimate the change in the dependent variable over the given interval from the domain of the independent variable. Estimate the rate of change.

2.

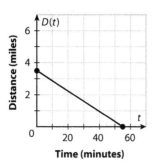

Given interval: $20 \leq t \leq 40$

Change in $D(t)$: _____

Rate of change: _____

3.

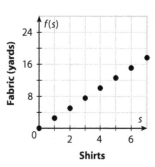

Given interval: $3 \leq s \leq 5$

Change in $f(s)$: _____

Rate of change: _____

Graph each linear function and answer the question. Explain your answer.

4. A plumber charges $50 for a service call plus $75 per hour. The total of these costs (in dollars) is a function $C(t)$ of the time t (in hours) on the job. For how many hours will the cost be $200? $300?

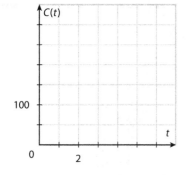

_____

_____

_____

_____

5. A bamboo plant is 10 centimeters tall at noon and grows at a rate of 5 centimeters every 2 hours. The height (in centimeters) is a function $h(t)$ of the time t it grows. When will the plant be 20 centimeters tall?

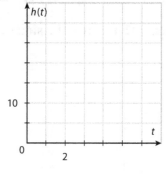

_____

_____

_____

_____

79

The Slope-Intercept Form

The **slope-intercept form** of the equation of a line is $y = mx + b$, where m is the **slope** and b is the **y-intercept.** The y-intercept of a graph is the point where the line crosses the y-axis. The ordered pair for the y-intercept is $(0, y)$.

To graph a linear equation using the slope-intercept form, first make sure the equation is in the slope-intercept form. Determine the slope and the y-intercept. Plot the y-intercept as $(0, y)$ and use the slope to plot another point. Then draw a line connecting the two points.

Remember, the slope formula is the ratio of the vertical change to the horizontal change.

$$\text{slope} = \frac{\text{rise}}{\text{run}} = \frac{y_2 - y_1}{x_2 - x_1}$$

Graph the equation

$y = \frac{1}{2}x + 3.$

$y = mx + b$

y-intercept: $b = 3$

slope: $m = \frac{1}{2}$

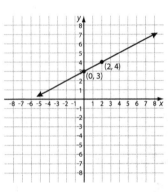

Plot the y-intercept as $(0, 3)$. Since the slope is $\frac{1}{2}$, move up 1 and right 2 and mark the point. Draw the line connecting the two points.

Graph the equation

$1 = 3x + y.$

First, put the equation in slope-intercept form.

$y = -3x + 1$

y-intercept:

$b = 1$

slope: $m = -3$

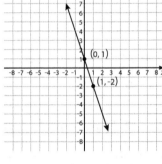

Plot the y-intercept as $(0, 1)$. Since the slope is -3 or $-\frac{3}{1}$, move down 3 and right 1 and mark the point. Draw the line connecting the two points.

Graph each equation using the slope-intercept form.

1. $y = \frac{2}{3}x - 2$

2. $y + \frac{1}{3}x = 4$

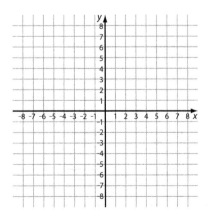

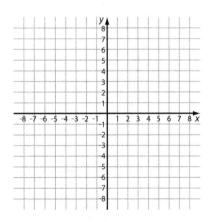

80

Graphing Slope-Intercept Form

Graph each linear function.

1. $f(x) = 3x - 4$

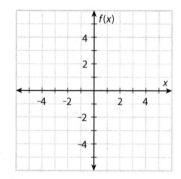

2. $f(x) = -\frac{1}{2}x + 2$

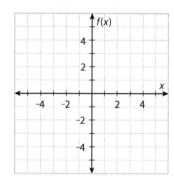

3. $f(x) = -1$

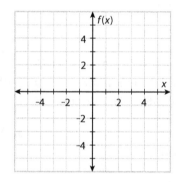

4. $f(x) = \frac{4}{3}x$

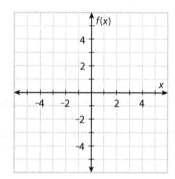

5. $f(x) = \frac{1}{4}x - 3$

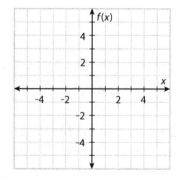

6. $f(x) = -5x + 1$

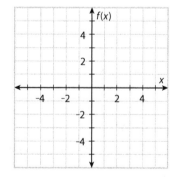

Changing the values of *m* and *b* in *f(x)* = *mx* + *b*

1. A salesperson earns a base monthly salary of $2,000 plus a 10% commission on sales. The salesperson's monthly income *I* (in dollars) is given by the function $I(s) = 0.1s + 2000$, where *s* is the sales (in dollars) that the salesperson makes. Sketch a graph to illustrate each situation using the graph of $I(s) = 0.1s + 2000$ as a reference.

   a. The salesperson's base salary is increased to $2,100.

   b. The salesperson's commission rate is decreased to 5%.

   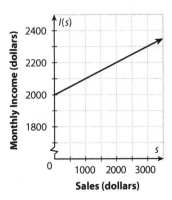

2. Mr. Resnick is driving at a speed of 40 miles per hour to visit relatives who live 100 miles away from his home. His distance *d* (in miles) from his destination is given by the function $d(t) = 100 - 40t$, where *t* is the time (in hours) since his trip began. Sketch a graph to illustrate each situation.

   a. He increases his speed to 50 miles per hour.

   b. He encounters a detour that increases the driving distance to 120 miles.

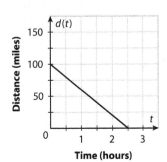   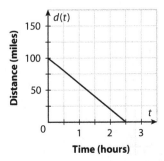

3. Use the graph of $d(t) = 100 - 40t$ in Exercise 2 to identify the domain and range of the function. Then tell whether the domain, the range, neither, or both are affected by the changes described in each part.

   _____

   _____

Exploring Transformations

Given a linear function $f(x) = mx + b$, you can create new linear functions by using a constant k in combination with the rule for $f(x)$. For instance, you can create the functions $g(x) = f(x) + k$ and $h(x) = f(kx)$. The graph of each of these new functions is geometrically related to the graph of f through transformations.

For Exercises 1 and 2, use the following information.

Consider the function $f(x) = x + 1$ as well as the related functions $g(x) = f(x) + 2$ and $h(x) = f\left(\frac{x}{2}\right)$. In the case of g, adding 2 is performed on the *output* of f. In the case of h, dividing by 2 is performed on the *input* of f. Each of these cases is illustrated below using -2, 0, and 2 as a few sample inputs of f.

Input of f	Output of f			Input of f	Output of f
		Input of g	Output of g		
				Input of h	Output of h

Input of f → Output of f → (+2) Input of g → Output of g:
-2 → -1 → 1
0 → 1 → 3
2 → 3 → 5

Input of f → (÷2) → Output of f / Input of h → Output of h:
-4 → -2 → -1
0 → 0 → 1
4 → 2 → 3

1. The graphs of f and g are shown along with arrows to indicate what happened to the points on the graph of f with x-coordinates -2, 0, and 2. The graph of g is a *vertical translation* of the graph of f. Is the slope or the y-intercept of f affected by the vertical translation? Show that this is true by writing the rule for $g(x) = f(x) + 2$.

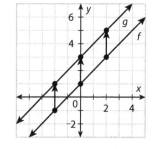

_____

2. The graphs of f and h are shown along with arrows to indicate what happened to the points on the graph of f with x-coordinates -2, 0, and 2. The graph of h is a *horizontal stretch* of the graph of f by a factor of 2. Is the slope or the y-intercept of f affected by the horizontal stretch? Show that this is true by writing the rule for $h(x) = f\left(\frac{x}{2}\right)$.

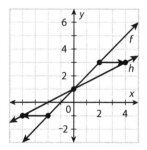

_____

83

Graphing Quadratic Equations

Graph each quadratic function.

1. $f(x) = 3x^2$

2. $f(x) = -\frac{3}{4}x^2$

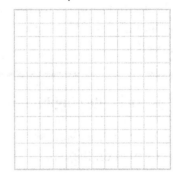

3. $f(x) = 0.6x^2$

4. $f(x) = -1.5x^2$

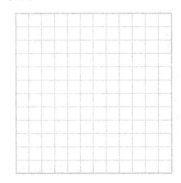

5. $f(x) = \frac{1}{5}x^2$

6. $f(x) = -2.5x^2$

7. $f(x) = 4x^2$

8. $f(x) = -0.2x^2$

Unit 6
Core Skills Algebra

Stretching, Shrinking, and Reflecting the Graph of $f(x) = x^2$

Write the equation for each quadratic function based on the graph shown.

1.
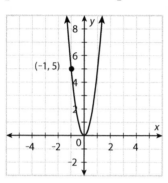

_____

2.
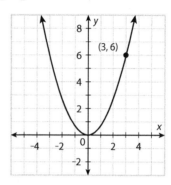

_____

3.
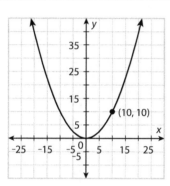

_____

4.
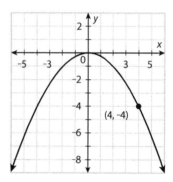

_____

5. A quadratic function has a *minimum value* when the function's graph opens up, and it has a *maximum value* when the function's graph opens down. In each case, the minimum or maximum value is the y-coordinate of the vertex of the function's graph. Under what circumstances does the function $f(x) = ax^2$ have a minimum value? A maximum value? What is the minimum or maximum value in each case?

_____

_____

6. A function is called *even* if $f(-x) = f(x)$ for all x in the domain of the function. Show that the function $f(x) = ax^2$ is even for any value of a.

_____

_____

More Graphing Quadratic Equations

Graph each quadratic function.

1. $f(x) = x^2 + 4$

2. $f(x) = x^2 - 5$

3. $f(x) = (x - 2)^2$

4. $f(x) = (x + 3)^2$

5. $f(x) = (x - 5)^2 - 2$

6. $f(x) = (x - 1)^2 + 1$

7. $f(x) = (x + 4)^2 + 3$

8. $f(x) = (x + 2)^2 - 4$

Translating the Graph of $f(x) = x^2$

Write a rule for each quadratic function based on the graph shown.

1.

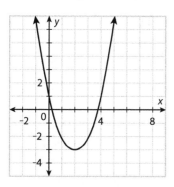

_____

2.

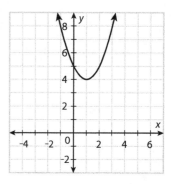

_____

3.

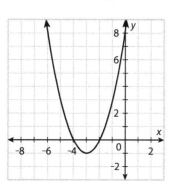

_____

4.

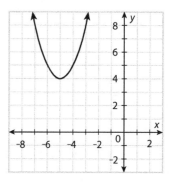

_____

Determine the domain and range of each function.

5. $f(x) = (x - 3)^2$

_____

_____

6. $f(x) = x^2 + 4$

_____

_____

7. $f(x) = (x + 5)^2$

_____

_____

8. $f(x) = x^2 - 7$

_____

_____

9. $f(x) = (x + 1)^2 - 6$

_____

_____

10. $f(x) = (x - 2)^2 + 8$

_____

_____

11. A function is called *even* if $f(-x) = f(x)$ for all x in the domain of the function. For instance, if $f(x) = x^2$, then $f(-x) = (-x)^2 = x^2 = f(x)$. In other words, you get the same value when you square $-x$ as you do when you square x. So, $f(x) = x^2$ is an even function.

a. Is $f(x) = x^2 - 1$ an even function? Explain.

_____

b. Is $f(x) = (x - 1)^2$ an even function? Explain.

_____

Combining Transformations of the Graph of $f(x) = x^2$

Graph each quadratic function.

1. $f(x) = 2(x - 2)^2 + 3$

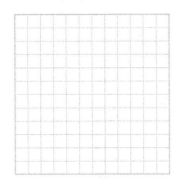

2. $f(x) = -(x - 1)^2 + 2$

3. $f(x) = \frac{1}{2}(x - 2)^2$

4. $f(x) = -\frac{1}{3}x^2 - 3$

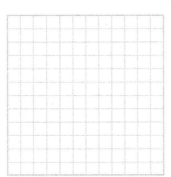

5. A roofer working on a roof accidentally drops a hammer, which falls to the ground. The hammer's height above the ground (in feet) is given by a function of the form $f(t) = a(t - h)^2 + k$ where t is the time (in seconds) since the hammer was dropped.

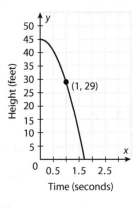

Because $f(t)$ is a quadratic function, its graph is a parabola. Only the portion of the parabola that lies in Quadrant I and on the axes is shown because only nonnegative values of t and $f(t)$ make sense in this situation. The vertex of the parabola lies on the vertical axis.

a. Use the graph to find an equation for $f(t)$.

_____

b. Explain how you can use the graph's t-intercept to check the reasonableness of your equation.

_____

_____

Writing Quadratic Functions in Vertex Form

Graph each function by first writing it in vertex form. Then give the maximum or minimum of the function and identify its zeros.

1. $f(x) = x^2 - 6x + 9$

_____

2. $f(x) = x^2 - 2x - 3$

_____

3. $f(x) = -7x^2 - 14x$

_____

4. $f(x) = 3x^2 - 12x + 9$

_____

5. $f(x) = -x^2 - 4x - 5$

_____

6. $f(x) = x^2 + 4x + 5$

_____

Graphing Functions of the Form $f(x) = ax^2 + bx + c$

Write the rule for each quadratic function in the form you would use to graph it. Then graph the function.

1. $f(x) = x^2 + 4x + 3$

_____

2. $f(x) = x^2 - 6x + 11$

_____

3. $f(x) = -x^2 + 2x - 2$

_____

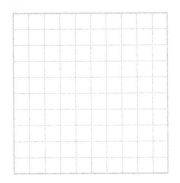

4. $f(x) = \frac{1}{2}x^2 - 4x + 5$

_____

5. A model rocket is launched from a 12-foot platform with an initial upward velocity of 64 feet per second.

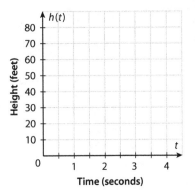

   a. Write a quadratic function in standard form that models the height of the rocket.

   _____

   b. Write the quadratic function in vertex form that models the height of the rocket.

   _____

   c. Graph the function.

   d. State the domain and range of the function in the context of the situation.

_____

Unit 6
Core Skills Algebra

Unit 6 Review

Graph each equation or function.

1. Make a table of 3 solutions and graph the solution by drawing a straight line through the points of $2x + y = 8$.

x	y

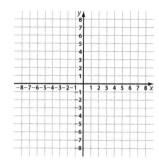

2. $x + 3y = 9$

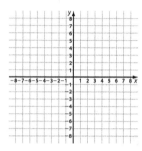

3. $f(x) = -\frac{2}{3}x + 4$

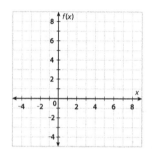

4. A pitcher with a maximum capacity of 4 cups contains 1 cup of apple juice concentrate. A faucet is turned on filling the pitcher at a rate of 0.25 cup per second. The amount of liquid in the pitcher (in cups) is a function $A(t)$ of the time t (in seconds) that the water is running.

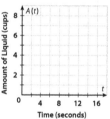

A gym charges a one-time joining fee of \$50 and then a monthly membership fee of \$25. The total cost, C, of being a member of the gym is given by the function $C(t) = 25t + 50$, where t is the time (in months) since joining the gym. For each situation described below, use the given graph of the function as a reference.

5. The gym decreases its one-time joining fee to \$25. What change would you make to the original graph?

_____

6. The gym increases its membership fee to \$30. What change would you make to the original graph?

_____

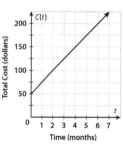

7. Graph the function: $f(x) = x^2 + 2$

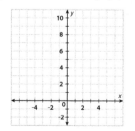

8. Write the equation for this quadratic function.

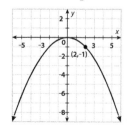

_____

91

Solving Linear Systems by Graphing

Solve each system by graphing. Check your answer.

1. $x - y = -2$
   $2x + y = 8$

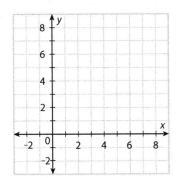

2. $x - y = -5$
   $2x + 4y = -4$

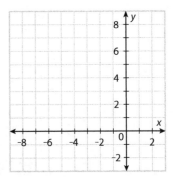

3. $x + 2y = -8$
   $-2x - 4y = 4$

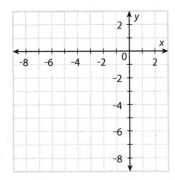

4. $2x + y = 1$
   $y = -3$

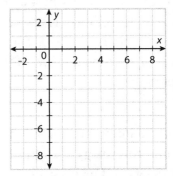

5. $x + 2y = 6$
   $x = 2$

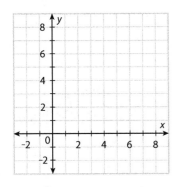

6. $2x - y = -6$
   $4x - 2y = -12$

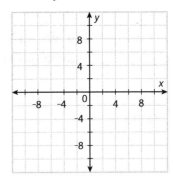

Systems of Equations

Systems of equations are two or more equations that are solved together or at the same time. Sometimes there is a solution that satisfies both equations.

Suppose you have two linear equations for lines that intersect. Each equation has 2 variables, x and y. Since both sides of an equation have the same value, you can create a new equation by adding the two equations together or by subtracting one equation from the other. The goal of combining equations in this way is to eliminate one of the variables in order to solve for the other variable. The solution to both equations will be a single ordered pair.

Solve: $x + y = 13$
$\qquad\;\; x - y = 1$

Add. $\quad x + y = 13$
$\qquad\;\; \underline{x - y = \;\; 1}$
$\qquad\;\; 2x + 0 = 14$
$\qquad\qquad\;\; x = \;\; 7$

Substitute the value of x into one of the original equations and solve for y.

$\qquad 7 + y = 13$
$\qquad\qquad y = 6$

Check: Substitute the values of x and y into the original equations.

$x + y = 13 \qquad x - y = 1$
$7 + 6 = 13 \qquad 7 - 6 = 1$

The solution to the system of equations is (7, 6).

Solve each system of equations. Check by substitution.

1. $a + b = 15$
$\quad a - b = 5$

_____

2. $a + b = 13$
$\quad a - b = 5$

_____

3. $a + b = 14$
$\quad a - b = 6$

_____

4. $x + y = 17$
$\quad x - y = 7$

_____

5. $m + n = 27$
$\quad m - n = 17$

_____

6. $d + e = 51$
$\quad d - e = 9$

_____

7. $x + y = 37$
$\quad x - y = 7$

_____

8. $b + c = -55$
$\quad b - c = 17$

_____

9. $a + b = 23$
$\quad a - b = 9$

_____

10. $m + n = 35$
$\qquad m - n = 15$

_____

11. $a + b = -44$
$\qquad a - b = 10$

_____

12. $x + y = 25$
$\qquad x - y = 15$

_____

93

Larger Coefficients

Systems of equations with coefficients greater than 1 are solved in exactly the same way as before.

Solve: $3x + 2y = 26$
$3x - 2y = 10$

Add. $3x + 2y = 26$
$\underline{3x - 2y = 10}$
$6x + 0 = 36$
$x = 6$

Substitute the value of x into one of the original equations and solve for y.
$3(6) + 2y = 26$
$y = 4$

Check: Substitute the values of x and y into the original equations.
$3x + 2y = 26 \qquad 3x - 2y = 10$
$3(6) + 2(4) = 26 \quad 3(6) - 2(4) = 10$
$18 + 8 = 26 \qquad 18 - 8 = 10$

The solution is (6, 4).

Solve each system of equations. Check by substitution.

1. $2a + 3b = 28$
$2a - 3b = 4$

2. $3x + 2y = 14$
$3x - 2y = 10$

3. $5a + 4b = 23$
$5a - 4b = 7$

_____   _____   _____

4. $8y + 6z = 40$
$8y - 6z = -8$

5. $3r + 7s = 57$
$3r - 7s = -27$

6. $9x + 5y = 67$
$9x - 5y = -13$

_____   _____   _____

Solving Linear Systems by Adding or Subtracting

Solve each system by adding or subtracting. Check your answer.

1. $-5x + y = -3$
   $5x + 3y = -1$

2. $2x + y = -6$
   $-5x + y = 8$

_____

3. $2x - 3y = -2$
   $2x + y = 14$

4. $6x - 3y = 15$
   $4x + 3y = -5$

_____

5. $-4x + y = -3$
   $4x - y = -2$

6. $x - 6y = 7$
   $-x + 6y = -7$

_____

7. If a linear system has no solution, what happens when you try to solve the system by adding or subtracting?

_____

_____

8. If a linear system has infinitely many solutions, what happens when you try to solve the system by adding or subtracting?

_____

_____

Changing the Coefficients

Recall that multiplying both sides of an equation by the same number does not change its solution. When you are solving a system of equations, you may need to change the form of one or both equations. By multiplying, you can change the coefficients so that the system can be solved.

The following example shows this method. Step 1 shows multiplying the second equation by 2 so that both equations will have the variable x with a coefficient of 2. In Step 2, the new equation is subtracted from the first equation. This eliminates the terms with x so the equation can be solved for y. Then, in Step 3, the value of y is substituted into one of the original equations. When you use this method, remember to check the solution in both original equations.

Solve: $2x + 3y = 9$
$x - 2y = 1$

Step 1:
Multiply by 2.

Step 2:
Subtract.

Step 3:
Substitute.

Check: Substitute the values of x and y into the original equations.

$2(x - 2y) = 2(1)$
$2x - 4y = 2$

$$\begin{array}{r} 2x + 3y = 9 \\ -(2x - 4y = 2) \\ \hline 7y = 7 \\ y = 1 \end{array}$$

$x - 2y = 1$
$x - 2(1) = 1$
$x = 3$

$2x + 3y = 9$ $x - 2y = 1$
$2(3) + 3(1) = 9$ $3 - 2(1) = 1$
$9 = 9$ $1 = 1$

The solution is (3, 1).

Solve each system of equations. Check.

1. $5a + 2b = -16$
$a + 3b = 15$

_____

2. $5d - 3e = 5$
$d - e = -1$

_____

3. $x + 4y = -9$
$2x - 4y = 6$

_____

4. $x + y = 4$
$2x + 3y = 10$

_____

5. $x - y = -4$
$2x - 3y = -14$

_____

6. $x + y = 4$
$3x - 2y = 7$

_____

7. $2x - y = 0$
$4x + 2y = 16$

_____

8. $5x + y = 8$
$2x - 3y = -7$

_____

9. $3x - y = 1$
$4x - 2y = -2$

_____

96

Changing Coefficients in Both Equations

Sometimes it is necessary to change coefficients in both equations in order to solve the equations. Do this by multiplying each equation by a factor that will allow one of its variables to have the same coefficient as the corresponding variable in the other equation. Remember, multiplying both sides of an equation by the same number will not change the solution.

Solve: $2x + 3y = 9$
$\qquad 3x + 2y = 11$

Step 1:
Multiply the first equation by 3.

$3(2x + 3y) = 3(9)$
$\qquad 6x + 9y = 27$

Step 2:
Multiply the second equation by 2.

$2(3x + 2y) = 2(11)$
$\qquad 6x + 4y = 22$

Step 3:
Subtract the new equations.

$\qquad 6x + 9y = 27$
$- \ (6x + 4y = 22)$
$\overline{\qquad\qquad\quad 5y = 5}$
$\qquad\qquad\quad y = 1$

Step 4:
Substitute $y = 1$ in either equation.

$6x + 9(1) = 27$
$\qquad 6x = 18$
$\qquad\quad x = 3$

Check: Substitute the values of x and y into the original equations.

The solution is (3, 1).

$2(3) + 3(1) = 9$
$\qquad 6 + 3 = 9$
$\qquad\qquad 9 = 9$

$3(3) + 2(1) = 11$
$\qquad 9 + 2 = 11$
$\qquad\quad 11 = 11$

Solve each system of equations.

1. $5a - 2b = 3$
$\quad 2a + 5b = 7$

2. $2a + 3b = 14$
$\quad 3a - 2b = 8$

3. $3x - 2y = 11$
$\quad 4x - 3y = 14$

_____   _____   _____

Solving Linear Systems by Multiplying

Solve each system and write the answer as an ordered pair. Check your answer.

1. $-2x + 2y = 2$
$5x - 6y = -9$

_____

2. $3x + 3y = 12$
$-6x - 11y = -14$

_____

3. $4x + 3y = 11$
$2x - 2y = -12$

_____

4. $6x + 3y = -24$
$7x - 5y = 6$

_____

5. $3x + 8y = 17$
$-2x + 9y = 3$

_____

6. $11x + 6y = -20$
$15x + 9y = -33$

_____

7. $2x + 3y = -6$
$10x + 15y = -30$

_____

8. $12x - 6y = 12$
$8x - 16y = -16$

_____

9. $5x + 9y = -3$
$-4x - 7y = 3$

_____

10. $3x - 4y = -1$
$-6x + 8y = 3$

_____

11. A linear system has two equations, $Ax + By = C$ and $Dx + Ey = F$. A student multiplies the x- and y-coefficients in the second equation by a constant k to get $kDx + kEy = kF$. The student then adds the result to $Ax + By = C$ to write a new equation.

   a. What is the new equation that the student wrote?

   _____

   b. If the ordered pair (x_1, y_1) is a solution of the original system, will it also be a solution of $Ax + By = C$ and the new equation? Why or why not?

   _____

   _____

98

Solving in Terms of One Variable

Sometimes it is helpful to isolate one of the variables in an equation that has two variables. To isolate a variable, change the form of the equation by adding, subtracting, multiplying, or dividing both sides by the same number or expression. When necessary, multiply both sides of an equation by -1 to change the signs.

Solve: $2x + 3y = 6$ **for** y **in terms of** x

$$2x + 3y = 6$$
$$2x + 3y - 2x = 6 - 2x$$
$$3y = 6 - 2x$$
$$\tfrac{1}{3}(3y) = \tfrac{1}{3}(6 - 2x)$$
$$y = 2 - \tfrac{2}{3}x$$

Solve: $y - x = 2$ **for** x **in terms of** y

$$y - x = 2$$
$$y - x - y = 2 - y$$
$$-x = 2 - y$$
$$-1(-x) = -1(2 - y)$$
$$x = -2 + y$$
$$x = y - 2$$

Solve each equation for y in terms of x.

1. $12x - 4y = 48$

2. $6x + 2y = 10$

3. $3x + 4y = 60$

_____   _____   _____

4. $-x + 2y = 8$

5. $x + 3y = 6$

6. $4x + 2y = -1$

_____   _____   _____

Solve each equation for x in terms of y.

7. $x - 3y = -1$

8. $-2x + 4y = 8$

9. $3x + y = 9$

_____   _____   _____

10. $3x - 2y = 3$

11. $2x - 2y = 20$

12. $7x + 4y = 28$

_____   _____   _____

The Substitution Method

Another way to solve systems of equations is to use the **substitution method.**
This method substitutes for one variable in terms of the other variable.

Solve: $x + 2y = 7$
$3x + y = 11$

Step 1:

Solve for x in terms of y in either equation.

$x + 2y = 7$
$x + 2y - 2y = 7 - 2y$
$x = 7 - 2y$

Step 2:

Substitute $7 - 2y$ for x in the second equation.

$3x + y = 11$
$3(7 - 2y) + y = 11$
$21 - 6y + y = 11$
$-5y = -10$
$y = 2$

Step 3:

Substitute 2 for y in either equation.

$x + 2(2) = 7$
$x = 3$

Check:

$x + 2y = 7$
$3 + 2(2) = 7$
and
$3x + y = 11$
$3(3) + 2 = 11$

The solution is (3, 2).

Use the substitution method to solve each system of equations. Write the answer as an ordered pair.

1. $x + 4y = 12$
$2x - y = 6$

_____

2. $x - y = 1$
$5x + 3y = 45$

_____

3. $3x + 2y = 13$
$x + y = 5$

_____

4. $x + y = 4$
$x + 3y = 10$

_____

5. $x - y = 2$
$4x + y = 23$

_____

6. $2x + 3y = 9$
$x - 2y = 1$

_____

7. $x + 2y = 9$
$x - y = 3$

_____

8. $x + 3y = 10$
$x + y = 6$

_____

9. $x + 3y = 11$
$x + y = 7$

_____

10. $x + 5y = 10$
$x - 2y = 3$

_____

11. $2x + y = 8$
$x + 2y = 7$

_____

12. $3x - y = 9$
$2x + y = 11$

_____

100

Solving Linear Systems by Substitution

Solve each system by substitution. Check your answer.

1. $x + y = 3$
   $2x + 4y = 8$

   _____

2. $x + 2y = 7$
   $4x + 3y = 3$

   _____

3. $-4x + y = 3$
   $5x - 2y = -9$

   _____

4. $8x - 7y = -2$
   $-2x - 3y = 10$

   _____

5. $2x - 2y = 5$
   $4x - 4y = 9$

   _____

6. $2x + 7y = 2$
   $4x + 2y = -2$

   _____

7. $2x - y = 7$
   $2x + 7y = 31$

   _____

8. $x - 2y = -4$
   $4y = 2x + 8$

   _____

For each linear system, tell whether it is more efficient to solve for *x* and then substitute or to solve for *y* and then substitute. Explain your reasoning. Then solve the system.

9. $6x - 3y = 15$
   $x + 3y = -8$

   _____

   _____

   _____

10. $\frac{x}{2} + y = 6$
    $\frac{x}{4} + \frac{y}{2} = 3$

    _____

    _____

    _____

Choose a Method

You have used several methods to solve systems of equations. Study each system of equations and decide which method is best to use. Then solve.

1. $2x + 3y = 16$
$3x - y = 2$

2. $5x - 2y = 6$
$2x + 5y = 14$

3. $6x + 5y = 6$
$3x + 5y = -12$

_____

4. $x + y = 5$
$x - 3y = 1$

5. $4x + 3y = 14$
$2x + 3y = 10$

6. $3x - y = 3$
$2x - 3y = -19$

_____

7. $10x + 7y = 45$
$3x + 7y = 38$

8. $2a - b = 5$
$7a + b = 49$

9. $a + b = -8$
$a - 2b = 1$

_____

102

Solving Problems with Systems of Equations

Some word problems can be solved by using systems of equations.

The sum of two numbers is 13. Their difference is 1. What are the numbers?

Let x = one number.
Let y = the other number.
Then, $x + y = 13$ (the sum)
$x - y = 1$ (the difference)

Add. $\quad x + y = 13$
$\quad\quad\quad \underline{x - y = \ 1}$
$\quad\quad\quad\ \ 2x = 14$
$\quad\quad\quad\ \ \ x = \ 7$

Substitute. $\ x + y = 13$
$\quad\quad\quad\quad\ 7 + y = 13$
$\quad\quad\quad\quad\quad\quad\ y = 6$

Check: $\ x + y = 13$
$\quad\quad\quad\ 7 + 6 = 13$

$\quad\quad\quad\ x - y = 1$
$\quad\quad\quad\ 7 - 6 = 1$

The two numbers are 7 and 6.

Use a system of equations to solve each problem.

1. Find the numbers whose sum is 15, if twice the first number minus the second number equals 6.

2. The sum of two numbers is 18. Twice the first number plus three times the second number equals 40. Find the numbers.

3. Four times a number increased by three times a second number is 25. Four times the first number decreased by three times the second number is 7. Find the two numbers.

4. The difference of two numbers is -1. If twice the first number is added to three times the second number, the result is 13. What are the numbers?

5. Three times the first of two numbers decreased by the second number equals 9. Twice the first number increased by the second number equals 11. Find the two numbers.

6. The first of two numbers decreased by five times the second number equals -10. The first number decreased by two times the second number equals -1. Find the numbers.

7. The first of two numbers added to two times the second number equals 9. The first number decreased by the second number is 3. Find the numbers.

8. Find the numbers whose sum is 9, if three times the first number increased by two times the second number equals 22.

9. The difference of two numbers is -3. Twice the first number increased by three times the second number is 29. Find the numbers.

10. Three times a number increased by two times another number equals 28. Two times the first number increased by three times the second number equals 27. Find the two numbers.

Systems of Equations with Fractional Coefficients

The methods for solving systems of equations with fractional coefficients are the same as for solving systems of equations with integer coefficients.

Solve: $\frac{1}{2}a + b = 5$
$\frac{1}{2}a - b = 1$

Add.

$\frac{1}{2}a + b = 5$
$\frac{1}{2}a - b = 1$
_____
$1a + 0 = 6$
$a = 6$

Substitute the value of a into one of the original equations and solve for b.

$\frac{1}{2}(6) + b = 5$
$b = 2$

The solution is $(6, 2)$.

Check: Substitute the values of a and b into the original equations.

$\frac{1}{2}a + b = 5$ $\frac{1}{2}a - b = 1$
$\frac{1}{2}(6) + 2 = 5$ $\frac{1}{2}(6) - 2 = 1$
$3 + 2 = 5$ $3 - 2 = 1$

Solve each system of equations.

1. $\frac{1}{4}m - n = 1$
$\frac{1}{4}m + n = 3$

2. $\frac{1}{2}x + y = 6$
$\frac{1}{2}x - y = 2$

3. $\frac{3}{4}x + y = 6$
$\frac{1}{2}x - 2y = -4$

_____

_____

_____

4. $\frac{3}{5}x + y = 11$
$\frac{2}{5}x - y = -1$

5. $\frac{2}{3}x + y = 0$
$\frac{2}{3}x - y = 8$

6. $\frac{3}{4}x + y = 11$
$\frac{3}{4}x - 3y = 3$

_____

_____

_____

System Problems with Fractional Coefficients

Use a system of equations with fractional coefficients to solve each problem.

1. One half of a number added to a second number equals 4. One half of the first number decreased by the second number equals zero. Find the two numbers.

2. One half of a number increased by a second number equals 8. One half of the first number decreased by the second number equals -2. Find the two numbers.

3. Four tenths of a number increased by the second number equals 19. One tenth of the first number decreased by the second number is equal to 1. What are the two numbers?

4. One third of a number increased by a second number equals 7. One third of the first number decreased by the second number is equal to -3. What are the numbers?

5. Two thirds of the first of two numbers added to the second number equals 6. One third of the first number decreased by the second number is equal to zero. Find the numbers.

6. Three fourths of a number increased by a second number equals 6. Three fourths of the first number decreased by three times the second number equals -6. What are the two numbers?

Graphing Systems of Linear and Quadratic Equations

Estimate the solutions to each system of equations by graphing. Confirm the solutions by substituting the values into the equations.

1. $f(x) = x^2$
   $g(x) = 4$

2. $y = x^2 - 1$
   $y = 0.5x - 3$

_____

_____

3. $f(x) = (x - 1)^2 + 3$
   $g(x) = 2x$

4. $f(x) = 3(x - 1)^2 + 4$
   $g(x) = -4x + 9$

_____

_____

Solve each system of equations using the Intersect feature of a graphing calculator. Round your answers to the nearest tenth.

5. $y = -x^2 + 6x + 7$
   $y = 2x + 6$

6. $f(x) = -x^2 + x - 2$
   $g(x) = 2x - 3$

_____

_____

© Houghton Mifflin Harcourt Publishing Company

Unit 7
Core Skills Algebra

Solving Systems of Linear and Quadratic Equations

The graph of a system of equations is shown. State how many solutions the system has. Then estimate the solution(s).

1. _____

_____

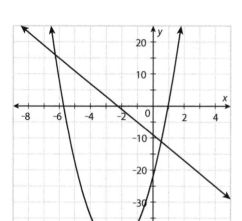

2. _____

_____

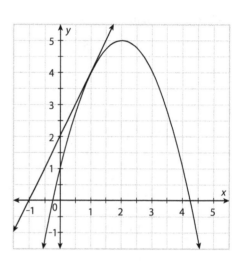

Solve each system of equations algebraically. Round to the nearest tenth, if necessary.

3. $y = x^2 - 2$

$y = -2$

_____

4. $y = (x - 3)^2$

$y = x$

_____

5. $y = -2x^2 - 4x + 1$

$y = -\frac{1}{2}x + 3$

_____

6. $y = x^2$

$y = 1$

_____

7. $y = x^2 + 4x - 5$

$y = 3x - 2$

_____

8. $y = -16x^2 + 15x + 10$

$y = 14 - x$

_____

Unit 7 Review

Solve each equation for y in terms of x.

1. $2y + 10x = 18$ **2.** $12x - 3y = 24$ **3.** $8x = -4y - 32$

_____   _____   _____

Solve each system of equations.

4. $x + y = 12$ **5.** $a + 5b = 14$ **6.** $x + 5y = 13$

   $x - y = 2$ $a - 5b = 4$ $2x - 3y = 0$

_____   _____   _____

7. $5x + 3y = 45$ **8.** $\frac{3a}{8} - b = 2$ **9.** $2x + 3y = 7$

   $x - y = 1$ $\frac{7a}{8} + b = 18$ $3x + 2y = 3$

_____   _____   _____

Solve.

10. The sum of two numbers is 17. Twice the first number decreased by the second number is 7. What are the numbers?

11. One half of a number increased by a second number equals 5. One half of the first number decreased by the second number equals 1. Find the two numbers.

_____   _____

12. Solve the system of equations by graphing.

   $f(x) = -8x + 48$

   $g(x) = -2(x - 2)^2 + 32$

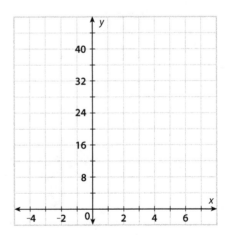

_____

108

Exploring Inequalities

Tell whether the given value is a solution of each inequality. Explain.

1. $x = 36;\ 3x < 100$ **2.** $m = 12;\ 5m + 4 > 50$ **3.** $b = 5;\ 60 - 10b \leq 20$

_____   _____   _____

4. Brent is ordering books for a reading group. Each book costs $11.95. If he orders at least $200 worth of books, he will get free shipping.

  a. Complete the verbal model for the situation.

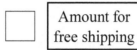

| Price per book | ☐ | Number of books | ☐ | Amount for free shipping |

  b. Choose a variable for the unknown quantity. Include units.

    Let _____ represent the _____.

  c. Write an inequality from the verbal model.

    _____

  d. Complete the table to find some numbers of books Brent can order and receive free shipping.

Books	Substitute	Compare	Solution?
15	$11.95(15) \overset{?}{\geq} 200$	$179.25 \overset{?}{\geq} 200$	No
16			
17			
18			

5. Farzana has a prepaid cell phone that costs $1 per day plus $.10 per minute she uses. She has a daily budget of $5 for phone costs.

  a. Write an inequality to represent the situation.

    _____

  b. What is the maximum number of minutes Farzana can use and still stay within her daily budget? Show your reasoning.

    _____

  c. Describe the solution set of the inequality.

    _____

Solving Inequalities with Addition and Subtraction

Inequalities are solved in much the same way equations are. You can add or subtract the same amount from both sides of an inequality without changing its solution. If you exchange the left and right sides of an inequality, you must reverse the direction. For example, $7 < 9$ is equivalent to $9 > 7$. Study the following examples.

Solve: $x - 2 > 12$

$x - 2 + 2 > 12 + 2$

$x > 14$

Solve: $3 \leq x + 15$

$3 - 15 \leq x + 15 - 15$

$-12 \leq x$

or

$x \geq -12$

Solve: $-x + 16 \leq -2x - 8$

$-x + 16 - 16 \leq -2x - 8 - 16$

$-x \leq -2x - 24$

$-x + 2x \leq -2x + 2x - 24$

$x \leq -24$

Solve.

1. $x - 7 > 15$

2. $x - 4 \leq 11$

3. $14 > x - 6$

4. $x + 9 \leq 10$

5. $20 < x + 5$

6. $8 \leq x + 12$

7. $x - 10 \geq -4$

8. $-17 < x + 7$

9. $x - 3 > -11$

10. $11 + x < 7$

11. $-15 + x < 16$

12. $-12 \geq 4 + x$

13. $2x + 3 < x - 1$

14. $4x + 2 > 4 + 3x$

15. $6x - 1 \leq 5x - 5$

16. $7 + 2x \leq x + 8$

17. $15 - 4x > 9 - 5x$

18. $22 + 9x \leq -12 + 8x$

Solving Inequalities with Multiplication and Division

As with equations, you can multiply or divide both sides of an inequality by the same number without changing the solution. However, if you multiply or divide by a negative number, you must change the direction of the inequality sign.

Solve: $\frac{x}{2} \geq 3$

Multiply both sides by 2.

$$2\left(\frac{x}{2}\right) \geq 2(3)$$

$$x \geq 6$$

Solve: $-2x < 6$

Divide both sides by -2 and reverse the sign.

$$\frac{-2x}{-2} > \frac{6}{-2}$$

$$x > -3$$

Solve: $-2x + 3 \leq 5x + 17$

$$-2x + 3 - 3 \leq 5x + 17 - 3$$

$$-2x \leq 5x + 14$$

$$-2x - 5x \leq 5x - 5x + 14$$

$$-7x \leq 14$$

$$\frac{-7x}{-7} \geq \frac{14}{-7}$$

$$x \geq -2$$

Solve.

1. $\frac{x}{5} > 2$

2. $\frac{x}{2} \leq -6$

3. $3 \leq \frac{x}{-4}$

4. $4x < 8$

5. $-10 \geq 2x$

6. $-6x \leq -18$

7. $3x + 2 > 8$

8. $8x - 13 > 19$

9. $-2 - 3x > 7$

10. $9x - 10 > 7x - 4$

11. $2 - 5x < 11 + 4x$

12. $3x - 2 \geq x + 18$

13. $-7x + 13 > -2x + 9$

14. $3x - \frac{2}{5} \leq 5x + \frac{3}{5}$

15. $4 + 2x < 6 + 6x$

Solving Problems with Inequalities

Some problems can be solved using inequalities.

Margaret is 2 years older than Sam, and their combined age is, at most, 20. What is the oldest Sam could be? What is the oldest Margaret could be?

Let x = Sam's age.

$x + 2$ = Margaret's age

$\underbrace{\text{Their combined age}}\ \underbrace{\text{is, at most,}}\ \underbrace{20.}$

$$x + (x + 2) \quad \leq \quad 20$$
$$2x + 2 \leq 20$$
$$2x \leq 18$$
$$x \leq 9$$

The oldest Sam could be is 9 years old.

The oldest Margaret could be is $x + 2$ or $9 + 2 = 11$ years old.

Solve using inequalities.

1. A jockey must weigh in at less than 130 pounds. This includes the jockey's weight plus the weight of the blanket, saddle, and bridle. If the combined weight of the equipment is $\frac{1}{8}$ of the jockey's weight, what is the maximum the jockey can weigh?

_____

2. The Rodriguez family has a fixed income of $4,000 a month. Their fixed expenses are $1,800 a month. They save at least one fourth of the remaining income each month. What is the minimum amount saved by the Rodriguez family in a year?

_____

3. The sum of three consecutive integers is less than 186. What is the maximum value for the first integer?

_____

4. The sum of four consecutive odd integers is greater than 48. What is the minimum value for the first integer?

_____

Exploring Graphs of Inequalities

Graph each inequality.

1. $y > x - 2$

2. $y < 3 - x$

3. $y \leq 2x$

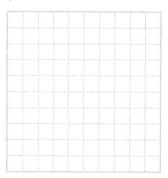

Use the graph of $y > x + 5$ for Exercises 4–6.

4. Name an ordered pair that is a solution of the inequality.

_____

5. Is $(3, 5)$ a solution of $y > x + 5$?

_____

6. Name an ordered pair that is a solution of $y \leq x + 5$.

_____

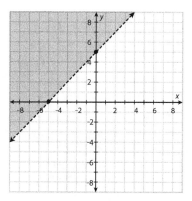

A box of chalk costs \$0.60. One eraser is \$0.40. Use the graph for Exercises 7 and 8. In the graph, (6, 1) means a purchase of 6 erasers and 1 boxes of chalk.

7. Ms. Woo can spend up to \$3.00 for chalk and erasers. If she buys no erasers, how many boxes of chalk can she buy?

_____

8. In what three ways can Ms. Woo spend exactly \$3.00? Write the answers as ordered pairs.

_____

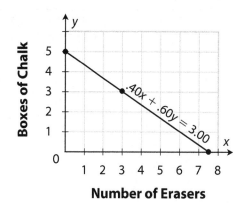

113

Liner Inequalities in Two Variables

Graph each inequality.

1. $y \geq 2$

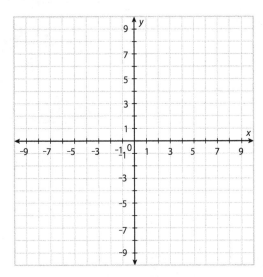

2. $x < ^-3$

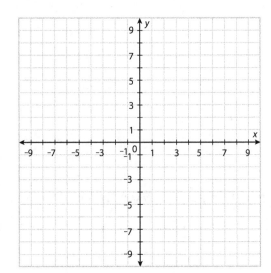

3. $x + 4y < 9$

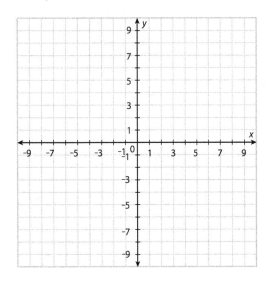

4. $2x - 2y \geq 5$

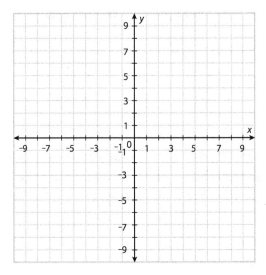

114

Name _____   Date _____

Solving Linear Inequalities

1. Given the function $f(x) = 16 - 9x$, for what values of x is $f(x) \leq 7$? Use the properties of inequality and other properties to justify your solution.

_____

_____

_____

_____

2. Given the functions $f(x) = 3(x - 4)$ and $g(x) = 2(x - 3)$, for what values of x is $f(x) > g(x)$? Use the properties of inequality and other properties to justify your solution.

_____

_____

_____

_____

Solve each linear inequality and justify your solution. Write your answer in set notation. Graph the solution on the number line.

3. $7x - 1 > 13$

_____

_____

_____

_____

4. $12 - 3x \leq 6$

_____

_____

_____

_____

5. $7(3x + 4) < 10 - 3x$

_____

_____

_____

_____

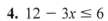

6. $-\frac{1}{3}(x + 2) \geq 7x + 3$

_____

_____

_____

_____

Solving Systems of Linear Inequalities

Solve each system of linear inequalities by graphing. Check your answers.

1. $x + y \leq -2$
$-x + y > 1$

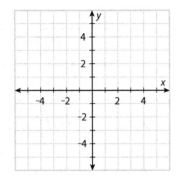

2. $x + 2y \geq 8$
$x - 2y < -4$

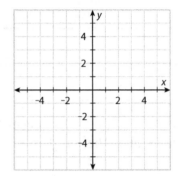

3. $y \geq -2$
$4x + y \geq 2$

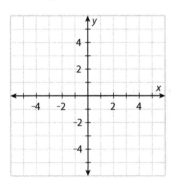

4. $x < 1$
$2x + y > 1$

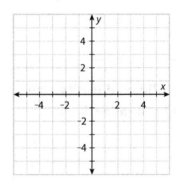

5. $x - y \leq -3$
$x - y > 3$

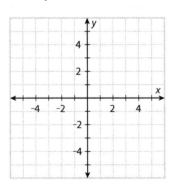

6. $4x + y \geq 4$
$4x + y > -4$

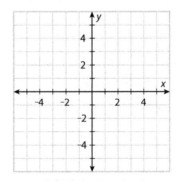

Square Roots

The sign $\sqrt{}$ tells you to find the **square root** of the number under the sign. The expression $\sqrt{9}$ is called a **radical**. The 9 is called a **radicand**, and the $\sqrt{}$ is called a **radical sign.**

The square root of a number is the factor which when multiplied by itself gives the number. The factor can be positive or negative ($\pm$).

Here are three examples:

$$\sqrt{4} = \pm 2 \qquad \sqrt{9} = \pm 3 \qquad \sqrt{81} = \pm 9$$

To take the square root of a monomial, first take the square root of the coefficient. Next, take the square root of each variable expression. The following examples use the positive square root of the coefficient.

$\sqrt{4x^2} = 2x$ $\qquad\qquad$ $\sqrt{9x^4} = 3x^2$ $\qquad\qquad$ $\sqrt{x^4y^2} = x^2y$

Check: $\qquad\qquad\qquad$ Check: $\qquad\qquad\qquad$ Check:

$2x \cdot 2x = 4x^2$ $\qquad$ $3x^2 \cdot 3x^2 = 9x^4$ $\qquad$ $x^2y \cdot x^2y = x^4y^2$

Find each positive square root.

1. $\sqrt{121} =$ $\qquad$ 2. $\sqrt{49} =$ $\qquad$ 3. $\sqrt{144} =$ $\qquad$ 4. $\sqrt{25} =$ $\qquad$ 5. $\sqrt{169} =$

6. $\sqrt{225} =$ $\qquad$ 7. $\sqrt{81} =$ $\qquad$ 8. $\sqrt{16} =$ $\qquad$ 9. $\sqrt{324} =$ $\qquad$ 10. $\sqrt{196} =$

11. $\sqrt{a^2} =$ $\qquad$ 12. $\sqrt{a^4} =$ $\qquad$ 13. $\sqrt{x^6} =$ $\qquad$ 14. $\sqrt{y^8} =$ $\qquad$ 15. $\sqrt{b^4} =$

16. $\sqrt{a^2b^2} =$ $\quad$ 17. $\sqrt{x^4y^4} =$ $\quad$ 18. $\sqrt{x^2y^2} =$ $\quad$ 19. $\sqrt{a^2b^2c^2} =$ $\quad$ 20. $\sqrt{x^4b^2c^4} =$

21. $\sqrt{9a^2} =$ $\quad$ 22. $\sqrt{16b^4} =$ $\quad$ 23. $\sqrt{36a^2b^2} =$ $\quad$ 24. $\sqrt{64x^2y^4} =$ $\quad$ 25. $\sqrt{81a^2b^4c^8} =$

26. $\sqrt{169x^{10}y^4} =$ $\quad$ 27. $\sqrt{289x^{12}} =$ $\quad$ 28. $\sqrt{324b^4c^6} =$ $\quad$ 29. $\sqrt{400a^2b^6} =$ $\quad$ 30. $\sqrt{100x^4y^2z^6} =$

117

Equations with Squares

Some equations have variables that are squared. To solve such an equation, first isolate the squared variable and then find the square root of both sides of the equation. An equation such as $x^2 = 9$ has two solutions. The solutions to $x^2 = 9$ are 3 and -3 because $(-3)(-3) = 9$ and $(3)(3) = 9$. These solutions can be written as ± 3. The symbol $\pm$ means positive or negative.

Solve: $2a^2 - 7 = 43$

$2a^2 - 7 + 7 = 43 + 7$

$2a^2 = 50$

$\frac{2a^2}{2} = \frac{50}{2}$

$a^2 = 25$

$\sqrt{a^2} = \sqrt{25}$

$a = \pm 5$

Check both solutions:

$2(5)^2 - 7 = 43$
$2(5)(5) - 7 = 43$
$50 - 7 = 43$
$43 = 43$

and

$2(-5)^2 - 7 = 43$
$2(-5)(-5) - 7 = 43$
$50 - 7 = 43$
$43 = 43$

Solve.

1. $2x^2 = 200$

2. $7x^2 = 175$

3. $3x^2 = 147$

4. $2x^2 = 32$

_____

_____

_____

_____

5. $x^2 + 15 = 40$

6. $x^2 - 12 = 24$

7. $x^2 + 17 = 81$

8. $x^2 - 15 = 85$

_____

_____

_____

_____

9. $3a^2 + 7 = 34$

10. $5a^2 - 9 = 116$

11. $2a^2 - 6 = 44$

12. $4a^2 + 3 = 19$

_____

_____

_____

_____

Combine like terms and solve.

13. $3x^2 - 7 = x^2 + 1$

14. $5x^2 + 3 = 2x^2 + 30$

15. $7x^2 - 15 = 5x^2 + 17$

_____

_____

_____

Using Equations with Squares

Recall that the area of a rectangle is equal to the length times the width, or $A = lw$. The area is always in square units. If you know the area and something about the length or width, you can use the formula to find both dimensions.

The area of a rectangle is 200 square feet. The length is twice the width. Find the dimensions.

Let x = width.   Since $A = 200$ square ft,   Check: $(2x)x = 200$

Let $2x$ = length. $2x^2 = 200$ $(20)10 = 200$

Then $A = (2x)x$ $x^2 = 100$ $200 = 200$

$A = 2x^2$ $x = \pm 10$

x

$2x$

The width (x) is 10 ft, and the length ($2x$) is 20 ft. The negative value of $x = -10$ is not a solution because dimensions cannot be negative.

Solve.

1. Find the dimensions of a rectangle with an area of 288 square centimeters. The length is twice the width.

2. Find the dimensions of a rectangle with an area of 128 square inches and the length 8 times the width.

3. The area of a rectangle is 100 square meters. The length is 4 times the width. What are the dimensions of the rectangle?

4. The length of a rectangle is six times the width, and the area is 2,166 square inches. Find the dimensions of the rectangle.

5. Find the dimensions of a rectangle with an area of 125 square centimeters if the width is one fifth of the length.

6. If the width of a rectangle is one third the length and the area is 48 square feet, find the dimensions of the rectangle.

Cube Roots

The sign $\sqrt[3]{}$ tells you to find the **cube root** of the number under the sign. The cube root of a number is used as a factor three times to give the number. Study the following examples.

$\sqrt[3]{8} = 2$

$\sqrt[3]{125} = 5$

$\sqrt[3]{1,000} = 10$

The cube root of 8 is 2, because $2 \cdot 2 \cdot 2 = 8$.

The cube root of 125 is 5, because $5 \cdot 5 \cdot 5 = 125$.

The cube root of 1,000 is 10, because $10 \cdot 10 \cdot 10 = 1,000$.

To take the cube root of a monomial, first take the cube root of the coefficient. Then take the cube root of each variable expression. Use the chart if needed.

$\sqrt[3]{216x^3} = 6x$

$\sqrt[3]{1,000x^6y^3} = 10x^2y$

Check:
$6x \cdot 6x \cdot 6x = 216x^3$

Check:
$10x^2y \cdot 10x^2y \cdot 10x^2y = 1,000x^6y^3$

Cube Root	Cube
1	1
2	8
3	27
4	64
5	125
6	216
7	343
8	512
9	729
10	1,000
11	1,331
12	1,728
13	2,197
14	2,744
15	3,375
16	4,096
17	4,913
18	5,832
19	6,859
20	8,000

Find each cube root. Use the chart above if needed.

1. $\sqrt[3]{27} =$

2. $\sqrt[3]{64} =$

3. $\sqrt[3]{1,728} =$

4. $\sqrt[3]{1} =$

5. $\sqrt[3]{4,096} =$

6. $\sqrt[3]{y^3} =$

7. $\sqrt[3]{y^6} =$

8. $\sqrt[3]{b^9} =$

9. $\sqrt[3]{c^{12}} =$

10. $\sqrt[3]{z^{15}} =$

11. $\sqrt[3]{8y^3} =$

12. $\sqrt[3]{2,744x^6} =$

13. $\sqrt[3]{1,331z^9} =$

14. $\sqrt[3]{8,000a^3} =$

15. $\sqrt[3]{4,096b^{12}} =$

16. $\sqrt[3]{343a^3b^3} =$

17. $\sqrt[3]{729x^6y^{15}} =$

18. $\sqrt[3]{8c^{12}d^9} =$

19. $\sqrt[3]{216x^3y^6} =$

20. $\sqrt[3]{3,375z^{27}} =$

21. $\sqrt[3]{512a^3b^3c^6} =$

22. $\sqrt[3]{1,000x^3y^6z^9} =$

23. $\sqrt[3]{2,197r^9s^9} =$

24. $\sqrt[3]{5,832t^{30}} =$

25. $\sqrt[3]{125x^{15}y^{15}} =$

Radicals and Rational Exponents

Write each radical expression in rational exponent form. Assume all variables are positive.

1. $\sqrt[5]{d}$ _____

2. $\sqrt[3]{b^2}$ _____

3. $\sqrt[4]{m^3}$ _____

Simplify each expression. Assume all variables are positive.

4. $\sqrt[3]{y^3z}$ _____

5. $\sqrt{x^4y}$ _____

6. $\sqrt{49x^2y^4}$ _____

7. $\sqrt[3]{x} \cdot \sqrt[4]{x}$ _____

8. $\sqrt{(3x)(12x^3)}$ _____

9. $\sqrt{xy} \cdot \sqrt{x^3y^5}$ _____

10. $\dfrac{\sqrt[3]{x}}{\sqrt[6]{x}}$ _____

11. $\sqrt[3]{\dfrac{8x^6}{y^9}}$ _____

12. $\sqrt[4]{\dfrac{x}{y^8}}$ _____

13. $(8x^3)^{\frac{2}{3}}$ _____

14. $\left(\dfrac{x^{\frac{3}{4}}}{y^{\frac{1}{4}}}\right)^{12}$ _____

15. $\left(\dfrac{4x^2}{y^6}\right)^{\frac{1}{2}}$ _____

16. $(216a^9)^{\frac{1}{3}}$ _____

17. $(a^4b^{-8})^{-\frac{3}{4}}$ _____

18. $(16b^{-2})^{-\frac{1}{2}}$ _____

19. Explain why the expression $x^{\frac{1}{2}}$ is undefined when $x < 0$.

_____

_____

20. Use the properties of exponents to show that $\sqrt[n]{\dfrac{a}{b}} = \dfrac{\sqrt[n]{a}}{\sqrt[n]{b}}$.

_____

_____

21. Show that $\sqrt[n]{a^m} = (\sqrt[n]{a})^m$.

_____

22. A student simplified the expression $\sqrt[3]{x^2} \cdot \sqrt{x}$ by writing $\sqrt[3]{x^2} \cdot \sqrt{x} = x^{\frac{3}{2}} \cdot x^{\frac{1}{2}} = x^{\frac{3}{2} + \frac{1}{2}} = x^{\frac{4}{2}} = x^2$.
Describe and correct the student's error.

_____

23. In the expression $\sqrt[n]{a^m}$, suppose m is a multiple of n. That is, $m = kn$ where k is an integer. Show how to obtain the simplified form of $\sqrt[n]{a^m}$. If a is a nonzero rational number, is $\sqrt[n]{a^m}$ rational or irrational? Explain.

_____

_____

_____

The Meaning of Proportion

Consider this situation. On Monday, Stan earned $48 for working 4 hours. On Tuesday, he earned $84 for working 7 hours.

The ratio of Monday's hours to Tuesday's hours is $\frac{4}{7}$. The ratio of Monday's earnings to Tuesday's earnings is $\frac{48}{84}$. Because these ratios are equal, you can write an equation.

Monday's hours $\rightarrow$ $\dfrac{4}{7} = \dfrac{48}{84}$ $\leftarrow$ Monday's dollars
Tuesday's hours $\rightarrow$ $\phantom{\dfrac{4}{7}}$ $\phantom{\dfrac{48}{84}}$ $\leftarrow$ Tuesday's dollars

An equation formed by two fractions is called a **proportion.** The fractions can be ratios or rates. A rate is a kind of ratio that has different units.

Monday's dollars $\rightarrow$ $\dfrac{48}{4} = \dfrac{84}{7}$ $\leftarrow$ Tuesday's dollars
Monday's hours $\rightarrow$ $\phantom{\dfrac{48}{4}}$ $\phantom{\dfrac{84}{7}}$ $\leftarrow$ Tuesday's hours

To solve a proportion that contains an unknown, cross-multiply and solve the resulting equation.

Kathryn earns $32 for working 2 hours. How much would she earn for working 6 hours?

Let x = the amount earned in 6 hours.   Solve by cross-multiplication.   Check:

$\dfrac{32}{x} = \dfrac{2}{6}$

$$32(6) = x(2)$$
$$192 = 2x$$
$$96 = x$$

$\dfrac{32}{96} = \dfrac{2}{6} = \dfrac{1}{3}$

Kathryn would earn $96 for working 6 hours.

Solve each proportion. Use cross-multiplication.

1. $\dfrac{x}{4} = \dfrac{5}{10}$ 2. $\dfrac{x}{6} = \dfrac{2}{3}$ 3. $\dfrac{2}{x} = \dfrac{6}{9}$ 4. $\dfrac{8}{x} = \dfrac{4}{8}$

_____   _____   _____   _____

5. $\dfrac{3}{25} = \dfrac{x}{100}$ 6. $\dfrac{4}{5} = \dfrac{x}{20}$ 7. $\dfrac{3}{7} = \dfrac{6}{x}$ 8. $\dfrac{7}{5} = \dfrac{21}{x}$

_____   _____   _____   _____

Solve.

9. If Rolando earned $28.50 in 2 hours, how much would he earn in 8 hours?

10. If it takes 3 hours for a horse to walk 10 miles, how far will the horse walk in 9 hours?

_____   _____

Fractions and Cross-Multiplication

For equations that contain only one fractional term on each side, a faster method is to **cross-multiply**. With this shortcut, each numerator is multiplied by the opposite denominator.

Solve: $\dfrac{2x}{3} = \dfrac{12}{9}$

$$9(2x) = 3(12)$$
$$18x = 36$$
$$x = 2$$

Check: $\dfrac{2(2)}{3} = \dfrac{12}{9}$

$\dfrac{4}{3} = \dfrac{4}{3}$

Solve: $\dfrac{x}{2} = \dfrac{3}{4}$

$$4x = 2(3)$$
$$4x = 6$$
$$x = \dfrac{3}{2}$$

Check: $\dfrac{3}{2}\left(\dfrac{1}{2}\right) = \dfrac{3}{4}$

$\dfrac{3}{4} = \dfrac{3}{4}$

Solve: $\dfrac{3}{x} = \dfrac{6}{4}$

$$4(3) = x(6)$$
$$12 = 6x$$
$$2 = x$$

Check: $\dfrac{3}{2} = \dfrac{6}{4}$

$\dfrac{3}{2} = \dfrac{3}{2}$

Solve. Check.

1. $\dfrac{x}{3} = \dfrac{2}{5}$

2. $\dfrac{x}{4} = \dfrac{1}{3}$

3. $\dfrac{x}{5} = \dfrac{3}{4}$

4. $\dfrac{2x}{9} = \dfrac{2}{3}$

_____ _____ _____ _____

5. $\dfrac{3x}{10} = \dfrac{3}{5}$

6. $\dfrac{5c}{12} = \dfrac{5}{6}$

7. $\dfrac{4x}{7} = \dfrac{3}{5}$

8. $\dfrac{2a}{5} = \dfrac{3}{8}$

_____ _____ _____ _____

9. $\dfrac{x}{6} = \dfrac{7}{12}$

10. $\dfrac{x}{7} = \dfrac{5}{8}$

11. $\dfrac{3}{4} = \dfrac{x}{8}$

12. $\dfrac{4}{5} = \dfrac{16}{m}$

_____ _____ _____ _____

13. $\dfrac{3x}{7} = \dfrac{4}{9}$

14. $\dfrac{10}{x} = \dfrac{5}{2}$

15. $\dfrac{3}{x} = \dfrac{3}{5}$

16. $\dfrac{5}{x} = \dfrac{2}{8}$

_____ _____ _____ _____

Unit 8 Review

Tell whether each value is a solution to the inequality. Explain each answer.

1. $b = 24; 3b > 100$

2. $w = 16; 4w + 5 < 70$

3. $k = 20; 37 - 3k \geq -23$

_____   _____   _____

_____   _____   _____

Graph.

4. $2x - 3y \geq 6$

5. $7x - y < 13$
$y + 3 \geq -3x$

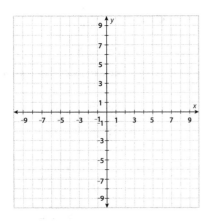

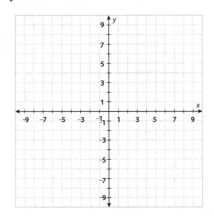

6. Graph the solution of $3x - 5 > 4$. Write the solution set using set notation, and graph your solution on a number line.

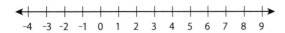

Find each square or cube root.

7. $\sqrt{49}$ _____

8. $\sqrt{64x^8y^4z^2}$ _____

9. $\sqrt{x^2y^4}$ _____

10. $\sqrt{256b^4c^{10}}$ _____

Simplify each expression.

11. $\sqrt[3]{(xy)^6}$ _____

12. $\sqrt{x} \cdot \sqrt[3]{x}$ _____

13. $\dfrac{\sqrt{x}}{\sqrt[4]{x}}$ _____

Solve.

14. $x^2 - 36 = 28$

15. $4x^2 - 6 = 3x^2 + 19$

16. $4w^2 + 20 = -8w^2 - 464$

_____   _____   _____

17. There are some pencils and erasers in a box. If there are 12 pencils and the ratio of pencils to erasers is 3:2, how many erasers are in the box?

18. The sum of three consecutive integers is less than 178. What is the maximum value for the first integer?

_____   _____

19. Find the dimensions of a rectangle with an area of 256 square feet if the width is $\frac{1}{4}$ the length.

_____

Cumulative Review

Simplify.

1. $(65 - 11) \div 9 + 100 =$

2. $46xy + 52xy - 17xy =$

3. $\frac{-36m^2n^2}{18n^3} =$

_____

_____

_____

4. $\sqrt{a^2b^2} =$

5. $\left(\frac{a}{2} + 3y\right) - \left(\frac{a}{2} + 6y\right) =$

6. $\frac{4r^2s^2}{5r} \div \frac{6rs}{10r^2} =$

_____

_____

_____

At what points does the line cross the *x*- and *y*-axes?

7. $y = 3x + 2$

8. $2x = y - 6$

9. $-4x + 10 = 2y$

_____

_____

_____

Solve.

10. $3(2a - 6) = 24 + 6$

11. $3k - 3 \geq 15$

12. $4 - 2x \leq 10$

_____

_____

_____

Solve each system of equations.

13. $x + 2y = 7$
   $x - 2y = 3$

14. $\frac{1}{2}x + y = 4$
   $\frac{1}{2}x - 2y = 7$

15. $3x + 2y = 25$
   $x - 3y = -21$

_____

_____

_____

Graph.

16. $2x - 2y = 10$

17. $f(x) = -x^2$

18. $2x > y + 2$

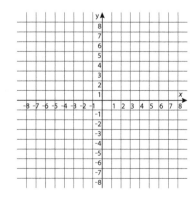

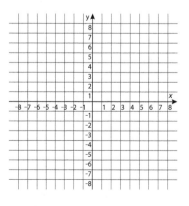

Proofs with Linear and Exponential Functions

1. Complete the proof that linear functions grow by equal differences over equal intervals.

Given: $x_2 - x_1 = x_4 - x_3$ and f is a linear function of the form $f(x) = mx + b$.

Prove: $f(x_2) - f(x_1) = f(x_4) - f(x_3)$

Proof:

$x_2 - x_1 = x_4 - x_3$	Given
$m(x_2 - x_1) = \boxed{}(x_4 - x_3)$	Mult. Prop. of Equality
$mx_2 - \boxed{} = mx_4 - \boxed{}$	Distributive Property
$mx_2 + b - mx_1 - b = mx_4 + \boxed{} - mx_3 - \boxed{}$	Add. and Subt. Prop. of Equality
$(mx_2 + b) - (mx_1 + b) = $ _____	Distributive Property
$f(x_2) - f(x_1) = $ _____	Definition of $f(x)$

2. Complete the proof that exponential functions grow by equal factors over equal intervals.

Given: $x_2 - x_1 = x_4 - x_3$ and g is an exponential function of the form $g(x) = ab^x$.

Prove: $\dfrac{f(x_2)}{f(x_1)} = \dfrac{f(x_4)}{f(x_3)}$

Proof:

$x_2 - x_1 = x_4 - x_3$	Given
$b^{x_2 - x_1} = b^{x_4 - x_3}$	If $x = y$, then $b^x = b^y$.
$\dfrac{b^{x_2}}{b^{x_1}} = \dfrac{b^{x_4}}{\boxed{}}$	Quotient of Powers Prop.
$\dfrac{ab^{x_2}}{ab^{x_1}} = \dfrac{ab^{x_4}}{\boxed{}}$	Mult. Prop. of Equality
$\dfrac{f(x_2)}{f(x_1)} = \dfrac{\boxed{}}{\boxed{}}$	Definition of $f(x)$

Comparing Linear and Exponential Functions

For Exercises 1–3, tell whether each quantity is changing at a *constant rate* per unit of time, at a *constant percent* rate per unit of time, or *neither*.

1. Amy's salary is $40,000 in her first year on a
   job with a $2,000 raise every year thereafter.   _____

2. Carla's salary is $50,000 in her first year on
   a job plus a 1% commission on all sales.   _____

3. Enrollment at a school is 976 students initially
   and then it declines 2.5% each year thereafter.   _____

4. Companies X and Y each have 50 employees. If Company X increases its workforce by 2 employees
   per month, and Company Y increases its workforce by 2% per month, will Company Y ever have
   more employees than Company X? If so, when?

   _____

5. Centerville and Easton each have 2500 residents. Centerville's population decreases by 80 people
   per year, and Easton's population decreases by 3% per year. Will Centerville ever have a greater
   population than Easton? If so, when? Explain your reasoning.

   _____

   _____

   _____

**Complete each statement with the correct function from the table
at the right.**

x	$f(x)$	$g(x)$
0	50	100
1	54	104
2	58	108
3	63	112
4	68	116
5	73	120

6. _____ grows at a constant rate per unit interval.

7. _____ grows at a constant percent rate per unit interval.

8. An equation for the linear function is as follows:

   _____

9. An equation for the exponential function is as follows:

   _____

Graphing Exponential Functions

Make a table of values and a graph for each function.

1. $f(x) = 2^x$

x	$f(x)$
-3	
-2	
-1	
0	
1	
2	
3	

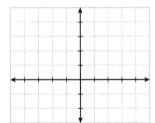

2. $f(x) = 2\left(\frac{3}{4}\right)^x$

x	$f(x)$
-3	
-2	
-1	
0	
1	
2	
3	

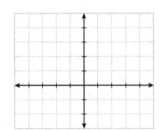

3. $f(x) = 0.9(0.6)^x$

x	$f(x)$
-3	
-2	
-1	
0	
1	
2	
3	

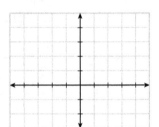

4. When an exponential function has a base greater than _____, the function

_____ as x increases.

5. When an exponential function as a base less than _____, the function

_____ as x increases.

6. Describe the shape of an exponential function with a base of 1.

_____

Writing Exponential Equations

Use two points to write an equation for each function shown.

1.

x	-3	-2	-1	0
f(x)	8	4	2	1

_____

2.

x	1	2	3	4
f(x)	8	6.4	5.12	4.096

_____

3.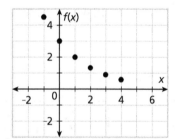

_____

4.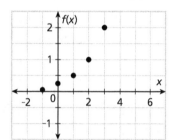

_____

5.

x	-1	0	1	2
f(x)	$\frac{2}{3}$	$\frac{1}{3}$	$\frac{1}{6}$	$\frac{1}{12}$

_____

6.

x	-1	0	1	2
f(x)	$\frac{3}{2}$	3	6	12

_____

Discrete Exponential Functions

1. The area of the top surface of an 8.5 inch by 11 inch piece of paper is a function of the number of times it is folded in half.

   a. Write an equation for the function that models this situation. Explain why this is an exponential function.

   _____

   b. Identify the value of a. What does it represent in this situation?

   _____

   c. What is the area of the top surface after 4 folds? Round to the nearest tenth of a square inch.

   _____

   d. What would the equation be if the original piece of paper had dimensions 11 inches by 17 inches? Compare this equation with the equation in part a.

   _____

2. Suppose you do a favor for 3 people. Then you ask each of them to do a favor for 3 more people, passing along the request that each person who receives a favor does a favor for 3 more people. Suppose you do your 3 favors on Day 1, each recipient does 3 favors on Day 2, and so on.

Day n	Favors $f(n)$
1	3
2	9
3	
4	
5	

   a. Complete the table for the first five days.

   b. Write an equation for the exponential function that models this situation.

   _____

   c. Describe the domain and range of this function.

   _____

   _____

   d. According to the model, how many favors will be done on Day 10? _____

   e. How is the number of favors done on Day 10 related to the number done on Day 5? Explain your reasoning.

   _____

   _____

   f. What would the equation be if everyone did a favor for 4 people rather than 3 people?

   _____

130

Exponential Growth Functions

Complete the table for each function.

	Function	Initial Amount	Growth Rate	Growth Factor
1.	$y = 1250(1 + 0.02)^t$			
2.	$y = 40(1 + 0.5)^t$			
3.	$y = 50(1.06)^t$			

Write an equation for each exponential growth function.

4. Eva deposits $1,500 in an account that earns 4% interest each year.

_____

5. Lamont buys a house for $255,000. The value of the house increases 6% each year.

_____

6. Brian invests $2,000. His investment grows at a rate of 16% per year.

_____

7. a. Suppose you invest $1,600 on your 16th birthday and your investment earns 8% interest each year. Write an equation to represent the value of your investment at any given time, t.

_____

b. What will be the value of the investment on your 30th birthday? Explain your reasoning.

_____

c. On which birthday will your investment be worth over $10,000? Explain your reasoning.

_____

_____

Analyzing Exponential Growth Functions

Sue is a coin collector. At the end of 2005, she bought a coin for $2.50 whose value had been growing 20% per year for 3 years. The value continued to grow at this rate until she sold the coin 4 years later.

1. Write an exponential growth equation for this situation, using the amount Sue paid as the value at time 0.

_____

2. Complete the table.

Time (years) t	Value ($) y
-3	
-2	
-1	
0	
1	
2	
3	
4	

3. Graph and connect the points.

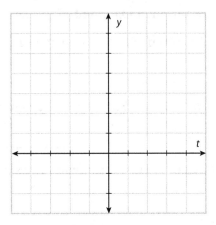

4. Describe the domain and range for this situation.

_____

_____

5. Identify the y-intercept. What does it represent?

_____

_____

6. What was the value of the coin at the end of 2003? at the time Sue sold the coin? Explain your reasoning.

_____

_____

Exponential Decay Functions

1. Identify the initial amount, the decay factor, and the decay rate for the function $y = 2.50(0.4)^t$. Explain how you found the decay rate.

_____

2. Mr. Nevin buys a car for $18,500. The value depreciates 9% per year. Write an equation for this function.

_____

3. You are given a gift of $2,500 in stock on your 16th birthday. The value of the stock declines 10% per year.

a. Write an exponential decay equation for this situation. _____

b. Complete the table. Round to the nearest dollar.   **c.** Graph and connect the points. Label the axes.

Time (years) t	Value ($) y
0	
1	
2	
3	
4	
5	

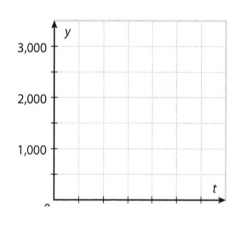

d. Predict the value of the stock on your 22nd birthday. Round to the nearest dollar.

_____

4. The value of two parcels of land has been changing exponentially in the years since they were purchased, as shown in the graph. Describe and compare the values of the two parcels of land.

_____

_____

_____

_____

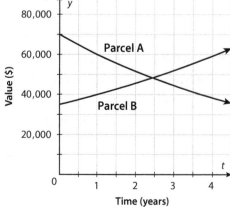

133

Changing the Values of *a* and *b* in *f*(x) = *ab*ˣ

1. Describe how the graph of $f(x) = ab^x$ compares with the graph of $f(x) = b^x$ for a given value of b when $a > 1$ and when $0 < a < 1$.

   _____

   _____

   _____

2. Describe how the graph of $f(x) = ab^x$ changes for a given positive value of a as you increase the value of b when $b > 1$. Discuss end behavior and the y-intercept.

   _____

   _____

   _____

   _____

3. Describe how the graph of $f(x) = ab^x$ changes for a given positive value of a as you decrease the value of b when $0 < b < 1$. Discuss end behavior and the y-intercept.

   _____

   _____

   _____

   _____

4. Consider the functions $Y_1 = (1.02)^x$ and $Y_2 = (1.03)^x$. Which function increases more quickly as x increases to the right of 0? How do the growth factors support your answer?

   _____

   _____

   _____

5. Consider the functions $Y_1 = (0.94)^x$ and $Y_2 = (0.98)^x$. Which function decreases more quickly as x increases to the right of 0? How do the decay factors support your answer?

   _____

   _____

   _____

Solving Equations Involving Exponents

Solve each equation.

1. $\frac{5}{2}(2)^x = 80$

$\boxed{} \cdot \frac{5}{2}(2)^x = \boxed{} \cdot 80$ Multiply to isolate the power $(2)^x$.

$(2)^x = 32$ Simplify.

$(2)^{\boxed{}} = 2^{\boxed{}}$ Write 32 as a power of 2.

$x = \boxed{}$ $b^x = b^y$ if and only if $x = y$.

2. $4\left(\frac{5}{3}\right)^x = \frac{500}{27}$

$\boxed{} \cdot 4\left(\frac{5}{3}\right)^x = \boxed{} \cdot \frac{500}{27}$ Multiply to isolate the power.

$\left(\frac{5}{3}\right)^x = \frac{125}{27}$ Simplify.

$\left(\frac{5}{3}\right)^x = \left(\frac{5}{3}\right)^{\boxed{}}$ Write the fraction as a power of $\frac{5}{3}$.

$x = \boxed{}$ $b^x = b^y$ if and only if $x = y$.

Solve each equation without graphing.

3. $5(3)^x = 405$

$x = $ _____

4. $\frac{1}{5}(5)^x = 5$

$x = $ _____

5. $10(4)^x = 640$

$x = $ _____

6. $7\left(\frac{1}{2}\right)^x = \frac{7}{8}$

$x = $ _____

7. $\frac{3}{4}\left(\frac{2}{3}\right)^x = \frac{4}{27}$

$x = $ _____

8. $3\left(\frac{3}{10}\right)^x = \frac{27}{100}$

$x = $ _____

Solve each equation by graphing. Round to the nearest hundredth.

9. $6^x = 150$

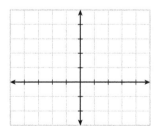

$x \approx $ _____

10. $5^x = 20$

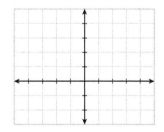

$x \approx $ _____

11. $(2.5)^x = 40$

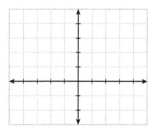

$x \approx $ _____

135

Applications of Exponential Equations

1. Last year a debate club sold 972 fund-raiser tickets on their most successful day. This year the 4 club officers plan to match that number on a single day as follows:

   To start off, on Day 0, each of the 4 officers of the club will sell 3 tickets and ask each buyer to sell 3 more tickets the next day. Every time a ticket is sold, the buyer of the ticket will be asked to sell 3 more tickets the next day.

   If the plan works, on what day will the number of tickets sold be 972?

   a. Write an equation in one variable to model the situation. _____

   b. If the plan works, on what day will the number sold be 972? _____

2. There are 175 deer in a state park. The population is increasing at the rate of 12% per year. At this rate, when will the population reach 300?

   a. Write an equation in one variable to model the situation.

   _____

   b. How long will it take for the population to reach 300?

   _____

   c. Suppose there are 200 deer in another state park and that the deer population is increasing at a rate of 10% per year. Which park's deer population will reach 300 sooner? Explain.

   _____

   _____

3. A city has 642,000 residents on July 1, 2011. The population is decreasing at the rate of 2% per year. At that rate, in what month and year will the population reach 500,000? Explain how you found your answer.

   _____

   _____

Exponential Functions

Graph each exponential function.

1. $f(x) = 3^{2x}$

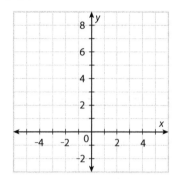

2. $f(x) = 3^{-2x}$

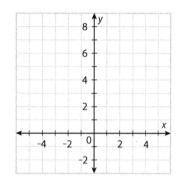

3. $f(x) = 4^{\frac{1}{2}x}$

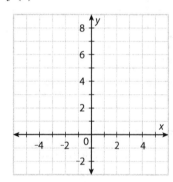

4. $f(x) = 4^{-\frac{1}{2}x}$

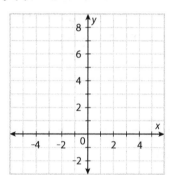

The graph of $f(x) = 3^x$ is shown. Write the function rules for $g(x)$ and $h(x)$ based on the descriptions given. Then sketch the graphs of $g(x)$ and $h(x)$ on the same coordinate plane.

5. The graph of $g(x)$ is a horizontal stretch of the graph of $f(x)$ by a factor of 4.

_____

6. The graph of $h(x)$ is a horizontal shrink of the graph of $f(x)$ by a factor of $\frac{1}{4}$.

_____

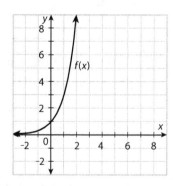

Write the equation for each transformation of the graph of $f(x) = \left(\frac{1}{2}\right)^x$.

7. The graph of $g(x)$ is a horizontal shrink of the graph of $f(x)$ by a factor of $\frac{1}{2}$ and a translation up by 4 units. _____

8. The graph of $h(x)$ is a horizontal stretch of the graph of $f(x)$ by a factor of 1.2, a vertical stretch by a factor of 3, and a translation 8 units down.

_____

137

Analyzing Exponential Functions

Write two equations for the exponential function whose graph is shown by choosing two different bases.

1.

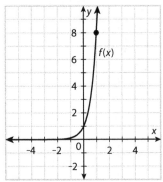

_____

_____

2. Leah plans to deposit $625 in one of the accounts shown in the table. She chooses the account with the greater effective rate. In which account will she invest? How much money will she have in her account after 4 years?

	Account A	Account B
Nominal Interest Rate	2.24%	2.23%
Compounding Period	Quarterly	Daily

_____

3. Provided $c \neq 0$, can changing the value of c in $f(x) = b^{cx}$ affect the range of the function? Explain.

_____

4. Provided $c \neq 0$, can changing the value of c in $f(x) = b^{cx}$ affect the end behavior of the function? Explain.

_____

5. Tyrell makes an investment that earns an annual interest rate of 8%. He wants to know the approximate equivalent monthly interest rate.

   a. One way to find the equivalent monthly interest rate is to recognize that in this situation the effective rate R is 8% and the number, n, of compounding periods is 12. Use the formula $R = \left(1 + \frac{r}{n}\right)^n - 1$ to solve for $\frac{r}{n}$.

   _____

   b. Another way to find the equivalent monthly interest rate is to rewrite the function $A(t) = (1.08)^t$, where $A(t)$ is the annual interest rate, so that the exponent is $12t$. What must you do to the base to compensate for making the exponent $12t$? Carry out the rewriting of $A(t) = (1.08)^t$ to find the equivalent monthly interest rate.

   _____

Unit 9 Review

Solve each equation.

1. $\frac{2}{3}(4)^x = \frac{128}{3}$

2. $3\left(\frac{5}{7}\right)^x = \frac{1875}{2401}$

3. $25(2)^x = 800$

_____   _____   _____

One of the functions defined by the table shows a growth at a constant rate per unit interval (linear). The other function shows a growth at a constant percent rate per unit interval (exponential).

	$f(x)$	$g(x)$
0	20	73
1	25	110
2	30	164
3	35	246
4	40	370
5	45	554

4. Write the equation for the linear function. _____

5. Write the equation for the exponential function. _____

6. Graph the function $f(x) = 4^x$.

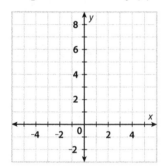

7. Make a table and a graph for the function $f(x) = 2\left(\frac{2}{3}\right)^x$ for the domain $\{-2, -1, 0, 1, 2, 3\}$.

x	$f(x)$

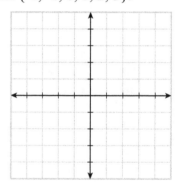

8. Complete the table and draw the graph for the exponential decay equation representing the cost of a car at $12,000, which loses 15% of its value each year. The exponential decay equation is $y = 12{,}000(1 - 0.15)^t$. Round to the nearest dollar.

Time (years) t	0	1	2	3	4	5	6
Value ($) y							

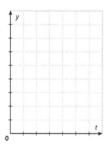

9. Arturo plans to deposit $850 in one of the accounts shown in the table. He chooses the account with the greater effective rate. How much money will he have in his account after 5 years?

	Account X	Account Y
Nominal Interest Rate	2.5%	2.48%
Compounding Period	Quarterly	Daily

Graphing Absolute Value Functions

Graph each absolute value function.

1. $g(x) = |x| + 5$

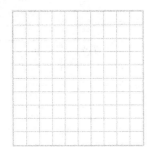

2. $g(x) = |x| - 6$

3. $g(x) = |x| - 4$

4. $g(x) = |x| + 3$

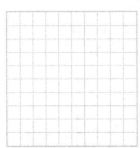

5. $g(x) = |x + 3|$

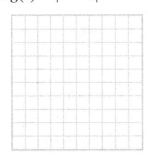

6. $g(x) = |x - 2|$

7. $g(x) = |x + 1|$

8. $g(x) = |x - 5|$

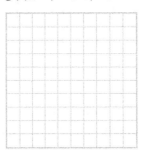

9. $g(x) = |x + 1| + 1$

10. $g(x) = |x - 4| + 2$

11. $g(x) = |x - 3| - 5$

12. $g(x) = |x + 7| - 1$

Translating the Graph of $f(x) = |x|$

Write the equation of each absolute value function whose graph is shown.

1.

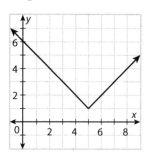

_____

2.

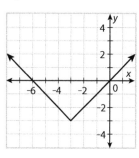

_____

3.

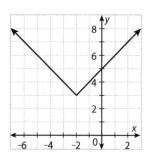

_____

4.

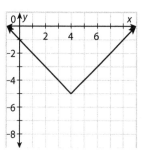

_____

Determine the domain and range of each function.

5. $g(x) = |x| - 7$

_____

_____

6. $g(x) = |x - 2|$

_____

_____

7. $g(x) = |x + 3| - 1$

_____

_____

8. $g(x) = |x + 2| + 2$

_____

_____

9. $g(x) = |x| + 1$

_____

_____

10. $g(x) = |x - 9| + 6$

_____

_____

11. A student says that the graph of $g(x) = |x + 3| - 1$ is the graph of the parent function, $f(x) = |x|$, translated 3 units to the right and 1 unit down. Explain what is incorrect about this statement.

_____

_____

12. Suppose you translate the graph of $g(x) = |x - 2| + 1$ to the left 4 units and down 3 units. What is the equation of the resulting function $h(x)$? Explain.

_____

_____

Core Skills Algebra

More Graphing Absolute Value Functions

Graph each absolute value function.

1. $g(x) = 3|x|$

2. $g(x) = -2.5|x|$

3. $g(x) = \frac{1}{2}|x|$

4. $g(x) = -\frac{2}{3}|x|$

5. a. Complete the table and graph all the functions on the same coordinate plane.

x	-6	-3	0	3	6
$g(x) = \frac{1}{3}|x|$					
$g(x) = |\frac{1}{3}x|$					
$g(x) = -\frac{1}{3}|x|$					
$g(x) = |-\frac{1}{3}x|$					

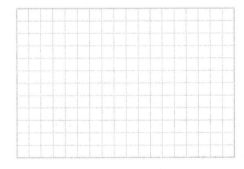

b. How do the graphs of $g(x) = a|x|$ and $g(x) = |ax|$ compare?

Unit 10
Core Skills Algebra

Stretching, Shrinking, and Reflecting the Graph of $f(x) = |x|$

Write the equation of each absolute value function whose graph is shown.

1.

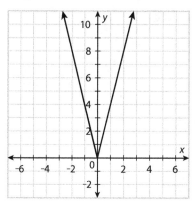

_____

2.

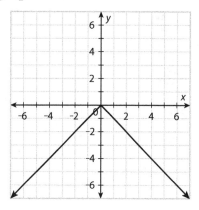

_____

3.

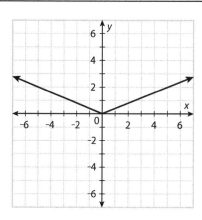

_____

4.

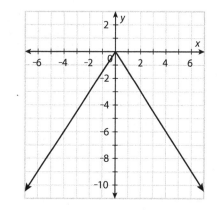

_____

5. From his driveway at point P, Mr. Carey's direct view of the traffic signal at point Q is blocked. In order to see the traffic signal, he places a mirror at point R and aligns it with the x-axis as shown.

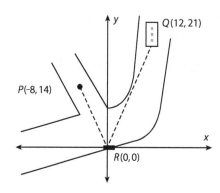

a. Use point Q to write an equation for a function of the form $g(x) = a|x|$ whose graph models the path that light from the traffic signal takes when it strikes the mirror at R.

_____

b. Explain why the mirror is positioned correctly.

_____

_____

Graphing Transformations of Absolute Value Functions

Graph each absolute value function.

1. $g(x) = \frac{3}{4}|x + 2|$

2. $g(x) = 2|x| - 4$

3. $g(x) = -\frac{1}{2}|x + 1|$

4. $g(x) = -3|x - 3| + 5$

5. $g(x) = 1.5|x - 2| - 3$

6. $g(x) = \frac{5}{3}|x + 3| - 5$

Combining Transformations of the Graph of $f(x) = |x|$

Write the equation for each absolute value function whose graph is shown.

1.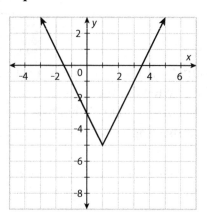

2.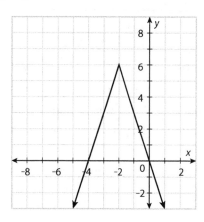

_____

3.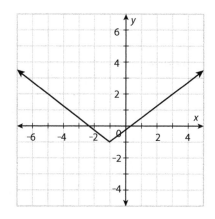

4.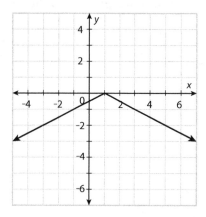

_____

5. The functions that you graphed in Exercises 1–6 on page 144 are listed in the table below. State the domain and range of each function.

Function	Domain	Range
$g(x) = \frac{3}{4}|x + 2|$		
$g(x) = 2|x| - 4$		
$g(x) = -\frac{1}{2}|x + 1|$		
$g(x) = -3|x - 3| + 5$		
$g(x) = 1.5|x - 2| - 3$		
$g(x) = \frac{5}{3}|x + 3| - 5$		

Analyzing Absolute Value Functions

1. Describe the domain and range of any function of the form $g(x) = a|x - h| + k$.

_____

_____

2. The definition of absolute value says that if a number x is positive, then $|x| = x$, and if it is negative, then $|x| = -x$. So, if two numbers a and b are both positive, then by the definition of absolute value, $|ab| = ab = |a||b|$. If a is negative and b is positive, then $|ab| = (-a)b = |a||b|$. What happens if a is positive and b is negative, or if a and b are both negative? What rule applies to $|ab|$ in all cases?

_____

_____

Before graphing, use the rule from Exercise 2 to write each function's equation in the form $g(x) = a|x - h| + k$. Then graph the function.

3. $g(x) = |2x + 8| - 1$

_____

4. $g(x) = |\frac{1}{2}x - 2| + 3$

_____

5. Does the value of a affect the location of the vertex for the graph of $g(x) = a|x - h| + k$? Why or why not?

_____

_____

_____

6. Suppose you vertically shrink the graph of $g(x) = 2|x + 3|$ by a factor of 0.5 and then translate the result 3 units right. What function has the resulting graph?

_____

Solving Absolute Value Equations

Solve each absolute value equation by graphing.

1. $-2|x + 1| + 4 = -4$

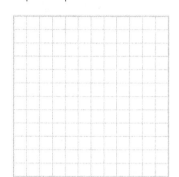

_____

2. $0.5|x - 3| + 2 = 4$

_____

3. $|x + 2| - 2 = -2$

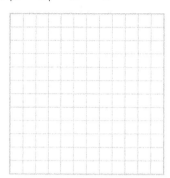

_____

Solve each absolute value equation using algebra.

4. $4|x + 3| - 7 = 5$

5. $0.8|x + 4| - 3 = 1$

6. $-3|x - 1| + 5 = 8$

_____   _____   _____

7. The number of shoppers in a store is modeled by $s(t) = -0.5|t - 288| + 144$ where t is the time (in minutes) since the store opened at 10:00 A.M.

a. For what values of t are there 100 shoppers in the store? _____

b. At what times are there 100 shoppers in the store? _____

c. What is the greatest number of shoppers in the store? _____

d. At what time does the greatest number of shoppers occur? _____

Piecewise Functions

Graph each function.

1. $f(x) = \begin{cases} -x + 1 & \text{if } x < 0 \\ x & \text{if } x \geq 0 \end{cases}$

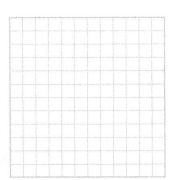

2. $f(x) = \begin{cases} -1 & \text{if } x < 1 \\ 2x - 2 & \text{if } x \geq 1 \end{cases}$

3. $f(x) = \begin{cases} x + 1 & \text{if } x \geq 0 \\ -x + 1 & \text{if } x < 0 \end{cases}$

Write the equation for each function whose graph is shown.

4.

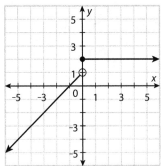

_____

5.

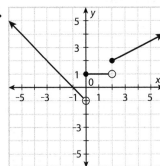

_____

6.

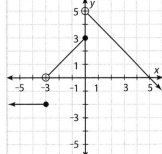

_____

7. Draw a piecewise function on the grid. Then write an equation for the function you drew.

_____

148

Working with Piecewise Functions

1. A garage charges the following rates for parking (with an 8-hour limit):

   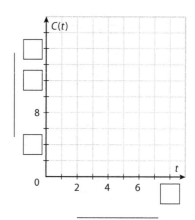

   $4 per hour for the first 2 hours
   $2 per hour for the next 4 hours
   No additional charge for the next 2 hours

   a. Write a piecewise function that gives the parking cost C (in dollars) in terms of the time t (in hours) that a car is parked in the garage.

   _____

   b. Graph the function. Include labels to show what the axes represent and to show the scales on the axes.

2. The cost to send a package between two cities is $8.00 for any weight less than 1 pound. The cost increases by $4.00 when the weight reaches 1 pound, and again each time the weight reaches a whole number of pounds after that.

   a. For a package having weight w (in pounds), write a function in terms of w to represent the shipping cost C (in dollars).

   _____

   b. Complete the table.

Weight (pounds) w	Cost (dollars) $C(w)$
0.5	
1	
1.5	
2	
2.5	

   c. Graph the function. Show the costs for all weights less than 5 pounds.

   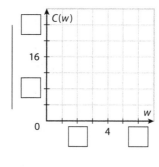

149

Unit 10 Review

Write the equation of each absolute value function whose graph is shown.

1.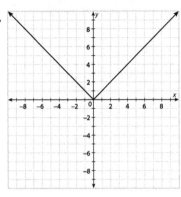

2.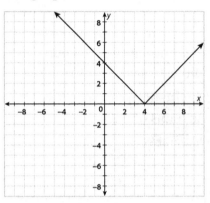

_____   _____

Give the domain and range of each function.

3. $f(x) = |x|$

4. $g(x) = |x - 4| + 2$

5. $g(x) = \frac{1}{2}|x - 3|$

_____   _____   _____

Graph each absolute value function.

6. $g(x) = \frac{1}{2}|x - 3|$

7. $g(x) = 3|x| - 7$

8. $g(x) = -\frac{3}{4}|x|$

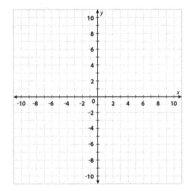 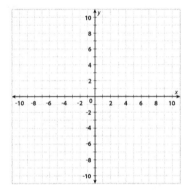 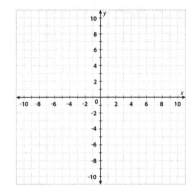

9. Solve the equation $2|x - 3| + 1 = 5$ by graphing.

10. Graph the function $f(x) = \begin{cases} -x & \text{if } x < 0 \\ 2x + 2 & \text{if } x \geq 0 \end{cases}$

_____

150

The Square of the Sum of Two Terms

Squaring a binomial is the same as multiplying a binomial by itself. Study the first example below. The first term of the answer is x^2, which is the square of the first term of the binomial. The middle term of the answer is $2xy$, which is twice the product of the two terms of the binomial. The last term of the answer is y^2, which is the square of the second term of the binomial. This leads to the following shortcut for finding the square of the sum of two terms.

Rule: The square of the sum of two terms is equal to the square of the first term, plus twice the product of the first and the second terms, plus the square of the second term.

Find: $(x + y)^2$

$(x + y)^2 = (x + y)(x + y)$

$\qquad = x(x) + x(y) + x(y) + y(y)$

$\qquad = x^2 + 2xy + y^2$

Find: $(a + 2b)^2$

$(a + 2b)^2 = (a + 2b)(a + 2b)$

$\qquad = a(a) + 2ab + 2ab + 2b(2b)$

$\qquad = a^2 + 4ab + 4b^2$

Find the square of each binomial.

1. $(a + b)^2 =$ _____

2. $(b + a)^2 =$ _____

3. $(m + n)^2 =$ _____

4. $(r + s)^2 =$ _____

5. $(b + c)^2 =$ _____

6. $(c + d)^2 =$ _____

7. $(2a + b)^2 =$ _____

8. $(x + 2y)^2 =$ _____

9. $(2a + 2b)^2 =$ _____

10. $(2y + z)^2 =$ _____

11. $(x + 3y)^2 =$ _____

12. $(3x + y)^2 =$ _____

13. $(2x + 3y)^2 =$ _____

14. $(3x + 2y)^2 =$ _____

15. $(3x + 5)^2 =$ _____

16. $(2x + 7)^2 =$ _____

17. $(m + 4)^2 =$ _____

18. $(6 + g)^2 =$ _____

19. $(2x + 3)^2 =$ _____

20. $(4a + 3)^2 =$ _____

The Square of the Difference of Two Terms

The only difference between squaring the sum of two terms and squaring the difference of two terms is the operation for the middle term of the product. With the sum of two terms, the terms are all added. With the difference of two terms, the middle term is subtracted. Here is a shortcut for squaring the difference of two terms.

Rule: The square of the difference of two terms is equal to the square of the first term, minus twice the product of the first and the second terms, plus the square of the second term.

Find: $(x - y)^2$

$$(x - y)^2 = (x - y)(x - y)$$
$$= x(x) - x(y) - x(y) + y(y)$$
$$= x^2 - 2xy + y^2$$

Find: $(2x - 5y)^2$

$$(2x - 5y)^2 = (2x - 5y)(2x - 5y)$$
$$= 2x(2x) - 2x(5y) - 2x(5y) + 5y(5y)$$
$$= 4x^2 - 20xy + 25y^2$$

Find the square of each binomial.

1. $(x - 4)^2 = $ _____

2. $(x - 3)^2 = $ _____

3. $(x - 5)^2 = $ _____

4. $(x - 8)^2 = $ _____

5. $(3 - y)^2 = $ _____

6. $(7 - x)^2 = $ _____

7. $(a - 12)^2 = $ _____

8. $(a - 10)^2 = $ _____

9. $(c - 2d)^2 = $ _____

10. $(x - 3y)^2 = $ _____

11. $(x - 6y)^2 = $ _____

12. $(x - 10y)^2 = $ _____

13. $(3x - 7y)^2 = $ _____

14. $(2x - 9y)^2 = $ _____

15. $(3a - 2b)^2 = $ _____

16. $(8c - 4d)^2 = $ _____

17. $(7x - 6y)^2 = $ _____

18. $(10m - 3n)^2 = $ _____

19. $(6x - 2y)^2 = $ _____

20. $(5x - 4y)^2 = $ _____

152

Name _____ Date _____

Factoring the Square of the Sum of Two Terms

The square of a binomial is a **perfect square trinomial**. For example, $(a + b)^2 = a^2 + 2ab + b^2$. To factor a perfect square trinomial such as $a^2 + 2ab + b^2$, think of the reverse of multiplication. The first term of each binomial will be the square root of the first term of the perfect square trinomial. The second term of each binomial will be the square root of the second term of the polynomial. Since the operation for the middle term of the polynomial is addition, the operation for each binomial also will be addition. Thus, the factors of $a^2 + 2ab + b^2$ are $(a + b)(a + b)$, or $(a + b)^2$.

Factor: $x^2 + 2xy + y^2$

$= (x + y)(x + y)$

$= (x + y)^2$

Factor: $25 + 10x + x^2$

$= (5 + x)(5 + x)$

$= (5 + x)^2$

Factor: $4y^2 + 48y + 144$

$= (2y + 12)(2y + 12)$

$= (2y + 12)^2$

Factor.

1. $a^2 + 2ay + y^2 =$ _____

2. $m^2 + 2mn + n^2 =$ _____

3. $c^2 + 2cd + d^2 =$ _____

4. $r^2 + 2rs + s^2 =$ _____

5. $x^2 + 4xy + 4y^2 =$ _____

6. $4x^2 + 4xy + y^2 =$ _____

7. $m^2 + 6mn + 9n^2 =$ _____

8. $r^2 + 14rt + 49t^2 =$ _____

9. $x^2 + 8xy + 16y^2 =$ _____

10. $9x^2 + 24x + 16 =$ _____

11. $49y^2 + 56y + 16 =$ _____

12. $x^2 + 10xy + 25y^2 =$ _____

13. $9 + 6y + y^2 =$ _____

14. $4z^2 + 12z + 9 =$ _____

15. $4 + 4x + x^2 =$ _____

16. $16x^2 + 56xy + 49y^2 =$ _____

17. $64 + 16x + x^2 =$ _____

18. $49 + 14x + x^2 =$ _____

19. $9x^2 + 12xy + 4y^2 =$ _____

20. $4x^2 + 16xy + 16y^2 =$ _____

21. $81 + 36x + 4x^2 =$ _____

22. $64x^2 + 16x + 1 =$ _____

23. $100 + 20x + x^2 =$ _____

24. $36x^2 + 24x + 4 =$ _____

Factoring the Square of the Difference of Two Terms

The polynomial $a^2 + 2ab + b^2$ is a perfect square trinomial and factors into $(a + b)^2$. The polynomial $a^2 - 2ab + b^2$ is also a perfect square trinomial. To factor $a^2 - 2ab + b^2$, follow the same method used for factoring $a^2 + 2ab + b^2$, but use subtraction as the operation in the squared binomial. Since the only difference between $a^2 + 2ab + b^2$ and $a^2 - 2ab + b^2$ is the operation on the middle term, the only difference between their factors should be the operation. Thus, $a^2 - 2ab + b^2 = (a - b)(a - b)$, or $(a - b)^2$.

Factor: $r^2 - 2rs + s^2$

$= (r - s)(r - s)$

$= (r - s)^2$

Factor: $9a^2 - 24a + 16$

$= (3a - 4)(3a - 4)$

$= (3a - 4)^2$

Factor: $4p^2 - 12pq + 9q^2$

$= (2p - 3q)(2p - 3q)$

$= (2p - 3q)^2$

Factor.

1. $x^2 - 2xy + y^2 =$ _____

2. $c^2 - 2cd + d^2 =$ _____

3. $b^2 - 2bd + d^2 =$ _____

4. $m^2 - 2mn + n^2 =$ _____

5. $r^2 - 2rs + s^2 =$ _____

6. $y^2 - 2yz + z^2 =$ _____

7. $x^2 - 4x + 4 =$ _____

8. $4a^2 - 12a + 9 =$ _____

9. $a^2 - 8a + 16 =$ _____

10. $x^2 - 12x + 36 =$ _____

11. $9x^2 - 36x + 36 =$ _____

12. $x^2 - 14x + 49 =$ _____

13. $x^2 - 6xy + 9y^2 =$ _____

14. $16x^2 - 16xy + 4y^2 =$ _____

15. $x^2 - 12xy + 36y^2 =$ _____

16. $x^2 - 16xy + 64y^2 =$ _____

17. $25a^2 - 30ab + 9b^2 =$ _____

18. $x^2 - 14xy + 49y^2 =$ _____

19. $4m^2 - 20mn + 25n^2 =$ _____

20. $x^2 - 22xy + 121y^2 =$ _____

21. $9x^2 - 12x + 4 =$ _____

22. $16x^2 - 16x + 4 =$ _____

23. $36x^2 - 36x + 9 =$ _____

24. $49x^2 - 42x + 9 =$ _____

The Product of the Sum and Difference of Two Terms

The first example below shows the results of multiplying the sum of two terms by the difference of the same two terms. The first term of the product is x^2, which is the square of the first term of each binomial. The second term of the product is y^2, which is the square of the second term of each binomial. The two middle terms added together become zero, so the final product is the difference of the two squares. This leads to the following shortcut for finding the product of the sum and difference of two terms.

Rule: The product of the sum and difference of two terms is equal to the square of the first term of each binomial minus the square of the second term of each binomial.

Find: $(x + y)(x - y)$

$= x(x) + x(-y) + x(y) + y(-y)$

$= x^2 - xy + xy - y^2$

$= x^2 - y^2$

Find: $(2x + 1)(2x - 1)$

$= 2x(2x) + 2x(-1) + 2x(1) + 1(-1)$

$= 4x^2 - 2x + 2x - 1$

$= 4x^2 - 1$

Find each product.

1. $(a + b)(a - b) =$ _____

2. $(y + z)(y - z) =$ _____

3. $(x + 6)(x - 6) =$ _____

4. $(x - 7)(x + 7) =$ _____

5. $(x - 3)(x + 3) =$ _____

6. $(x + 8)(x - 8) =$ _____

7. $(5d + g)(5d - g) =$ _____

8. $(6 - b)(6 + b) =$ _____

9. $(2x + 3)(2x - 3) =$ _____

10. $(3m + 5)(3m - 5) =$ _____

11. $(8x - 2)(8x + 2) =$ _____

12. $(6x - z)(6x + z) =$ _____

13. $(5 - 3x)(5 + 3x) =$ _____

14. $(7 + 6x)(7 - 6x) =$ _____

15. $(3k + 7m)(3k - 7m) =$ _____

16. $(9a - 5b)(9a + 5b) =$ _____

17. $(3x - 4y)(3x + 4y) =$ _____

18. $(4m + 6n)(4m - 6n) =$ _____

Factoring the Difference of Two Squares

An expression such as $y^2 - 9$ is the difference of two squares. There are only two terms, and one of the terms is subtracted from the other. The factors of $y^2 - 9$ are $(y + 3)(y - 3)$, where the middle terms add to zero.

To factor the difference of two squares, use these steps.

Step 1. Find the square root of each term.

Step 2. Use the sum of these two square roots as one factor.

Step 3. Use the difference of these two square roots as the other factor.

Factor: $4x^2 - 25$

Step 1: $2x$ = the square root of $4x^2$
 5 = the square root of 25

Step 2: $2x + 5$ = sum of the two square roots

Step 3: $2x - 5$ = difference

The factors are $(2x + 5)(2x - 5)$.

Check: $(2x + 5)(2x - 5)$

$= 4x^2 + 10x - 10x - 25$

$= 4x^2 - 25$

Factor.

1. $x^2 - y^2 =$ _____

2. $x^2 - 36 =$ _____

3. $x^2 - 100 =$ _____

4. $a^2 - 81 =$ _____

5. $25 - a^2 =$ _____

6. $m^2 - 9 =$ _____

7. $225 - x^2 =$ _____

8. $x^2 - 121 =$ _____

9. $4x^2 - 49 =$ _____

10. $64 - a^2 =$ _____

11. $25a^2 - 16 =$ _____

12. $900 - z^2 =$ _____

13. $100x^2 - 9 =$ _____

14. $36x^2 - 64 =$ _____

15. $144x^2 - 100 =$ _____

16. $49a^2 - 49 =$ _____

17. $9a^2 - 16b^2 =$ _____

18. $36m^2 - 49n^2 =$ _____

19. $25x^2 - 25y^2 =$ _____

20. $16x^2 - 81y^2 =$ _____

The Product of Two Binomials with a Common Term

Sometimes two binomials share only one common term, as in $(x + 5)(x - 3)$. To multiply two binomials with one common term, use one of the methods below. Pay particular attention to the sign of the middle term in the product.

Method 1: Multiply each term separately.

Find: $(x + 5)(x - 3)$.

$= x(x) + (-3)(x) + 5(x) + (5)(-3)$

$= x^2 - 3x + 5x - 15$

$= x^2 + 2x - 15$

Method 2: Use the steps shown above.

Find: $(x + 5)(x - 3)$.

Step 1: $(x)(x) = x^2$ Square the common term.

Step 2: $x(5 + -3) = 2x$ Add the unlike terms and multiply by the common term.

Step 3: $(5)(-3) = -15$ Multiply the unlike terms.

Step 4: $x^2 + 2x - 15$ Combine the results from steps 1–3.

Find each product.

1. $(x + 5)(x + 4) =$ _____

2. $(x + 2)(x + 6) =$ _____

3. $(x + 1)(x + 3) =$ _____

4. $(x + 3)(x + 4) =$ _____

5. $(x + 7)(x + 2) =$ _____

6. $(x + 4)(x + 6) =$ _____

7. $(x + 10)(x + 1) =$ _____

8. $(x + 6)(x + 7) =$ _____

9. $(x + 4)(x - 1) =$ _____

10. $(x + 2)(x - 3) =$ _____

11. $(x + 8)(x - 2) =$ _____

12. $(x + 7)(x - 2) =$ _____

13. $(x - 7)(x + 2) =$ _____

14. $(x - 10)(x + 1) =$ _____

15. $(x - 5)(x - 1) =$ _____

16. $(x - 7)(x - 3) =$ _____

17. $(x - 4)(x - 5) =$ _____

18. $(x - 3)(x - 5) =$ _____

Factoring Two Binomials with a Common Term

When two binomials with a common term are multiplied, the product is a trinomial. For example, $x^2 + 8x - 20$ is a trinomial that can be factored into two binomials with a common term, $(x + 10)(x - 2)$. To factor such a trinomial, use these steps.

Step 1:   Find the square root of the first term.

Step 2:   Find all the factors of the third term.

Step 3:   Decide which of these factors can be added to find the coefficient of the middle term.

Factor: $x^2 + 2x - 15$

Step 1: x = the square root of the first term

Step 2:   (5)(-3)   These are factors of the third term.
           (-5)(3)   Note that one factor must be
           (-1)(15)   negative in this example because
           (1)(-15)   the third term (-15) is negative.

Step 3: $5 + (-3) = 2$ Only the factors 5 and -3 add to 2,
                           the coefficient of the middle term.

The two binomial factors are $(x + 5)(x - 3)$.

Check: $(x + 5)(x - 3)$
$= x(x) + 5x - 3x - 15$
$= x^2 + 2x - 15$

Factor.

1. $x^2 + 8x + 15 =$ _____

2. $x^2 + 5x + 6 =$ _____

3. $x^2 + 3x + 2 =$ _____

4. $x^2 + 8x + 12 =$ _____

5. $x^2 + 7x + 10 =$ _____

6. $x^2 + 9x + 8 =$ _____

7. $x^2 + 4x - 12 =$ _____

8. $x^2 - 9x + 18 =$ _____

9. $x^2 + 2x - 8 =$ _____

10. $x^2 + 5x - 24 =$ _____

11. $x^2 - 4x - 12 =$ _____

12. $x^2 - 8x - 20 =$ _____

13. $x^2 - 9x - 10 =$ _____

14. $x^2 - 10x - 24 =$ _____

15. $x^2 - 7x + 12 =$ _____

16. $x^2 - 9x + 20 =$ _____

Multiplying Binomials and the FOIL Method

Knowing the types of binomials multiplied together can allow the use of shortcuts to find the product. It is important to remember, however, that any two binomials can be multiplied together using a simple method.

F	=	First terms
O	=	Outer terms
I	=	Inner terms
L	=	Last terms

A general method for multiplying any two binomials is the **FOIL** method. The FOIL method shows how to multiply all terms in a certain order.

Find: $(2x + 4)(x - 3)$

$$
\begin{aligned}
(2x + 4)(x - 3) &= 2x(x) + 2x(-3) + 4(x) + 4(-3) \\
&= 2x^2 - 6x + 4x - 12 \\
&= 2x^2 - 2x - 12
\end{aligned}
$$

Find each product using the FOIL method.

1. $(x + 2)(2x + 3) =$ _____

2. $(2x + 1)(x + 2) =$ _____

3. $(2x + y)(x + 2y) =$ _____

4. $(2x + 3y)(x + y) =$ _____

5. $(x + 5y)(2x + y) =$ _____

6. $(x + 3y)(2x + y) =$ _____

7. $(x + 3)(2x - 1) =$ _____

8. $(2x + 3)(x - 1) =$ _____

9. $(x + 2y)(2x - y) =$ _____

10. $(2x + y)(x - 2y) =$ _____

11. $(3x + 1)(x - 2) =$ _____

12. $(2x - 4y)(x + 3y) =$ _____

13. $(x - 3)(2x - 1) =$ _____

14. $(x - 4)(2x - 1) =$ _____

15. $(x - 3y)(2x - y) =$ _____

16. $(2x - 3)(x - 1) =$ _____

17. $(2x - y)(x - 2y) =$ _____

18. $(3x - 3y)(2x - y) =$ _____

Factoring for Two Binomials with Like Terms

The challenge in factoring trinomials such as $2x^2 + 7x - 4$ lies in finding the proper combination of factors that will give the middle term. There are three important facts to keep in mind when factoring all kinds of trinomials.

1. When all the terms of the trinomial are added, the terms in both binomials will be added.
2. When only the middle term is subtracted, the terms in both binomials will be subtracted.
3. When the last term is subtracted, the terms in one binomial are added and the terms in the other binomial are subtracted.

Factor: $2x^2 + 7x - 4$

Since the last term is subtracted, the terms in one binomial will be added, and the terms in the other binomial will be subtracted. List the possible factors of the first and third terms (in pairs).

List possible pairs of binomial factors. Find the middle term for each pair of factors. Keep trying until a pair of factors yields $7x$ as the middle term.

So, $2x^2 + 7x - 4 = (2x - 1)(x + 4)$.

Factors for first term

$2x^2 = (2x)(x)$

Factors for third term

$-4 = (-2)(2)$
$-4 = (-4)(1)$
$-4 = (4)(-1)$

Possible factor pairs	Middle term	
$(2x - 2)(x + 2)$	$4x - 2x = 2x$	No
$(2x + 2)(x - 2)$	$-4x + 2x = -2x$	No
$(2x - 4)(x + 1)$	$2x - 4x = -2x$	No
$(2x + 1)(x - 4)$	$-8x + x = -7x$	No
$(2x + 4)(x - 1)$	$-2x + 4x = 2x$	No
$(2x - 1)(x + 4)$	$8x - x = 7x$	Yes

Factor.

1. $2x^2 + 5x + 2 =$ _____

2. $3x^2 + 5x + 2 =$ _____

3. $7x^2 - 15x + 2 =$ _____

4. $5x^2 + 11x + 2 =$ _____

5. $2x^2 - 7x + 3 =$ _____

6. $3x^2 - 8x + 4 =$ _____

7. $5y^2 - 26y + 5 =$ _____

8. $7x^2 - 16x + 4 =$ _____

9. $2x^2 + 3x - 2 =$ _____

10. $3x^2 + x - 2 =$ _____

11. $5y^2 - 7y - 6 =$ _____

12. $7x^2 - 10x - 8 =$ _____

Unit 11 Review

Find each product.

1. $(x - y)(x + y) =$

2. $(4 - 6t)^2 =$

3. $(2x - y)(x + 4y) =$

_____   _____   _____

4. $(3 + 2x)^2 =$

5. $(5x - 3)(2x - 7) =$

6. $(x + 7)(x - 3) =$

_____   _____   _____

7. $(3x - 2y)(x - y) =$

8. $(6x + 5)^2 =$

9. $(9x - 3)^2 =$

_____   _____   _____

Factor.

10. $x^2 + 2xy + y^2 =$

11. $25x^2 - 40x + 16 =$

12. $64 - 16x^2 =$

_____   _____   _____

13. $x^2 - 2x - 8 =$

14. $x^2 - 3x - 4 =$

15. $3x^2 + x - 2 =$

_____   _____   _____

16. $9x^2 + 12x + 4 =$

17. $3x^2 + x - 10 =$

18. $16a^2 - 48a + 36 =$

_____   _____   _____

19. $2x^2 + x - 28 =$

20. $x^2 + 3x - 40 =$

21. $4a^2 - 4ab + b^2 =$

_____   _____   _____

161

Solving Quadratic Equations Graphically

Solve each quadratic equation by graphing. Indicate whether the solutions are exact or approximate.

1. $(x + 2)^2 - 1 = 3$

_____

2. $2(x - 3)^2 + 1 = 5$

_____

3. $-\frac{1}{2}x^2 + 2 = -4$

_____

4. $-(x - 3)^2 - 2 = -6$

_____

5. As part of an engineering contest, a student who has designed a protective crate for an egg drops the crate from a window 18 feet above the ground. The height (in feet) of the crate as it falls is given by $h(t) = -16t^2 + 18$, where t is the time (in seconds) since the crate was dropped.

a. Write and solve an equation to find the elapsed time until the crate passes a window 10 feet directly below the window from which it was dropped.

_____

b. Write and solve an equation to find the elapsed time until the crate hits the ground.

_____

c. Is the crate's rate of fall constant? Explain.

_____

_____

_____

162

Solving Quadratic Equations Using Square Roots

1. Write the square roots of 64 in simplified form. _____

2. Write the square roots of 32 in simplified form. _____

3. Write the square roots of $\frac{8}{9}$ in simplified form. _____

4. Explain why the square roots of 37 cannot be simplified. _____

_____

Solve each quadratic equation. Simplify solutions when possible.

5. $x^2 = 18$

_____

6. $-4x^2 = -20$

_____

7. $x^2 + 4 = 10$

_____

8. $2x^2 = 200$

_____

9. $(x - 5)^2 = 25$

_____

10. $(x + 1)^2 = 16$

_____

11. $2(x - 7)^2 = 98$

_____

12. $-5(x + 3)^2 = -80$

_____

13. $0.5(x + 2)^2 - 4 = 14$

_____

14. $3(x - 1)^2 + 1 = 19$

_____

15. To study how high a ball bounces, students drop the ball from various heights. The function $h(t) = -16t^2 + h_0$ gives the height (in feet) of the ball at time t measured in seconds since the ball was dropped from a height h_0.

a. The ball is dropped from a height $h_0 = 8$ feet. Write and solve an equation to find the elapsed time until the ball hits the floor.

_____

b. Does doubling the drop height also double the elapsed time until the ball hits the floor? Explain why or why not.

_____

c. When dropped from a height $h_0 = 16$ feet, the ball rebounds to a height of 8 feet and then falls back to the floor. Find the total time for this to happen. (Assume the ball takes the same time to rebound 8 feet as it does to fall 8 feet.)

_____

Quadratic Equations and the Zero Product Property

A **quadratic equation** is an equation in which the greatest exponent of any term is 2. An example is $x^2 + 10x + 25 = 0$. The **roots** of the equation are the values of x that make the equation true. To find the roots of the equation, first factor the trinomial. Then use the **zero product property,** which states that any number multiplied by zero equals zero. Therefore, if $ab = 0$, then $a = 0$ or $b = 0$ or both. To use this property, write each factor equal to zero and solve. Check each solution, or root, by substituting it back into the original equation.

Solve: $x^2 + 10x + 25 = 0$

$(x + 5)(x + 5) = 0$

$x + 5 = 0 \qquad x + 5 = 0$

$\qquad x = -5 \qquad\qquad x = -5$

The root of the equation is –5.

Check: $(-5)^2 + 10(-5) + 25 = 0$

$\qquad\qquad 25 - 50 + 25 = 0$

$\qquad\qquad\qquad\qquad 0 = 0$

Solve: $8x + 16x^2 = -1$

$16x^2 + 8x + 1 = 0 \qquad$ Rearrange terms.

$(4x + 1)(4x + 1) = 0$

$4x + 1 = 0 \qquad\qquad 4x + 1 = 0$

$\qquad 4x = -1 \qquad\qquad\qquad 4x = -1$

$\qquad\quad x = -\frac{1}{4} \qquad\qquad\qquad x = -\frac{1}{4}$

The root of the equation is $-\frac{1}{4}$.

Check: $8(-\frac{1}{4}) + 16(-\frac{1}{4})^2 = -1$

$\qquad\qquad -\frac{8}{4} + \frac{16}{16} = -1$

$\qquad\qquad\qquad -2 + 1 = -1$

Solve each quadratic equation. Check.

1. $x^2 + 4x + 4 = 0$

2. $x^2 + 6x + 9 = 0$

3. $x^2 + 8x + 16 = 0$

_____

_____

_____

4. $x^2 + 14x + 49 = 0$

5. $9x^2 + 12x = -4$

6. $16x^2 + 24x = -9$

_____

_____

_____

7. $4x^2 + 12x = -9$

8. $9 + 18x + 9x^2 = 0$

9. $16 + 16x + 4x^2 = 0$

_____

_____

_____

More Quadratic Equations and Perfect Square Trinomials

Some quadratic equations involve factoring a perfect square trinomial where the middle term is subtracted. An example is $x^2 - 2x + 1 = 0$.

To solve, or find the roots, factor the trinomial and use the zero product property as before. Check each solution.

Solve: $x^2 - 2x + 1 = 0$

$(x - 1)(x - 1) = 0$

$\qquad x - 1 = 0 \qquad x - 1 = 0$

$\qquad\qquad x = 1 \qquad\qquad x = 1$

The root of the equation is 1.

Check: $\quad (1)^2 - 2(1) + 1 = 0$

$\qquad\qquad\qquad 1 - 2 + 1 = 0$

$\qquad\qquad\qquad\qquad\quad 0 = 0$

Solve: $4x^2 - 12x = -9$

$4x^2 - 12x + 9 = 0$

$(2x - 3)(2x - 3) = 0$

$\qquad\qquad 2x - 3 = 0 \qquad 2x - 3 = 0$

$\qquad\qquad\qquad 2x = 3 \qquad\qquad 2x = 3$

$\qquad\qquad\qquad\quad x = \frac{3}{2} \qquad\qquad\quad x = \frac{3}{2}$

The root of the equation is $\frac{3}{2}$.

Check: $\quad 4\left(\frac{3}{2}\right)^2 - 12\left(\frac{3}{2}\right) = -9$

$\qquad\qquad 4\left(\frac{9}{4}\right) - \left(\frac{36}{2}\right) = -9$

$\qquad\qquad\qquad\qquad 9 - 18 = -9$

$\qquad\qquad\qquad\qquad\quad -9 = -9$

Solve each quadratic equation.

1. $x^2 - 16x + 64 = 0$

2. $25 - 10x + x^2 = 0$

3. $16 - 8x + x^2 = 0$

_____

_____

_____

4. $36 - 12x + x^2 = 0$

5. $4x^2 - 16x = -16$

6. $-8x + 16x^2 = -1$

_____

_____

_____

7. $-12x + 4 = -9x^2$

8. $9x^2 - 6x + 1 = 0$

9. $25x^2 - 20x = -4$

_____

_____

_____

Quadratic Equations and the Difference of Two Squares

To find the roots of a quadratic equation involving the difference of two squares, first factor the difference of the squares. Then use the zero product property.

Solve: $y^2 - 100 = 0$

$(y - 10)(y + 10) = 0$

$\quad y - 10 = 0 \qquad y + 10 = 0$

$\qquad y = 10 \qquad\qquad y = -10$

The roots of the equation are 10 and -10.

Check:

$(10)^2 - 100 = 0 \qquad (-10)^2 - 100 = 0$

$100 - 100 = 0 \qquad\quad 100 - 100 = 0$

Solve: $4x^2 - 9 = 0$

$(2x - 3)(2x + 3) = 0$

$\quad 2x - 3 = 0 \qquad 2x + 3 = 0$

$\qquad 2x = 3 \qquad\qquad 2x = -3$

$\qquad x = \frac{3}{2} \qquad\qquad x = -\frac{3}{2}$

The roots of the equation are $\frac{3}{2}$ and $-\frac{3}{2}$.

Check: $\quad 4\left(\frac{3}{2}\right)^2 - 9 = 0 \qquad 4\left(-\frac{3}{2}\right)^2 - 9 = 0$

$\qquad\qquad 4\left(\frac{9}{4}\right) - 9 = 0 \qquad 4\left(\frac{9}{4}\right) - 9 = 0$

$\qquad\qquad\qquad 9 - 9 = 0 \qquad\qquad 9 - 9 = 0$

Solve each quadratic equation.

1. $a^2 - 49 = 0$

2. $a^2 - 64 = 0$

3. $a^2 - 81 = 0$

_____

_____

_____

4. $x^2 - 144 = 0$

5. $x^2 - 400 = 0$

6. $x^2 - 16 = 0$

_____

_____

_____

7. $16x^2 - 100 = 0$

8. $4x^2 - 16 = 0$

9. $81x^2 - 36 = 0$

_____

_____

_____

10. $4x^2 - 36 = 0$

11. $25x^2 - 100 = 0$

12. $9x^2 - 36 = 0$

_____

_____

_____

Quadratic Equations and Factoring Trinomials

Some quadratic equations involve factoring a trinomial that is the product of two binomials with a common term. To find the roots of the equation, factor the trinomial and use the zero product property.

Solve: $x^2 - 5x - 14 = 0$

$(x - 7)(x + 2) = 0$

$x - 7 = 0 \qquad x + 2 = 0$

$x = 7 \qquad\quad x = -2$

The roots of the equation are 7 and -2.

Check:

$(7)^2 - 5(7) - 14 = 0 \quad (-2)^2 - 5(-2) - 14 = 0$

$49 - 35 - 14 = 0 \qquad 4 + 10 - 14 = 0$

$49 - 49 = 0 \qquad\qquad 14 - 14 = 0$

Solve: $x^2 + x = 12$

$x^2 + x - 12 = 0$

$(x - 3)(x + 4) = 0$

$x - 3 = 0 \qquad x + 4 = 0$

$x = 3 \qquad\quad x = -4$

The roots of the equation are 3 and -4.

Check:

$(3)^2 + 3 - 12 = 0 \quad (-4)^2 + (-4) - 12 = 0$

$9 + 3 - 12 = 0 \qquad 16 - 4 - 12 = 0$

$12 - 12 = 0 \qquad\qquad 16 - 16 = 0$

Solve each quadratic equation.

1. $x^2 + 7x + 12 = 0$

2. $x^2 + 7x + 6 = 0$

3. $x^2 + 9x + 20 = 0$

_____

_____

_____

4. $x^2 - 2x - 8 = 0$

5. $x^2 - 5x = 6$

6. $x^2 - 9x = 10$

_____

_____

_____

7. $x^2 - 8x = 33$

8. $x^2 - 7x - 44 = 0$

9. $x^2 - 10x - 39 = 0$

_____

_____

_____

10. $x^2 - 7x = -6$

11. $x^2 - 5x + 4 = 0$

12. $x^2 - 12x = -20$

_____

_____

_____

167

Solving $x^2 + bx + c = 0$ by Factoring

Complete the factorization of each polynomial.

1. $t^2 + 6t + 5 = (t + 5)(t + \boxed{})$

2. $z^2 - 121 = (z + 11)(z \boxed{}\boxed{})$

3. $d^2 + 5d - 24 = (d + \boxed{})(d - \boxed{})$

4. $x^4 - 4 = (x^2 + \boxed{})(\boxed{} - 2)$

Factor each polynomial.

5. $y^2 + 3y - 4$

_____

6. $x^2 - 2x + 1$

_____

7. $p^2 - 2p - 24$

_____

8. $g^2 - 100$

_____

9. $z^2 - 7z + 12$

_____

10. $q^2 + 25q + 100$

_____

Solve.

11. $m^2 + 8m + 16 = 0$

_____

12. $n^2 - 10n = 24$

_____

13. $x^2 + 25x = 0$

_____

14. $y^2 - 30 = 13y$

_____

15. $z^2 - 9 = 0$

_____

16. $p^2 = 54 - 3p$

_____

17. $x^2 + 11x - 42 = 0$

_____

18. $g^2 - 14g = 51$

_____

19. $n^2 - 81 = 0$

_____

20. $y^2 = 25y$

_____

21. $f(x) = x^2 + 11x + 30$

_____

22. $f(x) = x^2 - x - 20$

_____

23. $f(x) = x^2 + 6x - 7$

_____

24. $f(x) = x^2 + 2x + 1$

_____

Quadratic Equations and Coefficients Other Than 1

Sometimes a quadratic equation might have a squared term with a coefficient other than 1. To find the roots of the equation, follow the same factoring method used for finding two binomials with a like term.

Solve: $2x^2 - 10x + 12 = 0$

$(2x - 4)(x - 3) = 0$

$2x - 4 = 0 \qquad x - 3 = 0$

$\qquad x = 2 \qquad\qquad x = 3$

The roots of the equation are 2 and 3.

Check: $2(2)^2 - 10(2) + 12 = 0$

$8 - 20 + 12 = 0$

$-12 + 12 = 0$

and

$2(3)^2 - 10(3) + 12 = 0$

$18 - 30 + 12 = 0$

$-12 + 12 = 0$

Solve each quadratic equation.

1. $2x^2 + 5x + 2 = 0$

2. $2x^2 + 11x + 5 = 0$

3. $5x^2 - 14x - 3 = 0$

_____

_____

_____

4. $7x^2 + 13x - 2 = 0$

5. $3x^2 - 14x - 5 = 0$

6. $2x^2 - 5x + 3 = 0$

_____

_____

_____

7. $5x^2 + 9x - 2 = 0$

8. $2x^2 - 3x - 2 = 0$

9. $2x^2 + x - 3 = 0$

_____

_____

_____

10. $3x^2 - 2x - 5 = 0$

11. $5x^2 - 3x - 2 = 0$

12. $3x^2 + 14x - 5 = 0$

_____

_____

_____

Solving $ax^2 + bx + c = 0$ by Factoring

Factor.

1. $2x^2 + 15x + 7$

   _____

2. $7z^2 - 30z + 27$

   _____

3. $8x^2 - 10x - 3$

   _____

4. $30d^2 + 7d - 15$

   _____

Solve by factoring.

5. $10g^2 + 23g + 12 = 0$

   _____

6. $5y^2 - 2y - 7 = 0$

   _____

7. $2n^2 + 15 = 11n$

   _____

8. $6a^2 + 10a = 3a + 10$

   _____

9. $12x^2 - x = 20$

   _____

10. $9z^2 - 25 = 0$

    _____

11. $36h^2 - 12h + 1 = 0$

    _____

12. $12n^2 + 48 = 80n$

    _____

13. $18x^2 + 24x = -8$

    _____

14. $12y^2 + 3y = 54$

    _____

15. A dolphin bounces a ball off its nose at an initial upward velocity of 6 m/s to a trainer lying on a 1-meter-high platform. The function $h(t) = -5t^2 + vt$ models the ball's height (in meters) above the water, where v is the initial upward velocity of the ball in meters per second.

    a. Write an equation to find the time when $h(t) = 1$.

    $$-5t^2 + \boxed{}\, t = \boxed{}$$

    b. Solve the equation to find the two values for t.

    $t =$ _____ or $t =$ _____

    c. Explain the two values for t in the context of the situation.

    _____

    _____

    _____

Mixed Practice Solving Quadratic Equations

You have seen five general types of products of two binomials.

- The square of the sum of two terms: $(x + y)^2 = x^2 + 2xy + y^2$
- The square of the difference of two terms: $(x - y)^2 = x^2 - 2xy + y^2$
- The product of the sum and difference of two terms: $(x + y)(x - y) = x^2 - y^2$
- The product of two binomials with a common term: $(x + a)(x + b) = x^2 + abx + ab$
- The product of two binomials with like terms: $(x + a)(bx + c) = bx^2 + abcx + ac$

Solve each quadratic equation.

1. $x^2 - 49 = 0$

2. $x^2 - 4x + 4 = 0$

3. $x^2 + 4x - 5 = 0$

_____

_____

_____

4. $x^2 + 10x + 25 = 0$

5. $x^2 - 64 = 0$

6. $x^2 - 15x + 50 = 0$

_____

_____

_____

7. $x^2 - 2x = -1$

8. $x^2 - 7x = 30$

9. $2x^2 + 5x + 3 = 0$

_____

_____

_____

10. $2x^2 + 5x = -2$

11. $3x^2 + 2x = 5$

12. $x^2 - 16x = -64$

_____

_____

_____

13. $x^2 - 20x = -75$

14. $x^2 + 6x + 9 = 0$

15. $3x^2 - 6x - 9 = 0$

_____

_____

_____

Writing and Solving Quadratic Equations

Write an equation and find the solutions.

1. Find the number which when added to the square of the number equals 30.

2. The product of two consecutive integers is 90. Find the integers.

3. Find the number which when added to its square equals 20.

4. Find the number which when subtracted from its square equals 56.

5. The product of two consecutive even integers is 80. Find the integers. (Hint: Let x and $x + 2$ be the integers.)

6. The product of two consecutive odd integers is 99. What are the integers?

7. The square of a number added to twice the number equals 24. What is the number?

8. The length of a rectangle is 5 meters greater than the width. The area is 300 square meters. Find the dimensions. Remember, dimensions cannot be negative.

9. The length of a rectangle is 20 centimeters greater than the width. The area is 125 square centimeters. Find the dimensions of the rectangle.

10. The width of a rectangle is 10 meters less than the length. The area of the rectangle is 200 square meters. Find the length and width.

Completing the Square

One method for solving certain quadratic equations is called **completing the square.** The method works even when the trinomial cannot be factored. It involves changing the equation to make a perfect square trinomial on one side. Consider the equation $x^2 - 2x - 3 = 0$. First, rewrite the equation so that both terms containing variables are on one side of the equal sign and the constant (a number) is on the other. Then add the square of one-half the coefficient of x to both sides of the equation. This would be $\left(\frac{1}{2} \cdot 2\right)^2$, or 1. Finally, factor and find the roots, or solutions, of the equation. Sometimes the solutions will contain square roots.

Solve: $x^2 - 2x - 3 = 0$

$x^2 - 2x = 3$	Rearrange terms.	Check: $(3)^2 - 2(3) - 3 = 0$
$x^2 - 2x + 1 = 3 + 1$	Add $\left(\frac{1}{2} \cdot 2\right)^2$, which equals 1, to both sides.	$9 - 6 - 3 = 0$
$(x - 1)^2 = 4$		$9 - 9 = 0$
$\sqrt{(x - 1)^2} = \sqrt{4}$	Factor. Find the square root of	and
$x - 1 = \pm 2$	both sides.	$(-1)^2 - 2(-1) - 3 = 0$
$x - 1 = +2 \quad x - 1 = -2$		$1 + 2 - 3 = 0$
$x = 3 \qquad x = -1$	Solve each equation.	$3 - 3 = 0$

Solve. Use the method of completing the square.

1. $x^2 - 2x - 3 = 0$

2. $y^2 + 2y - 8 = 0$

3. $m^2 - 4m - 32 = 0$

_____ _____ _____

4. $p^2 - 4p - 5 = 0$

5. $x^2 - 4x = 3$

6. $m^2 = -6m - 7$

_____ _____ _____

173

Solving $x^2 + bx + c = 0$ by Completing the Square

1. The diagram represents the expression $x^2 + 4x + c$ with the constant term missing. Complete the square by filling in the bottom right corner with 1-tiles, and write the expression as a trinomial and in factored form.

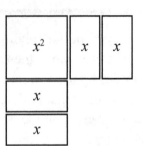

_____

Complete the square to form a perfect square trinomial. Then factor the trinomial.

2. $m^2 + 10m + \boxed{}$

_____

3. $g^2 - 20g + \boxed{}$

_____

4. $y^2 + 2y + \boxed{}$

_____

5. $w^2 - 11w + \boxed{}$

_____

Solve each equation by completing the square.

6. $s^2 + 15s = -56$

_____

7. $r^2 - 4r = 165$

_____

8. $y^2 + 19y + 78 = 0$

_____

9. $x^2 - 19x + 84 = 0$

_____

10. $t^2 + 2t - 224 = 0$

_____

11. $x^2 + 18x - 175 = 0$

_____

12. $g^2 + 3g = -6$

_____

13. $p^2 - 3p = 18$

_____

14. $z^2 = 6z - 2$

_____

15. $x^2 + 25 = 10x$

_____

174

Solving $ax^2 + bx + c = 0$ by Completing the Square

Solve each equation by completing the square.

1. $9z^2 + 48z = 36$

_____

2. $49x^2 + 28x = 60$

_____

3. $121r^2 - 44r = 5$

_____

4. $4x^2 + 20x - 11 = 0$

_____

5. $2x^2 + 9 = 9x$

_____

6. $3x^2 + 4x = 20$

_____

7. A carpenter is making the tabletop shown below. The area will be 24 square feet.

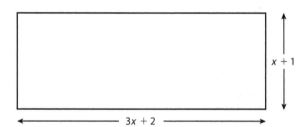

$x + 1$

$3x + 2$

a. Write an equation to represent this situation.

_____

b. Solve the equation. Which solution(s) make sense in this situation? Explain.

_____

_____

c. What are the dimensions of the tabletop?

_____

Deriving the Quadratic Formula

The formula $x = \dfrac{-b \pm \sqrt{b^2 - 4ac}}{2a}$ is called the quadratic formula. For any quadratic equation written in standard form, $ax^2 + bx + c = 0$, the quadratic formula gives the solutions of the equation.

Solve the general form of the quadratic equation, $ax^2 + bx + c = 0$, by completing the square to find the values of x in terms of a, b, and c.

Step 1: Subtract c from both sides of the equation.

$$ax^2 + bx = \boxed{}$$

Step 2: Multiply both sides of the equation by $4a$ to make the coefficient of x^2 a perfect square.

$$4a^2x^2 + \boxed{}\, x = -4ac$$

Step 3: Add b^2 to both sides of the equation to complete the square. Then write the trinomial as the square of a binomial.

$$4a^2x^2 + 4abx + b^2 = -4ac + \boxed{}$$

$$\left(\boxed{}\right)^2 = b^2 - 4ac$$

Step 4: Apply the definition of a square root and solve for x.

$$\boxed{} = \pm \sqrt{\boxed{}}$$

$$2ax = -\boxed{} \pm \sqrt{\boxed{}}$$

$$x = \underline{\hspace{4cm}}$$

Another method of deriving the quadratic formula is to first divide each term by a, and then complete the square. Complete the derivation in the space below.

The Quadratic Formula

The **quadratic formula** can be used to find the roots of a quadratic equation. It is particularly useful when a quadratic equation cannot be solved by factoring.

Every quadratic equation can be written in the general form $ax^2 + bx + c = 0$. Hence, in the equation $x^2 - 7x + 6 = 0$, $a = 1$, $b = -7$, and $c = 6$.

$$x = \frac{-b \pm \sqrt{b^2 - 4ac}}{2a}$$

Use the quadratic formula by first writing each equation in the form $ax^2 + bx + c = 0$. Then substitute for a, b, and c in the formula.

Solve: $x^2 - 7x + 6 = 0$

$ax^2 + bx + c = 0$

Substitute $a = 1$, $b = -7$, and $c = 6$ in the quadratic formula.

$x = \dfrac{-b \pm \sqrt{b^2 - 4ac}}{2a}$

$x = \dfrac{-(-7) \pm \sqrt{(-7)^2 - 4(1)(6)}}{2(1)}$

$x = \dfrac{7 \pm \sqrt{49 - 24}}{2}$

$x = \dfrac{7 \pm \sqrt{25}}{2} = \dfrac{7 \pm 5}{2}$

$x = \dfrac{7 + 5}{2} \qquad x = \dfrac{7 - 5}{2}$

$x = 6 \qquad\qquad x = 1$

The roots of the equation are 6 and 1.

Check: $(6)^2 - 7(6) + 6 = 0$

$36 - 42 + 6 = 0$

$-6 + 6 = 0$

and

$(1)^2 - 7(1) + 6 = 0$

$1 - 7 + 6 = 0$

$-6 + 6 = 0$

Use the quadratic formula to solve each quadratic equation.

1. $x^2 + 5x + 6 = 0$

2. $2x^2 + 5x + 2 = 0$

3. $4x^2 - 9x + 2 = 0$

_____

_____

_____

4. $2x^2 - 7x + 3 = 0$

5. $2x^2 - 13x + 6 = 0$

6. $5x^2 = x + 4$

_____

_____

_____

7. $2x^2 + x = 1$

8. $3x^2 = 20 - 7x$

9. $x^2 + 2x - 15 = 0$

_____

_____

_____

Using the Quadratic Formula

State how many real solutions each equation has. Do not solve the equations.

1. $3x^2 + 8x + 6 = 0$

_____

2. $z^2 = 9$

_____

3. $9d^2 + 16 = 24d$

_____

4. $-2x^2 = 25 - 10x$

_____

Solve each equation using the quadratic formula. Round to the nearest hundredth, if necessary.

5. $16 + r^2 - 8r = 0$

_____

6. $3x^2 = 10 - 4x$

_____

7. $2s^2 = 98$

_____

8. $z^2 = 2.5z$

_____

9. $3x^2 + 16x - 84 = 0$

_____

10. $34z^2 + 19z = 15$

_____

11. $6q^2 + 25q + 24 = 0$

_____

12. $7x^2 + 100x = 4$

_____

State what method you would use to solve each equation. Justify each answer. You do not need to solve the equations.

13. $4x^2 + 25 = 20x$

_____

14. $2z^2 = 20$

_____

15. $4x^2 + 25 = 18x$

_____

16. $g^2 - 3g - 4 = 0$

_____

17. A football player kicks a ball with an initial upward velocity of 47 feet per second. The initial height of the ball is 3 feet. The function $h(t) = -16t^2 + vt + h_0$ models the height (in feet) of the ball, where v is the initial upward velocity and h_0 is the initial height. If no one catches the ball, how long will it be in the air?

_____

More Practice with the Quadratic Formula

Solve: $2x^2 + x - 2 = 0$

Substitute $a = 2$, $b = 1$, and $c = -2$.

$$x = \frac{-b \pm \sqrt{b^2 - 4ac}}{2a}$$

$$x = \frac{-(1) \pm \sqrt{(1)^2 - 4(2)(-2)}}{2(2)}$$

$$x = \frac{-1 \pm \sqrt{1 + 16}}{4}$$

$$x = \frac{-1 + \sqrt{17}}{4} \qquad x = \frac{-1 - \sqrt{17}}{4}$$

The roots of the equation are $\frac{-1 + \sqrt{17}}{4}$ and $\frac{-1 - \sqrt{17}}{4}$.

Use the quadratic formula to solve each quadratic equation. Write the answer in simplest radical form.

1. $x^2 - 2x - 2 = 0$

2. $2x^2 - 8x + 3 = 0$

3. $2x^2 + 3x - 1 = 0$

_____

_____

_____

4. $3x^2 - 4x - 2 = 0$

5. $6x^2 = 5x + 3$

6. $3x^2 = 2x + 3$

_____

_____

_____

7. $3x^2 = 5x - 1$

8. $5x^2 - 3 = 3x$

9. $2x^2 + 5x = 1$

_____

_____

_____

Using the Quadratic Formula in Solving Problems

Some problems can be solved using the quadratic formula. Use guess and check or a calculator to find the square root of large numbers.

The square of a number added to three times the number is equal to 28.
What number or numbers satisfy these conditions?

Let x = the number.

Write an equation:

$x^2 + 3x = 28$.

Rearrange into $ax^2 + bx + c = 0$

$$x^2 + 3x - 28 = 0$$

Find a, b, c:
$a = 1$, $b = 3$, and $c = -28$.

Substitute into the quadratic formula.

$$x = \frac{-b \pm \sqrt{b^2 - 4ac}}{2a}$$

$$x = \frac{-(3) \pm \sqrt{(3)^2 - 4(1)(-28)}}{2(1)}$$

$$x = \frac{-3 \pm \sqrt{9 + 112}}{2} = \frac{-3 \pm \sqrt{121}}{2} = \frac{-3 \pm 11}{2}$$

$$x = \frac{-3 + 11}{2} = 4 \qquad x = \frac{-3 - 11}{2} = -7$$

Both -7 and 4 satisfy the conditions of the problem.

First write an equation. Then solve using the quadratic formula.

1. One-half the square of a number is equal to 16 more than twice the number. What is the number?

2. Find the two consecutive odd integers whose product is 143.

3. The product of two consecutive odd integers is 323. What are the integers?

4. Find the number which when subtracted from its square equals 72.

5. The length of a rectangle is 10 more than twice the width. The area of the rectangle is 672 square inches. Find the length and width. (Remember, dimensions cannot be negative.)

6. The width of a rectangle is one-half the length minus 11 centimeters. The area of the rectangle is 700 square centimeters. Find the length and width.

Name _____ Date _____

Unit 12 Review

Solve by factoring.

1. $x^2 + 10x + 25 = 0$

2. $x^2 + 16x = -64$

3. $4x^2 + 32x + 64 = 0$

_____

_____

_____

4. $4x^2 - 4x + 1 = 0$

5. $4x^2 - 64 = 0$

6. $x^2 + 5x + 4 = 0$

_____

_____

_____

Solve by completing the square.

7. $m^2 - 4m + 1 = 0$

8. $y^2 - 2y - 1 = 0$

9. $x^2 - 4x = 5$

_____

_____

_____

Solve using the quadratic formula.

10. $2x^2 + 7x + 6 = 0$

11. $x^2 - 6x = 2$

12. $x^2 - 8x = -3$

_____

_____

_____

Solve algebraically.

13. $2x^2 - 7 = 9$ _____

14. $-3(x - 6)^2 + 19 = 7$ _____

Solve by graphing.

15. $2(x - 4)^2 + 1 = 8$

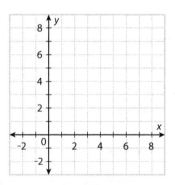

_____

16. The length of a rectangle is 10 inches greater than the width. The area of the rectangle is 75 square inches. Find the dimensions.

17. Find the number which when added to its square equals 12.

_____

_____

18. While practicing a tightrope walk at a height of 20 feet, a circus performer slips and falls into a safety net 15 feet below. The function $h(t) = -16t^2 + 20$, where t represents time measured in seconds, gives the performer's height above the ground (in feet) as he falls.

Write and solve an equation to find the elapsed time until the performer lands in the net. You can solve using a graphic calculator.

_____

Precision and Significant Digits

Choose the more precise measurement in each pair.

1. 18 cm; 177 mm

2. 3 yd; 10 ft

3. 40.23 kg; 40.3 kg

_____   _____   _____

4. One student measures the length of a rectangular wall to the nearest meter and finds that the length is 5 meters. Another student measures the height of the wall to the nearest tenth of a meter and finds that the height is 3.2 meters. Determine the number of significant digits in each measurement. What are the minimum and maximum possible values for the area of the wall?

_____

Determine the number of significant digits in each measurement.

5. 12,080 ft

6. 0.8 mL

7. 1.0065 km

_____   _____   _____

8. You measure a rectangular window to the nearest tenth of a centimeter and find that the length is 81.4 centimeters. A friend measures the width to the nearest centimeter and finds that the width is 38 centimeters. Use the correct number of significant digits to write the perimeter and area of the window.

_____

9. A student measured the length and width of a square rug to the nearest hundredth of a meter. He found that the length and width were 1.30 meters. The student was asked to report the area using the correct number of significant digits, and he wrote the area as 1.7 square meters . Explain the student's error.

_____

10. Measure the length and width of the rectangle to the nearest tenth of a centimeter. Then use the correct number of significant digits to write the perimeter and area of the rectangle.

_____

Use a Graph to Estimate

The graph shows the rate at which sound travels in air. Use the graph for Exercises 1–7.

1. About how many seconds does it take sound to travel 3 miles in air?

   _____

2. What is the approximate distance that sound travels in air in 4 seconds?

   _____

3. What does the point (10, 2) represent?

   _____

   _____

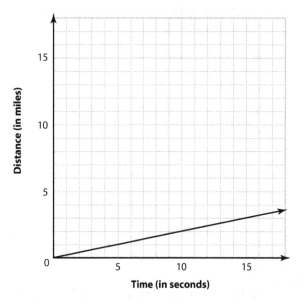

4. What is the slope of the line?

   _____

5. What is the y-intercept of the line?

   _____

6. Write the equation of the line.

   _____

7. Predict the approximate time it would take sound to travel 10 miles in the air.

   _____

Correlation

1. The table lists the heights and weights of the six wide receivers who played for the New Orleans Saints during the 2010 football season.

   a. Display the data on a scatter plot.

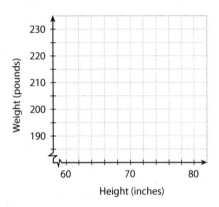

Wide Receiver	Height (inches)	Weight (pounds)
Arrington	75	192
Colston	76	225
Henderson	71	200
Meachem	74	210
Moore	69	190
Roby	72	189

   b. Describe the correlation and estimate the correlation coefficient using one of these values: -1, -0.5, 0, 0.5, 1.

   _____

2. Read the article shown at the right. Describe the correlation and decide whether correlation implies causation in this case. Explain your reasoning.

   _____

   _____

   _____

   _____

WALKING SPEED MAY PREDICT LIFE SPAN

Researchers who looked at data from nearly 35,000 senior citizens discovered that an elderly person's walking speed is correlated to that person's chance of living 10 more years. For instance, the researchers found that only 19 percent of the slowest-walking 75-year-old men lived for 10 more years compared with 87 percent of the fastest-walking 75-year-old men. Similar results were found for elderly women.

Fitting Lines to Data

The table lists the median age of males living in the United States based on the results of the U.S. Census over the past few decades.

Year	1970	1980	1990	2000	2010
Median Age of Males	26.8	28.8	31.6	34.0	35.5

1. Let t represent time (in years since 1970), and let a_M represent the median age of males. Make a table of paired values of t and a_M. Complete the labels for the x- and y-axes of the graph. Then draw a scatter plot.

t	a_M

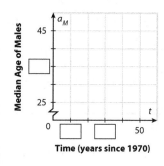

2. Draw a line of fit on the scatter plot and find an equation of the line.

_____

3. Calculate the residuals, complete the labels for the x- and y-axes of the graph, and make a residual plot.

t	a_M actual	a_M predicted	Residual

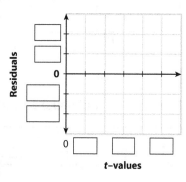

4. Evaluate the suitability of a linear fit and the goodness of the fit.

_____

5. Predict the median age of males in 1995 and 2015. Identify each prediction as an interpolation or an extrapolation.

_____

More Fitting Lines to Data

The table lists, for various lengths (in centimeters), the median weight (in kilograms) of male infants and female infants (ages 0–36 months) in the United States.

Length (cm)	50	60	70	80	90	100
Median Weight (kg) of Male Infants	3.4	5.9	8.4	10.8	13.0	15.5
Median Weight (kg) of Female Infants	3.4	5.8	8.3	10.6	12.8	15.2

1. Let l represent an infant's length in excess of 50 centimeters. (For instance, for an infant whose length is 60 cm, $l = 10$.) Let w_M represent the median weight of male infants, and let w_F represent the median weight of female infants. Make a table of paired values of l and either w_M or w_F (whichever you prefer).

l						
w						

2. Draw a scatter plot of the paired data.

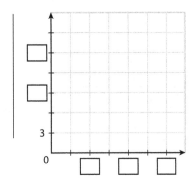

3. Draw a line of fit on the scatter plot and find the equation of the line. According to your model, at what rate does weight change with respect to length?

_____

_____

_____

_____

4. Calculate the residuals, and make a residual plot.

l	w actual	w predicted	Residual

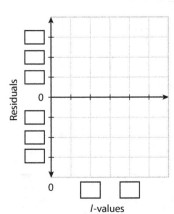

5. Evaluate the suitability of a linear fit and the goodness of the fit.

_____

Linear Regression

1. Women began competing in the discus throw in the 1928 Olympic Games. The table gives the distances (in meters) that a discus was thrown by women to win the gold medal at the Olympic Games from 1928 to 1964.

Year of Olympic Games	Women's Gold Medal Discus Throw (meters)
1928	39.62
1932	40.58
1936	47.63
1940	No Olympics
1944	No Olympics
1948	41.92
1952	51.42
1956	53.69
1962	55.10
1964	57.27

a. Find the equation of the line of best fit.

_____

b. Find the correlation coefficient.

_____

c. Evaluate the suitability and goodness of the fit.

_____

_____

_____

2. The table lists the median heights (in centimeters) of girls and boys from age 2 to age 10. Choose either the data for girls or the data for boys.

Age (years)	Median Height (cm) of Girls	Median Height (cm) of Boys
2	84.98	86.45
3	93.92	94.96
4	100.75	102.22
5	107.66	108.90
6	114.71	115.39
7	121.49	121.77
8	127.59	128.88
9	132.92	133.51
10	137.99	138.62

a. Identify the real-world variables that x and y will represent.

_____

b. Find the equation of the line of best fit.

_____

c. Find the correlation coefficient.

_____

d. Evaluate the suitability and goodness of the fit.

_____

_____

_____

Performing Exponential Regression

The first two columns of the table show the population of Arizona (in thousands) in census years from 1900 to 2000. Use a graphing calculator for Exercises 1–6.

1. Find an exponential function model for the data. Round to four significant digits.

   _____

2. Identify the parameters in the model, including the growth or decay rate, and explain what they represent.

   _____

   _____

   _____

3. Use the more precise model stored on your calculator to complete the third column of the table with population values based on the model. Round to three significant digits.

4. Use the results of Exercise 3 to complete the residuals column of the table.

5. Use your model from Exercise 1 to predict the population of Arizona in 1975 and in 2030, to the nearest thousand. Discuss the accuracy of the results. Which result is likely to be more accurate? Why?

Arizona Population, y, (in thousands) in Years, x, Since 1900			
x	y	y_m	$y - y_m$
0	123		
10	204		
20	334		
30	436		
40	499		
50	750		
60	1,302		
70	1,771		
80	2,718		
90	3,665		
100	5,131		

_____

_____

_____

6. Make a residual plot. Does the model fit the data well? Explain.

_____

_____

_____

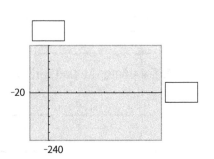

Measures of Center and Spread

The numbers of students in each of a school's six Algebra 1 classes are listed below.
Find each statistic for this data set.

28 30 29 26 31 30

1. Mean = _____

2. Median = _____

3. Range = _____

4. Lower Quartile = _____

5. Upper Quartile = _____

6. IQR = _____

7. Find the standard deviation of the Algebra 1 class data by completing the table and doing the calculations below it.

Data Value x	Deviation from Mean, $x - \bar{x}$	Squared Deviation, $(x - \bar{x})^2$
28		
30		
29		
26		
31		
30		

Mean of squared deviations = _____

Standard deviation ≈ _____

8. Suppose a student in the Algebra 1 class with 31 students transfers to the class with 26 students. The student claims that the measures of center and the measures of spread will all change. Correct the student's error.

_____

_____

_____

189

More Measures of Center and Spread

1. The table lists the heights (in centimeters) of 8 males and 8 females on the U.S. Olympic swim team, all randomly selected from swimmers on the team who participated in the 2008 Olympic Games held in Beijing, China.

Heights of Olympic Male Swimmers	196	188	196	185	203	183	183	196
Heights of Olympic Female Swimmers	173	170	178	175	173	180	180	175

a. Use a graphing calculator to complete the table below.

	Center		Spread	
	Mean	Median	IQR $(Q_3 - Q_1)$	Standard Deviation
Olympic Male Swimmers				
Olympic Female Swimmers				

b. Discuss the consistency of the measures of center for male swimmers and the measures of center for female swimmers, and then compare the measures of center for male and female swimmers.

_____

_____

_____

c. What do the measures of spread tell you about the variation in the heights of the male and female swimmers?

_____

_____

_____

Data Distributions and Outliers

1. **a.** Rounded to the nearest $50,000, the values (in thousands of dollars) of homes sold by a realtor are listed below. Use the number line to create a line plot for the data set.

      300   250   200   250   350

      400   300   250   400   300

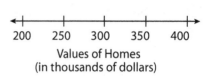

Values of Homes
(in thousands of dollars)

   b. Suppose the realtor sells a home with a value of $650,000. Which statistics are affected when 650 is included in the data set?

       _____

   c. Would 650 be considered an outlier? Explain.

       _____

       _____

2. In Exercise 1, find the mean and median for the data set with and without the data value 650. Why might the realtor want to use the mean instead of the median when advertising the typical value of homes sold?

       _____

       _____

3. Give an example of a data set with a symmetric distribution that also includes one or more outliers.

       _____

       _____

       _____

4. Suppose that a data set has an approximately symmetric distribution, with one outlier. What could you do if you wanted to use the mean and standard deviation to characterize the data?

       _____

       _____

       _____

More Data Distributions and Outliers

The table shows Chloe's scores on math tests in each quarter of the school year.

1. Use the number line below to create a line plot for Chloe's scores.

70 72 74 76 78 80 82 84 86 88 90

Chloe's Test Scores

Chloe's Scores			
I	II	III	IV
74	77	79	74
78	75	76	77
82	80	74	76
76	75	77	78
85	77	87	85

2. Complete the table below for the data set.

Mean	Median	Range	IQR	Standard Deviation

3. Identify any outliers in the data set.

_____

4. Complete the table below for the data set above if the outliers are removed.

Mean	Median	Range	IQR	Standard Deviation

5. Which of the statistics changed when the outliers were removed?

_____

6. Describe the shape of the distribution.

_____

7. Which measure of center and which measure of spread should be used to characterize the data? Explain.

_____

Histograms

1. The ages of the first 44 U.S. presidents on the date of their first inauguration are listed below.

42, 43, 46, 46, 47, 47, 48, 49, 49, 50, 51, 51, 51, 51, 51, 52, 52, 54, 54, 54, 54, 54, 55,
55, 55, 55, 56, 56, 56, 57, 57, 57, 57, 58, 60, 61, 61, 61, 62, 64, 64, 65, 68, 69

a. Complete the frequency table by organizing the data into six equal intervals.

Age Interval	Frequency
41–45	2

b. Use the frequency table to complete the histogram.

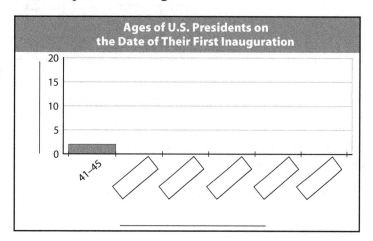

c. Describe the shape of the distribution. What measures of center and spread would you use to characterize the data? Why?

_____

_____

d. Use the histogram to estimate the median and IQR.

_____

2. Describe a way to estimate the standard deviation from a histogram.

_____

_____

Box Plots

The table shows the 2010 average salary for an MLB player by team for both the American League (AL) and the National League (NL).

1. Find the values for the five-number summary for each league.

	AL	NL
Min.		
Q_1		
Median		
Q_3		
Max.		

MLB Players' Average 2010 Salaries (in millions of dollars)			
American League		**National League**	
Team	**Salary**	**Team**	**Salary**
New York	8.3	Chicago	5.4
Boston	5.6	Philadelphia	5.1
Detroit	4.6	New York	5.1
Chicago	4.2	St. Louis	3.7
Los Angeles	3.6	Los Angeles	3.7
Seattle	3.5	San Francisco	3.5
Minnesota	3.5	Houston	3.3
Baltimore	3.1	Atlanta	3.1
Tampa Bay	2.7	Colorado	2.9
Kansas City	2.5	Milwaukee	2.8
Cleveland	2.1	Cincinnati	2.8
Toronto	2.1	Arizona	2.3
Texas	1.9	Florida	2.1
Oakland	1.7	Washington	2.0
		San Diego	1.5
		Pittsburgh	1.3

2. Complete the scale on the number line below. Then use the number line to create two box plots, one for each league. Show any outliers as individual dots.

MLB Player's Average 2010 Salaries (in millions of dollars)

1.0 ☐ ☐ ☐ ☐ ☐ ☐ ☐ ☐

3. Compare the center, spread, and shape of the two data distributions. Ignore any outliers.

_____

_____

_____

_____

194

Two-Way Frequency Tables

Antonio surveyed 60 of his classmates about their participation in school activities as well as whether they have a part-time job. The results are shown in the two-way frequency table below. Use the table to complete the exercises.

Job \ Activity	Clubs Only	Sports Only	Both	Neither	Total
Yes	12	13	16	4	
No	3	5	5	2	
Total					

1. Complete the table by finding the row totals, column totals, and grand total.

2. Create a two-way relative frequency table using decimals.

Job \ Activity	Clubs Only	Sports Only	Both	Neither	Total
Yes					
No					
Total					

3. Give each relative frequency as a percent.

   a. The joint relative frequency of students surveyed who participate in school clubs only and have part-time jobs:

   _____

   b. The marginal relative frequency of students surveyed who do not have a part-time job:

   _____

   c. The conditional relative frequency that a student surveyed participates in both school clubs and sports, given that the student has a part-time job:

   _____

4. Discuss possible influences of having a part-time job on participation in school activities. Support your response with an analysis of the data.

   _____

   _____

   _____

Unit 13 Review

Violet and Juan measure the length and width of a book cover. Their measurements are 16 cm for the width and 23.6 cm for the length.

1. Determine the minimum and maximum possible values for the actual width and length.

2. What are the minimum and maximum possible areas for the book cover?

_____   _____

Give the number of significant digits in each measurement.

3. 840.09 m _____   4. 36,000 miles _____   5. 0.010 kilogram _____

The table lists the latitude and average annual temperature for various cities in the Northern Hemisphere.

6. Make a scatter plot for the data.

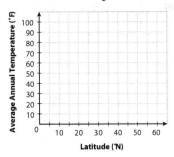

City	Latitude	Avg. Annual Temperature
Bangkok, Thailand	13.7 °N	82.6 °F
Cairo, Egypt	30.1 °N	71.4 °F
London, England	51.5 °N	51.8 °F
Moscow, Russia	55.8 °N	39.4 °F
New Delhi, India	28.6 °N	77.0 °F
Tokyo, Japan	35.7 °N	58.1 °F
Vancouver, Canada	49.2 °N	49.6 °F

7. Describe the correlation and estimate the correlation coefficient. _____

The April high temperatures in degrees Fahrenheit for five consecutive years in Boston are listed in the table.

77	86	84	93	90

8. Find the equation for the line of fit. _____

9. Find the mean.   10. Find the median.   11. Find the range.   12. Find the interquartile range.

_____   _____   _____   _____

13. Calculate the standard deviation. Use a calculator and round to the nearest tenth. _____

14. What can you conclude about the data in this line plot?

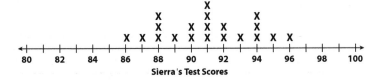

_____

Final Review

Evaluate each expression if $r = 8$, $s = 3$, and $t = 6$.

1. $r + st =$ **2.** $rs + \frac{t}{s} =$ **3.** $t - 2s =$ **4.** $r + 5s =$

_____   _____   _____   _____

Simplify.

5. $\frac{12b + 40}{4} =$ **6.** $m + 9 - (3m + 6) =$ **7.** $\frac{3}{8}(16c - 32) =$ **8.** $3r - 2(r + 5) =$

_____   _____   _____   _____

Solve.

9. $4x - 4 = 2x + 8$ **10.** $\frac{x}{2} + 4 = \frac{x}{3} + 5$ **11.** $6b - 4 = 2(2b + 1)$

_____   _____   _____

Simplify.

12. $(7xy^2)(-7x^2y) =$ **13.** $(r^3s^5)^2 =$ **14.** $\frac{-30mn^3}{15m^2n} =$ **15.** $\sqrt[3]{27a^6}$

_____   _____   _____   _____

16. $\sqrt{64x^2y^8z^4}$ **17.** $\sqrt{36b^4c^6d^{12}}$ **18.** $\sqrt{144z^{20}x^{10}w^8}$ **19.** $\sqrt{81r^2s^2t^2}$

_____   _____   _____   _____

Multiply or divide.

20. $(3x - 2y)(x - 3y)$ **21.** $(3a - b)(2c + b)$ **22.** $(2x^2 - y^2 - 3)(xy - y)$

_____   _____   _____

23. $(2x - y)^2$ **24.** $(2x^2 - xy - y^2) \div (2x + y)$ **25.** $(2a^2 - 8ab + 6b^2) \div (2a - 2b)$

_____   _____   _____

Solve each system of equations.

26. $x + 2y = 9$ **27.** $2x + 3y = 14$ **28.** $\frac{3x}{4} + \frac{y}{2} = 5$

    $x - y = 3$ $x + 2y = 18$ $\frac{x}{4} + \frac{y}{2} = 1$

_____   _____   _____

29. $3y = 6 - 2x$ **30.** $2x - 3y = -19$ **31.** $x - 2y = 5$

    $8x = 3y - 1$ $4x + 5y = 17$ $2x + 3y = 10$

_____   _____   _____

Write the equations and solve.

32. Carlos is three times as old as Maria. The sum of their ages is 56 years. How old is each?

33. The sum of three numbers is 180. The second number is twice the first, and the third number is three times the first. Find each number.

_____   _____

197

34. Two small pitchers and one large pitcher can hold 8 cups of water. One large pitcher minus one small pitcher constitutes 2 cups of water. How many cups of water can each pitcher hold?

_____

Factor.

35. $4x^2 - 49 =$

_____

36. $25 - 70x + 49x^2 =$

_____

37. $x^2 + 20x + 99$

_____

Solve.

38. $x^2 + 49 = -14x$

_____

39. $16x^2 - 24x + 9 = 0$

_____

40. $2x^2 + x - 3 = 0$

_____

41. $x^2 - 3x = 10$

_____

42. $2b^2 + 4 = 9b$

_____

43. $a^2 + 6a + 9 = 0$

_____

44. $\left(\frac{1}{2}\right)^x = 4$

_____

45. $5^x = 125$

_____

46. $\frac{7}{3}(3)^x = 63$

_____

47. Complete a table of solutions for 3 values of x and graph the equation of $4x - 2y = 6$.

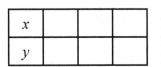

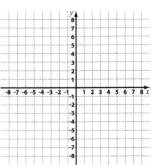

Solve the inequalities.

48. $2(b + 1) \le b - 4$ _____

49. $10x - 3(2x + 1) \ge 8x + 1$ _____

50. Graph the inequality $7x - y < 13$.

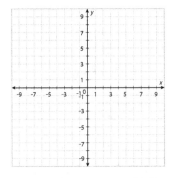

51. How will the graph of $7x - y < 13$ change if the inequality is changed to $7x - y \le 13$?

_____

52. How will the graph of $7x - y < 13$ change if the inequality is changed to $7x - y \ge 13$?

_____

Name _____ Date _____

Solve the systems of inequalities by graphing.

53. $4x + y < 2$
$y > -2$

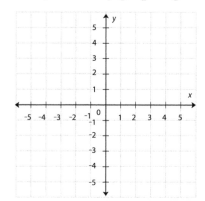

54. $3x + 2y \geq -2$
$x + 2y \leq 2$

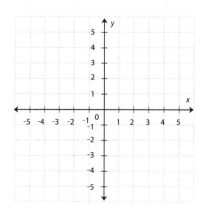

The graph shows the value of two different shares of stock over the period of four years since they were purchased. The values have been changing exponentially.

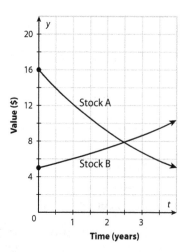

55. The model for the graph representing Stock A is an

exponential _____ model. The initial value is _____

and the decay factor is $12 \div 16 =$ _____.

56. The model for the graph representing Stock B is an

exponential _____ model. The initial value is _____
and the growth factor is _____ ÷ _____ = _____.

57. Explain why (3, 2) is not a solution for this graph of a system of linear equalities.

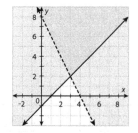

_____

58. What is the equation of the absolute value function shown in the graph?

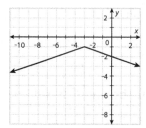

_____

For Exercises 59–61, refer to the graph of an absolute value function $f(x)$ shown below.

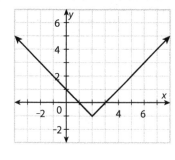

59. What is the equation for $f(x)$? _____

60. What are the domain and range of $f(x)$? _____

61. What are the solutions of $f(x) = g(x)$, where $g(x) = 1$?

_____

199

Name _____ Date _____

Graph the following functions.

62. $g(x) = 2x^2$

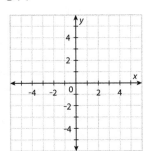

63. $g(x) = \frac{1}{2}x^2$

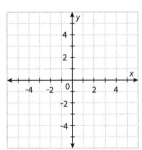

64. $g(x) = -2x^2$

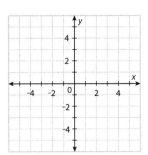

65. Describe the solution of a quadratic equation when the $\sqrt{b^2 - 4ac}$ is negative.

_____

Use the table below for Exercises 66–70.

Number of Internet Hosts							
Years since 2001	0	1	2	3	4	5	6
Number (millions)	110	147	172	233	318	395	490

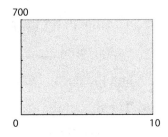

66. Enter the data from the table on a graphing calculator, with years since 2001 in List 1 and number of Internet hosts in List 2. Then set up a scatter plot of the data, as shown, and graph it.

67. Find the function, y, and the correlation coefficient, x. _____

68. What does the correlation coefficient suggest about the model? _____

69. Use your rounded function model to predict the number of Internet hosts in 2010 and in 2020.

Round to three significant digits. _____

70. Are these predictions likely to be accurate? Explain. _____

Use the frequency table of the monthly salaries of 20 people for Exercises 71 and 72.

71. What is the mean salary?

_____

72. What is the standard deviation of the data rounded to the nearest

whole number? _____

Salaries ($)	Frequency
3500	5
4000	8
4200	5
4300	2

73. Create a box plot and find the median, first quartile, and third quartile of the following data set:

2, 6, 7, 8, 8, 11, 12, 13, 14, 15, 22, 23

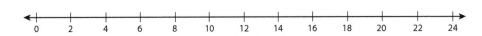

200

Answer Key

Page 1

1. 20
2. 6
3. 8
4. 10
5. $7,500
6. 81 °F
7. $-9x$
8. $4.5rt$
9. $3z$
10. $1\frac{3}{4}a$ or $\frac{7}{4}a$
11. $a = 4$
12. $b = -10$
13. $x = 8$
14. $a = -12$
15. $n = 5$
16. $w = 4$ inches, $l = 12$ inches
17. 72
18. $6ab^2c$
19. $-6x^3y^4$
20. a^3b^6
21. $2x$
22. $\frac{-2a^2}{b^2}$
23. $2a + 2b$
24. $3a - b$
25. $7a^2 - 5b^3$
26. 1
27. $\frac{1}{b}$
28. $4 + 5a$
29. $6x - 3y$
30. $2r^2 + 3rs + s^2$
31. $2a^3 - 6ab$
32. $2x^4 + 6x^3 + 14x^2$
33. $x^2 + 2xy + y^2$
34. $2x^2 - xy - 3y^2$

Page 2

35.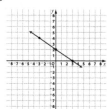
36. $(5, 1)$
37. $(6, 4)$
38. $(3, 1)$
39. $(1, 1)$
40. $(4, 2)$
41. $(8, 2)$
42. $4xy^2$
43. $5xy^2z^4$
44. $2x^2y^3z^5\sqrt{10}$
45. $(x + y)^2$

46. $(3x + 2y)^2$
47. $(2x - 1)(x + 4)$
48. $x = 6, x = 1$
49. $x = -\frac{1}{2}, x = -2$
50. $x = -4$
51. $w = 5$ inches, $l = 9$ inches
52. 24 and 25
53. $9r + 360$;
54. $x \geq -5$
55. $x > -3$

Page 3

56. yes; there is a unique value in the range for every value in the domain
57. no; 2 in the domain is pair to 4 and 6 in the range
58. no; 1, 2, and 3 in the domain are paired to more than one value in the range
59. $g(n) = \frac{-16 + n}{4}$
60. 3, 6, 9, 12
61. Shift the line down 25.
62. Change the slope from 25 to 50.
63. $f(x) = (x - 3)^2 + 2$
64.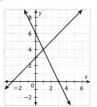
65.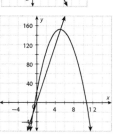
66.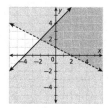

Page 4

67. x^2y^2
68. $\sqrt[6]{x}$
69. $\sqrt[4]{x}$
70. $9x^6$
71. $g(x) = 2\left(\frac{1}{2}\right)^x$
72. $g(x) = |x| + 2$
73. $t = 10$ and $t = 50$
74. 20%
75. 25%
76. About 36%

Page 5

1. Natural numbers, whole numbers, integers, rational numbers
2. Integers, rational numbers
3. Rational numbers
4. Whole numbers, integers, rational numbers
5. 7
6. 0
7. 17
8. 22
9. 12
10. 19
11. 11
12. 26
13. -23, 23
14. -14, 14
15. -32, 32
16. -29, 29

Page 6

1. Commutative Property of Multiplication
2. Distributive Property
3. Commutative Property of Addition
4. Associative Property of Addition
5. $15x + 5y$
6. $2n - 48$
7. $x + 16$
8. $14b + 3c - 3$
9. $4.86n + 7$; dollars
10. $5.25n + 2$; cups
11. When you simplify the expression $2(2x - 1) + 2(3x)$, you get $10x - 2$. The student forgot to distribute the 2 to the -1 inside the parentheses.

Page 7

1. yz
2. $e - f$
3. $p + q$ or $q + p$
4. $b \div 7$ or $\frac{b}{7}$
5. $r + 2$ or $2 + r$
6. $a - 6$
7. $12 \div n$ or $\frac{12}{n}$
8. $3n$
9. $n - 8$
10. $n + 1$ or $1 + n$
11. $100n$
12. $20 - n$
13. $32 - t$
14. $7n$
15. $28 \div g$ or $\frac{28}{g}$
16. $25 - n$

Page 8

1. Let a and b be rational numbers, $a = \frac{p}{q}$ and $b = \frac{r}{s}$ where $p, q, r,$ and s are integers, $q \neq 0$, and $s \neq 0$. Then $ab = \frac{p}{q} \cdot \frac{r}{s} = \frac{pr}{qs}$. The set of integers is closed under multiplication, so pr and qs are integers, and $q \neq 0$ and $s \neq 0$, so $qs \neq 0$. Therefore, ab is rational, so the set of rational numbers is also closed under multiplication.

2. Let a and b be rational numbers where $b \neq 0$. Write $a \div b$ as $a \cdot \frac{1}{b}$. If b is a rational number, then $\frac{1}{b}$ is also rational. The rational numbers are closed under multiplication, so $a \cdot \frac{1}{b}$ is rational.

3. Let $a \neq 0$ be rational, let b be irrational, and let $a \cdot b = c$. Assume that c is rational. Rewrite $a \cdot b = c$ as $b = \frac{1}{a} \cdot c$ by multiplying both sides by $\frac{1}{a}$. Because both $\frac{1}{a}$ and c are rational numbers and the set of rational numbers is closed under

201

multiplication, $\frac{1}{a} \cdot c$ must be rational. This contradicts the condition that b be irrational. So, the assumption that c is rational must be false, which means that c, the product of a rational number and an irrational number, must be an irrational number.

4a. Irrational because this is the sum of a rational number and an irrational number

4b. Irrational because you can write this as $3 + (-\sqrt{3})$, which is again the sum of a rational number and an irrational number

4c. Rational because
$(3 + \sqrt{3})(3 - \sqrt{3}) =$
$9 + 3\sqrt{3} - 3\sqrt{3} - 3 = 6$

Page 9

1. $l = 50$ feet
2. $l = 30$ meters
3. $l = 60$ centimeters
4. $l = 100$ yards
5. $w = 30$ feet
6. $w = 20$ feet
7. $w = 12$ inches
8. $w = 3.5$ meters
9. $w = 4$ miles

Page 10

1. 15 meters
2. 6 feet
3. 6 yards
4. 9 meters
5. 10 feet
6. 6 inches
7. 4 feet
8. 10 meters
9. 5 yards

Page 11

1. $2,304
2. $400
3. $1,200
4. 5%
5. 6%
6. 6%
7. 3 years
8. 5 years
9. 2 years

Page 12

1. 260 miles per hour
2. 416 miles per hour
3. 2,800 miles per hour
4. 500 miles per hour
5. 5 hours
6. 4 hours
7. 6 seconds
8. 2.5 seconds
9. 430 miles per hour
10. 55 miles per hour

Page 13

1. $a + 7z + 7$
2. $-x + 3y$
3. $4x - 5y - 9$
4. 16
5. 60
6. 50
7. 16
8. Associative Property of Addition
9. Distributive Property
10. 99
11. 9
12. 46
13. 4
14. 5
15. 56
16. 81
17. 2.5
18. 6 feet
19. $500
20. 45 °C
21. $3.78 c - 10$; dollars
22. $20 + 5w$

Page 14

1. $-7, 9, \frac{1}{10}, 14$
2. $5x, a, 2xy, \frac{1}{3}a, \frac{12}{z}$
3. 5
4. 4
5. π
6. -42
7. 1,250
8. 1.5
9. -9
10. $\frac{2}{3}$
11. $\frac{1}{2}$
12. $-\frac{3}{4}$
13. 1
14. $\frac{3}{2}$
15. 0.4
16. $\frac{1}{4}$
17. -1
18. $\frac{3}{5}$

Page 15

1. $20a$
2. $30b$
3. $54m$
4. $21a$
5. $21xy$
6. $36mn$
7. $12rs$
8. $64ab$
9. $20x$
10. $-28a$
11. $-27b$
12. $50c$
13. $12ab$
14. $50st$
15. $36xz$
16. $-14mnp$
17. $3y$
18. $2x$
19. $5at$
20. $12.5m$
21. $1.2rs$
22. $3bc$
23. $4tv$
24. $4.2z$
25. $36bc$
26. $105rt$
27. $108xyz$
28. $-120mn$
29. $-285rst$
30. $-768ef$
31. $700xyz$
32. $128rst$

Page 16

1. $64n$
2. $-4y$
3. $-15ab$
4. $7n$
5. $3ab$
6. $-9mn$
7. $24r$
8. $-4p$
9. $40st$
10. $-10x$
11. $-1.8jk$
12. $72x$
13. $0.9w$
14. $-84abc$
15. $-8x$
16. $-9pqr$
17. $0.65k$
18. $7fg$
19. $12b$
20. $-9cd$
21. $-5.5rs$
22. $-28hm$
23. $7g$
24. $-48hy$
25. $-21ij$
26. $0.4fg$
27. $6z$
28. $0.4r$
29. $-20t$
30. $5evw$
31. $56dv$
32. $18jkm$
33. $-18bpr$
34. $-7t$
35. $80djq$
36. $3dgn$
37. $-5s$
38. $-4m$
39. $-23n$
40. $6gt$

Page 17

1. $6y - 6$
2. $3r - rt$
3. $35 + 5n$
4. $-ax + 2x$
5. $-9r + 36$
6. $4c + 8$
7. $-7t - 7$
8. $6g + 4gs$
9. $-2gp + 7p$
10. $35y - 56$
11. $10a - 12$
12. $-16d - 8$
13. $-10k - 7kr$
14. $-14a - 14b$
15. $-4s - 8st$
16. $-24p + 16q$
17. $-mx - 3m$
18. $18x + 9y$
19. $-3ce + 9cg$
20. $m - 9$
21. $6b - 15c + 3d$
22. $-27x + 6xy$
23. $3jn - 8kn$
24. $3tx + 2t$
25. $10ab - 5a$
26. $-9b - 27ab$
27. $4m - 20n$
28. $-12rs + 2rt$
29. $-45s + 10t - 5v$
30. $-p - 2q + r$
31. $6xy - 8xz$
32. $2km + 6kn - 14k$

202

Page 18

1. $-28x + 12y - 8z$
2. $-8m - 18n + 3mn$
3. $-42ab + 56$
4. $3p - 3q$
5. $-6x - y + z$
6. $4r - 5s$
7. $14y - 3$
8. $9x - 15$
9. $x - 2y$
10. $4a - b$
11. $7x - 17y$
12. $11m - 11n$
13. $5s - t$
14. $2m - 3n$
15. $12x - 14y$
16. $5b + 13$
17. $11x - 9y$
18. $-5m + 2n$

Page 19

1. $-k$
2. $\frac{3}{7}x$
3. 0
4. $s - r$
5. $r - \frac{4}{3}y$
6. $c + 1\frac{3}{4}x$
7. $-r$
8. x
9. $-c - \frac{1}{3}y$
10. $-8p + 4$
11. $-2y - \frac{1}{3}$
12. $4a - 2$
13. $x + 3y$
14. $6a + \frac{b}{2}$
15. $-a$

Page 20

1. $\frac{-ab}{15}$
2. $\frac{rt}{32}$
3. $\frac{-pq}{56}$
4. $\frac{-nx}{4}$
5. $\frac{3hk}{35}$
6. $\frac{-x}{14}$
7. $\frac{3yz}{8}$
8. $\frac{3p}{10}$
9. $\frac{5n}{12}$
10. $\frac{-4ab}{15}$
11. $2xz$
12. $\frac{2ef}{3}$
13. $\frac{-5v}{12w}$
14. $\frac{-xy}{6}$
15. $\frac{3ab}{20}$

Page 21

1. $\frac{5}{3}$
2. -1
3. $\frac{1}{7}$
4. 3.5
5. $\frac{7}{3}$
6. 1
7. $\frac{-5}{2}$
8. $\frac{1}{5}$
9. $-51q$
10. $182st$
11. $-72xy$
12. $-12ky$
13. $3x$
14. $5rs$
15. $-9y$
16. $-35mn$
17. $9r - 27$

Page 22

18. $4w + 6mw$
19. $-64p - 32$
20. $-32ac - 6ad$
21. $\frac{7xy}{2}$
22. prs
23. $\frac{-sy}{6}$
24. $\frac{-5mn}{3}$
25. $-k + 2$
26. $7r - 13$
27. $21a + b$
28. $a + b$
29. $-9x + 15$
30. $6b + 10$

Page 22

1. no; $1.06(40) = 42.4$
2. no; $1.06(45) = 47.7$
3. yes; $1.06(50) = 53$
4. no; $1.06(55) = 58.3$
5a. $5 \cdot$ Ticket price + $5 \cdot$ Online fee = Total paid
5b. $5t + 5(1.50) = 60$; $5t + 7.50 = 60$
5c. \$10.5
6. $m - 0.15m = 26.35$ or $0.85m = 26.35$; the price before the discount was \$31.

Page 23

1. 8
2. 30
3. 5
4. 4
5. 4
6. 7
7. 16
8. 25
9. 300
10. 11
11. 15
12. 66
13. 9
14. -10
15. 1
16. 12
17. $\frac{1}{7}$
18. 44
19. 80
20. 515
21. $\frac{1}{2}$
22. $1\frac{1}{2}$
23. $4\frac{1}{3}$
24. 3

Page 24

1. 3
2. 18
3. 4
4. 31
5. 0
6. -5
7. 6
8. 63
9. -13
10. 0
11. -12
12. 2
13. 11
14. 10
15. -18
16. 81
17. -19
18. 24
19. -19
20. 6

Page 25

1. 28
2. 11
3. -22
4. 166
5. 6
6. 2
7. 132
8. $^-15$
9. -6
10. 2
11. 152
12. 31
13. -7
14. 40
15. -1
16. -3

Page 26

1. 6
2. -6
3. -9
4. $-\frac{10}{3}$
5. -8
6. 4
7. 6
8. -12
9. 2
10. 3
11. 4
12. -4
13. 2
14. 2
15. -6
16. 5

Page 27

1. 32
2. -6
3. 10
4. 90
5. 64
6. -81
7. 18
8. 0
9. 70
10. -40
11. -6
12. 1
13. -15
14. -80
15. 100
16. 72

Page 28

1. 13
2. 22
3. 10
4. 3
5. -1
6. -4
7. -6
8. 1
9. -6
10. 3
11. 27
12. -4
13. 15
14. -8
15. -2
16. 12
17. 45
18. $\frac{4}{3}$
19. 20
20. -1
21. -24
22. 5
23. -18
24. -5
25. -1
26. -12
27. 0
28. 12
29. $\frac{-8}{5}$
30. -26
31. -12
32. 108
33. -46
34. -7
35. 13
36. 90
37. -108
38. -59
39. $\frac{-1}{4}$
40. -8

Page 29

1. 21
2. 3
3. -24
4. 20
5. -20
6. 60
7. 42
8. 14
9. 20
10. 30
11. -16
12. 30
13. 40
14. -30
15. 10
16. -120

Page 30

1. -20
2. 6
3. 5
4. 5
5. 20
6. 5
7. -19
8. -2
9. 6
10. -55
11. 23
12. 5
13. 40
14. 13
15. 3
16. -12

Page 31

1. 48
2. 70
3. 45
4. 7
5. 60
6. 6

Page 32

1. Quanisha is 10 years old. Her father's age is 40.
2. Leroy has \$1.20. Aaron has \$6.00.
3. Tyrone has \$6.00, and Thomas has \$18.00.
4. Ling is 28 years old, and her sister is 14.
5. Deidra receives \$2,000. Shelby receives \$1,000.
6. From Kansas City to Denver is 600 miles. From Kansas City to St. Louis is 300 miles.

Page 33

1. 7
2. -4
3. 4
4. 3
5. -1
6. 3
7. 4
8. 1
9. 9
10. 4
11. -2
12. 2
13. -15
14. 3
15. -3
16. 2

203

Page 34

1. -5
2. -2
3. -1
4. 1
5. 4
6. 0
7. -4
8. 7
9. 4
10. 1
11. -9
12. 6
13. 2
14. 7
15. 3
16. 12

Page 35

1. 4
2. 4
3. 9
4. -1
5. 3
6. 1

Page 36

1. 5
2. 14
3. 10
4. -66
5. -20
6. 8
7. 27
8. 14
9. 12

Page 37

1. 4
2. 8
3. -4
4. 5
5. 4
6. 1
7. 6
8. -5
9. 4
10. 5
11. 4
12. 7
13. 6
14. 7
15. 9

Page 38

1. Length = 210 feet, width = 70 feet
2. First number = 42, second number = 43
3. Length = 140 meters, width = 70 meters
4. First number = 30, second number = 60, third number = 90
5. Length = 40 feet, width = 10 feet
6. First number = 20, second number = 80, third number = 400
7. Length = 50 centimeters, width = 10 centimeters
8. First number is 13, second number is 14, third number is 15

Page 39

1. $x = b - a$; -6
2. $x = \frac{b}{a}$; -5
3. $x = \frac{c}{a-b}$; 7

Page 40

1. $t = \frac{d}{r}$
2. $I = \frac{V}{R}$
3. $V = \frac{m}{D}$
4. $\frac{SA}{2\pi h} = r$
5. $\frac{SA - 2hl}{2l + 2h} = w$
6. $\frac{2A}{h} - a = b$

Page 41

1. $\frac{a - f}{6} = r$
2. $\frac{P}{2 + \pi} = x$
3. $\frac{2A}{n} - 2n = x$

Page 42

1. 100
2. 131
3. 15
4. 9
5. -7
6. $\frac{2}{5}$
7. 6
8. 12
9. 3
10. $\frac{1}{11}$
11. $\frac{3}{2}$
12. $\frac{1}{3}$
13. 2
14. 12
15. 4
16. 6
17. 3
18. 3
19. Leslie has $7.50, Lakita has $7.75.
20. Rosa is 8, and Marcos is 15.
21. no; 1.06(36) = 38.16
22. yes; 1.06(39) = 41.34
23. 4
24. $k = \frac{2E}{x^2}$

Page 43

1. a^8
2. b^7
3. c^{12}
4. d^{10}
5. 15,625
6. a^4b^3
7. m^7n^2
8. x^7y^4
9. a^2bc
10. x^3yz
11. rs^3t
12. de^6f
13. a^4xy^3
14. a^5b^3c
15. $2y^5$
16. $b^8d^2f^3$
17. $7m^8n^4$
18. $18a^6b^7$
19. $16b^4cd$
20. $25x^4y^6$
21. $-72ay^2$
22. $54ab^3c$
23. $12x^5y^3$
24. $-12m^2r^7$
25. $48yz^6$
26. $9q^3$
27. $-144yz^4$
28. $75r^9s$
29. $30ax^4y^3$
30. $50b^2c^4d^2$
31. $-36ax^4y^2$
32. $48abc^2d^3$

Page 44

1. 729
2. 256
3. 15,625
4. 46,656
5. $4a^8$
6. $81h^{12}$
7. $16n^{20}$
8. $125k^{21}$
9. $a^{16}b^4$
10. s^6t^6
11. $x^5y^{15}z^5$
12. $m^{16}n^8p^8$
13. a^8b^2
14. y^4z^2
15. m^3n^{12}
16. $p^{18}q^3$
17. m^4n^8
18. $p^{10}q^4$
19. r^6s^{12}
20. $x^{16}y^8$
21. $4c^4d^2e^6$
22. $16x^6y^4z^2$
23. $16m^4n^{20}p^{12}$
24. $125r^{12}s^6t^9$
25. a^5b^6
26. $m^{14}n^3$
27. j^8k^9
28. $x^{11}y^8$
29. $m^{11}n^{18}$
30. $g^{24}h^9$
31. $9x^6y^{10}$
32. $49p^{14}q^{24}$
33. $27x^5y^8$

Page 45

1. 1
2. d^3
3. b^4
4. m^5
5. c^4
6. x^2
7. y^2
8. a^2
9. m^5
10. s^3
11. x
12. a
13. c^3
14. c^6
15. 1
16. 2
17. $3a^2$
18. $5e^4$
19. 9
20. $2d^3$
21. $2x$
22. 10
23. $5b$
24. $2d^2$
25. $3b$
26. $2a$
27. $2y^2$
28. e^5
29. d^6
30. $4f^6$

Page 46

1. $\frac{1}{x^5}$
2. $\frac{1}{y}$
3. $\frac{1}{a^3}$
4. $\frac{1}{b}$
5. $\frac{1}{s^2}$
6. $\frac{1}{x^2}$
7. $\frac{1}{a}$
8. $\frac{1}{y^5}$
9. $\frac{1}{b}$
10. $\frac{1}{d^2}$
11. $\frac{-1}{y}$
12. $\frac{-1}{x^4}$
13. $\frac{-1}{z^2}$
14. $\frac{-1}{r^2}$
15. $\frac{-1}{d^3}$
16. $\frac{3}{c}$
17. $\frac{3}{x^2}$
18. $\frac{9}{b^3}$
19. $\frac{-9}{4r}$
20. $\frac{6}{e^2}$
21. $\frac{2}{x}$
22. $\frac{3}{y}$
23. $\frac{6}{a^4}$
24. $\frac{5}{b^4}$
25. $\frac{3}{z^3}$
26. $-3a^{-1}$
27. $-4b^{-2}$
28. $-9x^{-6}$
29. $-9r^{-2}$
30. $2z^{-1}$

Page 47

1. x
2. $\frac{b}{a}$
3. $\frac{a^2}{b^2}$
4. $\frac{x^2y^2}{z}$
5. $\frac{yz^2}{x}$
6. $\frac{3y^2}{x}$
7. $\frac{4y^3}{x}$
8. $\frac{1}{2a}$
9. $5a^2$
10. $\frac{a^2}{4bc^3}$
11. $\frac{3}{y}$
12. $\frac{-x}{2y}$
13. $\frac{4x}{y}$
14. $\frac{2y}{-x}$
15. $\frac{-y^2}{3x}$
16. $\frac{b}{-5a^2}$
17. $\frac{-3y}{x}$
18. $\frac{-4y^2}{x^2}$
19. $\frac{a}{-5b}$
20. $\frac{-6z^2}{x^2}$
21. $\frac{3}{xy}$
22. $\frac{yz}{6x}$
23. $\frac{x^2}{2y}$
24. $\frac{2b}{a}$
25. $\frac{5b^2}{a}$
26. $\frac{2a}{3y}$
27. $\frac{8y}{5x^2}$
28. $\frac{2b}{3a}$
29. $\frac{2c^2}{3a^2}$
30. $\frac{7a}{6bc^2}$

Page 48

1. $8a$
2. $6x$
3. $10m - 14n$
4. $8y + z$
5. $7x + y$
6. 0
7. $-10a$
8. $13r - 2s$
9. $3m + 2n$
10. $2r + 6st$
11. $b - 4cd$
12. $-12xy - 16z$
13. $8x - y$
14. $2cd + 2d$
15. $10ab - 15yz$
16. $3m - 7n$
17. 0
18. $28p - 33q$
19. $2xyz$
20. $5rst + 7t$
21. $5abc + 7ab$
22. $-2yz + 14y$
23. $11xy - 11z$
24. $-2abc + 10ab$

Page 49

1. $2y$
2. $-a + 5b$
3. $m + 11n$
4. $-2y$
5. $-3a - 3b$
6. $4m - 3n$
7. $2x - 2y$
8. $4b - 3c$
9. $-5r + s$

10. $3a - 2b - 5cd$
11. $3m + 7np$
12. $3rs - 7t$
13. $-3x + 6yz$
14. 0
15. $-8rs - 10t$
16. $9x - yz$
17. $9x + 2wy$
18. $-3mn$
19. -9
20. 0
21. $2rs - 2t$
22. $-9xyz + 9z$
23. $abc - 2c$
24. $-2rst + 2rs$

Page 50

1. $7x^3 + 7y^2$
2. $8a^2 + 9b^2$
3. $5b^2 + 12c^2$
4. $8m^2 - 5n^2$
5. $2x^2 - 2y$
6. $3a^2 - 3b$
7. $2b^2 + 2b$
8. $3m^2 + 4n^4$
9. $x^2 - 3y$
10. $10x^3 - y^2$
11. $8a^3 + b^2$
12. $9b^3 - 6b^2$
13. $-m$
14. $-8x^2 + 2y^3$
15. $11y^2$
16. $-8a^3 - 4a^2 - a$
17. $-3b^3 + 4b^2 - b$
18. $-6m^2 - 6m$
19. $-8x^4 - 2x^2 - 3$
20. $2b^2 + 1$
21. $-3x^2 - x + 6$
22. $-6x^4 - x^3 + 3x^2$
23. $6m^2 - 16m$
24. $12a^4$

Page 51

1. 1
2. $\frac{x}{9y}$
3. $\frac{30y}{b}$
4. $\frac{ax}{2}$
5. $\frac{a}{x^3}$
6. $\frac{72a^2}{b}$
7. $-8bx^4$
8. $\frac{-18a}{5}$
9. $-6b$
10. $\frac{x^3}{4a^2}$
11. $6a^2x^2$
12. $\frac{x}{4a}$
13. $2b$
14. $\frac{z^2}{6}$
15. $\frac{1}{p}$
16. 1
17. $2x + 2y$
18. $\frac{-1}{2x}$

Page 52

1. $\frac{a}{x^2}$
2. $\frac{1}{m^2n^2}$
3. bz^3
4. $\frac{5x}{2y}$
5. $\frac{4xy}{3ab}$
6. $\frac{x}{y}$
7. $\frac{xy}{18}$
8. $\frac{ab}{12x}$
9. $\frac{3x^2y^2}{ab}$
10. $\frac{2x}{3}$
11. $\frac{ab}{2}$
12. $\frac{ab}{4}$
13. $\frac{-3a^3}{5}$
14. $\frac{-3x}{2}$
15. $\frac{-4y}{3}$
16. $36a^2$
17. $\frac{15x^2y}{2}$
18. $28a^3b^2$
19. a
20. $\frac{2}{a}$
21. $2x$

Page 53

1. $x^2 + xy$
2. $2xy + y^2$
3. $x^4 + 2x^3y$
4. $2x^2 + 2xy$
5. $6x^2 + 9xy$
6. $12a^4 - 6a^3b$
7. $-4ab - 2b^2$
8. $-6ab - 2b^2$
9. $12ab^3 - 9b^4$
10. $4x^3 + 4xy$
11. $4b^3 - 2a^2b$
12. $15c^5 + 20c^2$
13. $6x^2 - 10xy - 4xz$
14. $4xy - 6y^2 + 8yz$
15. $15ab^2 + 12b^3 - 6b^2c$
16. $16a^2b - 20b^3 - 12bc^2$
17. $-14ab + 6b^5 + 2b$
18. $12c^4 + 9c^3 - 6c^2$
19. $10x^2y - 4xy^2 + 6xyz$
20. $x^2z + xyz - xz^2$
21. $8a^2b^2 + 8ab^3 + 8ab^2$
22. $-5x^2yz + 3xy^2z - 4xyz^2$
23. $2a^3bc + 2ab^3c + 2abc^3$
24. $-4x^2y^3z - 4xy^3z^2$

Page 54

1. monomial
2. binomial
3. polynomial
4. binomial
5. trinomial
6. binomial
7. $x^2 + 5x + 6$
8. $x^2 + 18x + 77$
9. $x^2 + 8x + 16$
10. $x^2 - 1$
11. $2x^2 + x - 78$
12. $6x^2 - 13x - 5$
13. $9x^2 - 48x + 64$
14. $81x^2 - 49$

Page 55

1. $a + 1$
2. $3xy - 2z$
3. $7y$
4. $2b + 3c + 4d$
5. $9x + 12y + 8z$
6. $ay + 2y^2 + 3y^3$
7. $-2a^2 + 5a + 1$
8. $3x^2 - 4x - 6$
9. $-5x^2 - 4x + 3$
10. $-3x^2 - 5x - 7$
11. $-3a^2 - 4ay - 5y^2$
12. $-2x^2 - 3xy - 4y$
13. $4x^2 + 3x + 5$
14. $2a^3 + 3a^2 + 2a$
15. $4x^2 + 2xy + 3y^2$
16. $2x + 6 - 4y$
17. $5x^2 - 4xy + 6y^2$
18. $3c + 4cd - 2d^2$

Page 56

1. $(7m)(n - 2p - 3q)$
2. $(5x)(x^2 - 2x + 3)$
3. $(4a)(x + 2y - 3z)$
4. $(6ab)(a^2 - 2ab + 3b^2)$
5. $(2x)(5x^2 + 4x - 1)$
6. $(3)(3a^2b^2 + 2ab + 5)$
7. $(4xy)(2x + 1 - 3y)$
8. $(2x)(5x^2 - 6x - 3)$
9. $(5ab)(4a^2 - 3ab + 2b^2)$
10. $(4xy^2)(4y - 3x + 5xy)$
11. $(3a^2)(1 - 5ay + 6a^2y^2)$
12. $(5ab)(4b^2 - 3ab - 5a^2)$

Page 57

1. $a^2 + 2ab + b^2$
2. $a^2b^2 - c^2$
3. $4x^2 + 4xy + y^2$
4. $9a^2 - 12ab + 4b^2$
5. $x^3y^2 + x^2yz - xyz - z^2$
6. $-2c^2 - 3cd + 2d^2$
7. $-3x^2 + 10xy + 8y^2$
8. $-a^2 + 4ab - 4b^2$
9. $-6a^2bc + 8abc + 3ad - 4d$
10. $-y^2 + 4z^2$
11. $3a^2 + 5ab - 12b^2$
12. $-36x^2 + 18xy - 2y^2$
13. $x^2y^2 + 2xyz + z^2$
14. $8a^2b^2 - 10abc + 3c^2$
15. $12x^4y^5 - 3x^2y^4 + 4x^3y^4 - xy^3$
16. $a^3c + a^2b - a^2d - ac^2 - bc + cd$
17. $2x^2 - 3xy + 2xz + y^2 - yz$
18. $g^2k - 2gk^2 - 2gk + 4k^2 - gm + 2km$
19. $2x^3 + 2x^2y - x^2 - xy + x + y$

205

Answer Key
Core Skills Algebra

20. $6d^2h + 2d^3 + 3h^2$
$+ dh - 6hw - 2dw$

21. $4x^3 - 6x^2y + xy^2 + y^3$

Page 58

1. $a - 2b$
2. $x - y$
3. $a + 2b$
4. $x + 1$
5. $3x - 2y$
6. $5a + 2b$
7. $5 + x$
8. $4 + 2x$
9. $2x + 3y$

Page 59

1. $6b^3 - 8b^2 + 12b$
2. $12x^3y - 6x^2y^2 - 9xy^3$
3. $40x^2 + 12x^2y^2$
4. $x^3 - x^2 - x + 10$
5. $4a^3 - 7ab^2 + 3b^3$
6. $6x^4 - 7x^3 + x$
7. $-4x^2 + 13x$
8. $6x^3 - 15x^2 + 12x - 2$
9. $-6a^2 + 4a$
10. $3x^2 + 6xz - 3y^2 + 3z^2$
11. $36x^2y^2 + 54x^2y - 6xy^2 - 9xy$
12. $-25b^3 + 6b^2$
13. $x + 4$
14. $2x + 1$
15. $y - 2$
16. 3
17. $18y - 6x + 6x^2$
18. $4y + 3xy - 2x^2y$
19. $x + 2$
20. $x - 3$
21. $2 + 3x$

Page 60

1. c^3d^3
2. $-25x^6y^4$
3. $x^3y^9z^{12}$
4. m^6
5. $-\dfrac{2a^2}{3c^2}$
6. $6xy + 2x$
7. $-2b - 6$
8. $-6m^3 - 15m^2 + 5m$
9. $\dfrac{b}{a}$
10. x^2yz
11. $\dfrac{-3x^2}{5}$
12. $x - 1$
13. $5xy + 2z$
14. $4a^3 - 3a - 1$
15. $x^2 - xy$
16. $4x^2y - 2y^2 - 6y$
17. $3a^2 - 14ab - 24b^2$
18. $a^3b - a^2b + 3ab + ab^3 - b^3 - 3b$
19. $2x^2 + 7x + 3$
20. $21x^2 - 38x + 5$
21. $36x^2 - 57x - 30$

22. $x - 2$
23. $x + 2y$
24. $2x - 3y$
25. $4z(3a - 2b + 4c)$
26. $3y(3f + 5g - 9)$

Page 61

1. 2
2. 27
3. 24
4. $2a + 7b$
5. $2y^3 - 10y^2 - 5x^2$
6. $16a^4x^2$
7. $6ab^3 + 3ac^2$
8. $5rs^2$
9. $a - \dfrac{1}{2}$
10. $5a^3b^8c^3$
11. $\dfrac{4}{3a^3}$
12. $\dfrac{1}{9}$
13. $3x$
14. $12a^2 + 2ab + 4ab^2 - 2b^2 + 2b^3$
15. $-27a^2$
16. $12x^2 + 10y^3z^6 - 5$
17. $x + 3$
18. $15q^2 + 4q - 35$
19. The numbers are 92, 93, and 94.
20. 5 feet
21. $1.15p$
22. $1.2c \le 50$; $c \le 41.67$

Page 62

1. Domain: {0, 2, -4};
Range: {-3, 2, 5}
2. Domain: {⁻9, 0, 3}; Range: {1, 3}
3. Domain: {-3, -1, 1, 9};
Range: {-5, -2}
4. Domain: {-8, -4, 4, 8};
Range: {-1}
5. Domain: {0, 1, 4, 6};
Range: {-4, -3, 0, 2}
6. Domain: {-4, -1, 1, 3};
Range: {-2, 1, 3, 5}
7. yes
8. no
9. yes
10. no

Page 63

1.

Set A	Set B
0	2
1	3
2	4
3	5
4	6
5	7

2. $n + 2$
3. Domain: {-2, -1, 0, 1, 2, 3};
Range: {-6, -3, 0, 3, 6, 9}
4.

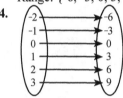

5.

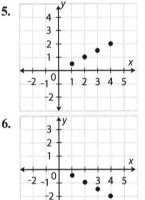

6.

Page 64

1. Function; Domain: {0, 1, 2, 3, 4, 5, 6, 7, 8, 9}, Range: {0, -1, -2, -3, -4, -5, -6, -7, -8, -9}
2. Function; Domain: {3, 5, 7, 9}, Range: {4, 6, 8, 10}
3. Not a function; each of the numbers 10, 11, and 12 has two or more factors, and functions must have exactly one output for each input.
4. Function; Domain: {2, 4, 6, 8, 10}, Range: {1, 2, 3, 4, 5}
5. Not a function; each input is paired with two outputs, not exactly one output.
6. Function; Domain: {-64, -27, -8, -1, 0, 1, 8, 27, 64}; Range: {-4, -3, -2, -1, 0, 1, 2, 3, 4}
7a. $0, 5 - 0 = 5, (0, 5)$; $1, 5 - 1 = 4$, $(1, 4)$; $2, 5 - 2 = 3, (2, 3)$; $3, 5 - 3 = 2, (3, 2)$; $4, 5 - 4 = 1$, $(4, 1)$; $5, 5 - 5 = 0, (5, 0)$; Check graph.

206

Answer Key
Core Skills Algebra

7b. Domain and Range: {0, 1, 2, 3, 4, 5}; unit of independent variable: number of downloads; unit of dependent variable: dollars

Page 65

1. $(0, 5)$
2. $(4, 3)$
3. $(2, 4)$
4. $(2, 0)$
5. $(0, 2)$
6. $(4, -2)$
7. $(3, -4)$
8. $(-1, 0)$
9. $(-5, 4)$

Page 66

1.
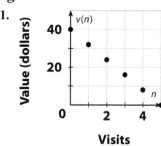
Visits

2. $40
3. -8 dollars per visit
4. Domain: {0, 1, 2, 3, 4, 5}; Range: {0, 8, 16, 24, 32, 40}
5. Yes, because it can be written in the form of a linear function [$v(n) = -8n + 40$] and the graph consists of individual points that lie along a line; Yes, because the function is discrete and linear and the outputs correspond to evenly spaced input values from the set of integers.

6.
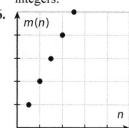

7. {2, 4, 6, 8, 10}
8. Yes, because it can be written in the form of a linear function [$m(n) = 2n$] and the graph consists of individual points that lie along a line; Yes, because the function is discrete and linear and the outputs correspond to evenly spaced input values from the set of integers.

Page 67

1. x-intercept: -1; y-intercept: 1
2. x-intercept: 2; y-intercept: -4
3. x-intercept: 3; y-intercept: 6
4. $(0, -3), (3, 0)$
5. $(0, -3), \left(\frac{3}{4}, 0\right)$
6. $(0, 5), (5, 0)$

Page 68

1a. The domain of $f(x)$ is the set of whole numbers from 0 to 5. The domain of $g(x)$ is the set of real numbers from 0 to 5. The initial values are both -2. The range of $f(x)$ is {-2, 1, 4, 7, 10, 13}. The range of $g(x)$ is {$g(x) \mid -2 \leq g(x) \leq 18$}.

1b. Sample answer: $f(x)$ is linear because there is a common difference of 3 per unit increase in x. $g(x)$ is linear because its graph is a line. $f(x)$ is discrete because its graph would consist of isolated points. $g(x)$ is continuous because its graph is unbroken over its domain.

2a. Domain for Grace: {10, 10.25, 10.5, 10.75, 11, . . ., 20}; Range for Grace: {90, 92.25, 94.50, 96.75, 99, . . ., 180}; Domain for Frances: {$t \mid 5 \leq t \leq 15$}; Range for Frances: {$f(t) \mid 50 \leq f(t) \leq 150$}.

2b. Grace earns $9 per hour and from $90 to $180 per week. Frances earns $10 per hour and from $50 to $150 per week.

Page 69

1. $f(x) = 4x + 1$
2. $f(x) = 6$
3. $f(x) = -\frac{2}{3}x + 5$
4. $f(x) = \frac{7}{4}x$
5. $f(x) = -x + 5$
6. $f(x) = \frac{3}{2}x - 3$
7. $f(x) = 6x - 7$
8. $f(x) = -\frac{4}{5}x + 2$
9. $f(x) = 2x - 1$
10. $f(x) = -\frac{1}{2}x + 3$

Page 70

1a. The t-intercept if the graph were extended to the t-axis.

1b. $g(t) = -2t + 10$

1c. Set $g(t)$ equal to 0 and solve for t; she can drive for 5 hours.

2a. Independent variable is time, t, measured in minutes; dependent variable is distance, d, measured in miles.

2b. $d_J(t) = \frac{1}{8}t$; $d_N(t) = \frac{1}{10}t + 1.5$

2c.
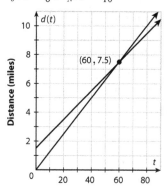
Time (minutes)
Jamal does not catch up with Nathan.

Page 71

1. $g(x) = x + 1$
2. $g(x) = -x + 4$
3. $g(x) = \frac{1}{2}x + \frac{3}{2}$ or $\frac{1}{2}(x + 3)$
4. $g(x) = \frac{3}{2}x - 9$ or $\frac{3}{2}(x - 6)$
5. $g(x) = \frac{1}{3}x + \frac{1}{4}$ or $\frac{1}{3}(x + \frac{3}{4})$
6. $g(x) = -\frac{2}{5}x - 3$
7. $F(C) = \frac{5}{9}C + 32$; the function converts degrees Celsius to degrees Fahrenheit.
8a. $h(t) = -0.5t + 10$;
    D = {$t \mid 0 \leq t \leq 20$};
    R = {$h \mid 0 \leq h \leq 10$}
8b. $t(h) = -2h + 20$;
    D = {$h \mid 0 \leq h \leq 10$};
    R = {$t \mid 0 \leq t \leq 20$}
8c. If you input the height of the candle, the inverse function tells you how long the candle has burned.
9. $g(x) = \frac{x - b}{m} = \frac{1}{m}x - \frac{b}{m}$; the slope is $\frac{1}{m}$, and the y-intercept is $-\frac{b}{m}$.
10. No; a constant function is a many-to-one pairing, so the inverse would have to be a one-to-many pairing, but a function must pair each input with a single output.

Page 72

1. 0, 1, 4, 9
2. 5, $5\frac{1}{2}$, $6\frac{1}{3}$, $7\frac{1}{4}$
3. 2, 1, 0.5, 0.25
4. 0, 1, $\sqrt{2}$, $\sqrt{3}$
5. 2, 12, 22, 32
6. 16, 8, 4, 2

207

7. 1, 3, 7, 15

8. 1, 1, 0, −1

9a. $42,000; $44,100; $46,305; $48,620.25

9b. $f(0) = 40,000$ and $f(n) = 1.05f(n − 1)$ for $n \geq 1$

9c. 56,284; Donna's salary 7 years after she began working if she keeps getting the same raise each year

10. 34

11. 312

Page 73

1a.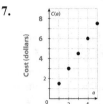

1b. 4, 9, 16, 25

1c. $f(n) = n^2$

1d. 100

2. $f(n) = n + 5$

3. $f(n) = 3n$

4. $f(n) = \frac{1}{n}$

5. $f(1) = 8$ and $f(n) = f(n − 1) + 1$ for $n \geq 2$

6. $f(1) = 2$ and $f(n) = 2f(n − 1)$ for $n \geq 2$

7. $f(1) = 27$ and $f(n) = f(n − 1) − 3$ for $n \geq 2$

Page 74

1. $h(x) = 2x − 8$

2. $h(x) = 5x − 6$

3. $h(x) = -10x + 12$

4. $j(x) = 8x + 4$

5a. $R(c) = 20c + 500$

5b. $E(c) = 6c$

5c. $P(c) = R(c) − E(c) = 14c + 500$

6a. $C(r) = 2r + 30$

6b. $P(r) = 5$

6c. $T(r) = P(r) \cdot C(r) = 10r + 150$

Page 75

1. Domain: {−6, 0, 2}; Range: {0, 4, 6}; yes

2. Domain: {−4, −1, 4}; Range: {−1, 1, 3, 5}; no

3. (3, −2)

4. (2, 4)

5. (−5, 3)

6.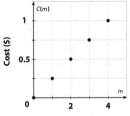

7.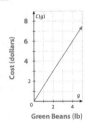

8. $f(x) = -2x + 3$

9. $f(x) = 3x − 1$

10. $g(x) = 2x + 2$

11. $g(x) = \frac{1}{2}x − \frac{1}{2}$ or $\frac{1}{2}(x − 1)$

12. 3, 5, 7, and 9

Page 76

1.

x	y
−4	6
0	3
4	0
8	−3

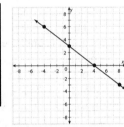

2.

x	y
−2	−7
0	−5
5	0
2	−3

3.

x	y
0	4
2	0
1	2
3	−2

Page 77

1. no

2. yes

3. Answers in table will vary for items 3–4.

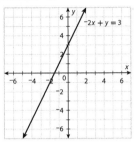

4.

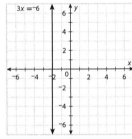

5. 0, 5, 4

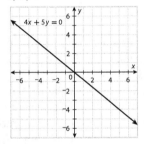

Page 78

1.

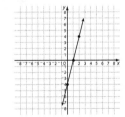

2.

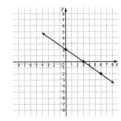

3.

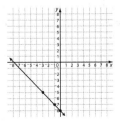

Page 79

1. $.75 per ticket
2. about −1.3 miles; about −0.065 mi/min
3. about 5 yards; about 2.5 yards/shirt
4.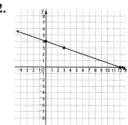

2 hours; about 3.3 hours

5.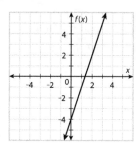

about 4:00 P.M.

Page 80

1.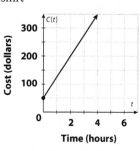

2.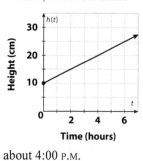

Page 81

1.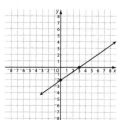

2.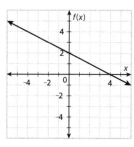

3.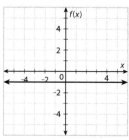

4.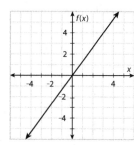

5.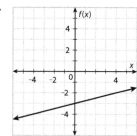

6.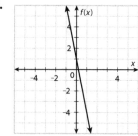

Page 82

1a.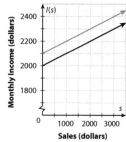

1b.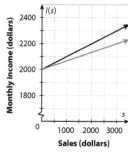

2a.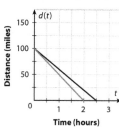

2b.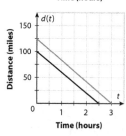

3. $D = \{t \mid 0 \le t \le 2.5\}$; $R = \{d(t) \mid 0 \le d(t) \le 100\}$; part (a): domain changes; part (b): both change

Page 83

1. y-intercept changes; $g(x) = x + 3$
2. slope changes; $h(x) = \frac{x}{2} + 1 = \frac{1}{2}x + 1$

Page 84

1.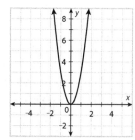

2.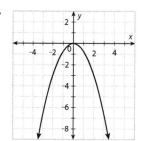

Answer Key
Core Skills Algebra

3.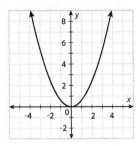

4.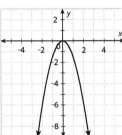

5.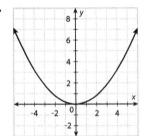

6.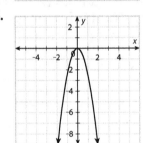

7.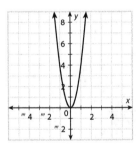

8.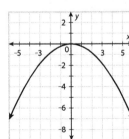

Page 85

1. $f(x) = 5x^2$
2. $f(x) = \frac{2}{3}x^2$
3. $f(x) = \frac{1}{10}x^2$
4. $f(x) = -\frac{1}{4}x^2$
5. Minimum value when $a > 0$; maximum value when $a < 0$; minimum or maximum value is 0.
6. $f(-x) = a(-x)^2 = ax^2 = f(x)$

Page 86

1.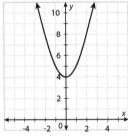

2.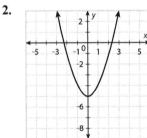

3.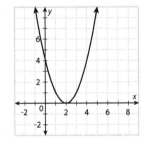

4.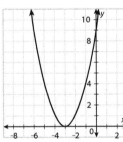

5.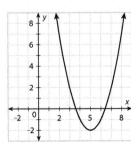

6.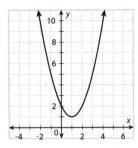

7.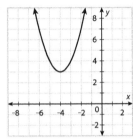

8.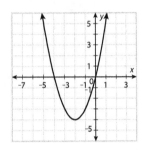

Page 87

1. $f(x) = (x - 2)^2 - 3$
2. $f(x) = (x - 1)^2 + 4$
3. $f(x) = (x + 3)^2 - 1$
4. $f(x) = (x + 5)^2 + 4$
5. D = {real numbers}; R = $\{y \mid y \geq 0\}$
6. D = {real numbers}; R = $\{y \mid y \geq 4\}$
7. D = {real numbers}; R = $\{y \mid y \geq 0\}$
8. D = {real numbers}; R = $\{y \mid y \geq -7\}$
9. D = {real numbers}; R = $\{y \mid y \geq -6\}$
10. D = {real numbers}; R = $\{y \mid y \geq 8\}$
11a. Yes; $f(-x) = (-x)^2 - 1 = x^2 - 1$ $= f(x)$
11b. No; $f(-x) = (-x - 1)^2 = (-(x + 1))^2 = (x + 1)^2 \neq f(x)$

210

Page 88

1.
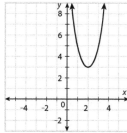

2.
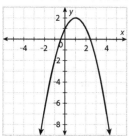

3.
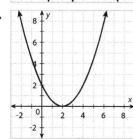

4.
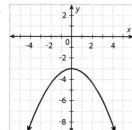

5a. $f(t) = -16t^2 + 45$

5b. The t-intercept is approximately 1.7 seconds; $f(1.7) = -1.24$, which is close to 0, so the equation agrees with the graph.

Page 89

1.
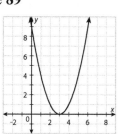

minimum: (3, 0); zero: (3, 0)

2.
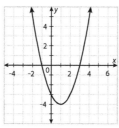

minimum: (-1, -4); zeros: (-1, 0) and (3, 0)

3.
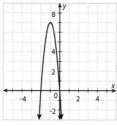

maximum: (-1, 7); zeros: (-2, 0) and (0, 0)

4.
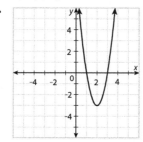

minimum: (2, -3); zeros: (1, 0) and (3, 0)

5.
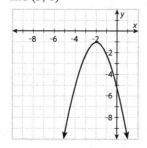

maximum: (-2, -1); zeros: none

6.
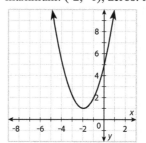

minimum: (-2, 1); zeros: none

Page 90

1. $f(x) = (x + 2)^2 - 1$
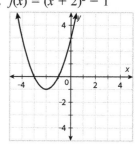

2. $f(x) = (x - 3)^2 + 2$
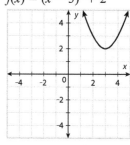

3. $f(x) = -(x - 1)^2 - 1$
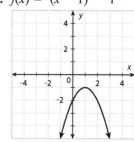

4. $f(x) = \frac{1}{2}(x - 4)^2 - 3$
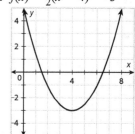

5a. $h(t) = -16t^2 + 64t + 12$

5b. $h(t) = -16(t - 2)^2 + 76$

5c.
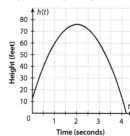

5d. Domain: $0 \leq t \leq 4.18$ (approximately);
Range: $0 \leq h(t) \leq 76$

211

Answer Key
Core Skills Algebra

Page 91

1.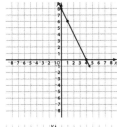

2.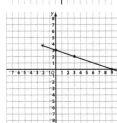

3.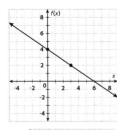

4.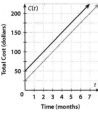

5.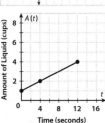

Shift the graph down 25.

6.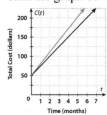

Increase the slope, but leave the vertical intercept the same.

7.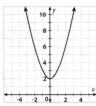

8. $f(x) = -\frac{1}{4}x^2$

Page 92

1. (2, 4)
2. (–4, 1)
3. no solution
4. (2, –3)
5. (2, 2)
6. infinitely many solutions

Page 93

1. (10, 5)
2. (9, 4)
3. (10, 4)
4. (12, 5)
5. (22, 5)
6. (30, 21)
7. (22, 15)
8. (–19, –36)
9. (16, 7)
10. (25, 10)
11. (–17, –27)
12. (20, 5)

Page 94

1. (8, 4)
2. (4, 1)
3. (3, 2)
4. (2, 4)
5. (5, 6)
6. (3, 8)

Page 95

1. $(\frac{2}{5}, -1)$
2. (–2, 2)
3. (5, 4)
4. (1, –3)
5. no solution
6. infinitely many solutions
7. When the equations are added or subtracted, the result is a false statement, such as 0 = 5; this means there is no solution.
8. When the equations are added or subtracted, the result is a true statement, such as 0 = 0; this means there are infinitely many solutions.

Page 96

1. (–6, 7)
2. (4, 5)
3. (–1, –2)
4. (2, 2)
5. (2, 6)
6. (3, 1)
7. (2, 4)
8. (1, 3)
9. (2, 5)

Page 97

1. (1, 1)
2. (4, 2)
3. (5, 2)

Page 98

1. (3, 4)
2. (6, –2)
3. (–1, 5)
4. (–2, –4)
5. (3, 1)
6. (2, –7)
7. infinitely many solutions
8. (2, 2)
9. (–6, 3)
10. no solution
11a. $(A + kD)x + (B + kE)y = C + kF$
11b. Yes; the solution is a solution for the original equation and any multiple of either original equation.

Page 99

1. $y = 3x - 12$
2. $y = -3x + 5$
3. $y = -\frac{3}{4}x + 15$
4. $y = \frac{1}{2}x + 4$
5. $y = -\frac{1}{3}x + 2$
6. $y = -2x - \frac{1}{2}$
7. $x = 3y - 1$
8. $x = 2y - 4$
9. $x = \frac{-y}{3} + 3$
10. $x = \frac{2}{3}y + 1$
11. $x = 10 + y$
12. $x = \frac{-4}{7}y + 4$

Page 100

1. (4, 2)
2. (6, 5)
3. (3, 2)
4. (1, 3)
5. (5, 3)
6. (3, 1)
7. (5, 2)
8. (4, 2)
9. (5, 2)
10. (5, 1)
11. (3, 2)
12. (4, 3)

Page 101

1. (2, 1)
2. (–3, 5)
3. (1, 7)
4. (–2, –2)
5. no solution
6. $(-\frac{3}{4}, \frac{1}{2})$
7. (5, 3)
8. infinitely many solutions
9. Solve for x first; if solving for y first, each side would have to be divided by a constant after isolating the y-term; (1, –3)
10. Solve for y first; if solving for x first, each side would have to be

Answer Key
Core Skills Algebra

multiplied by a constant after isolating the *x*-term; infinitely many solutions

Page 102

1. (2, 4)
2. (2, 2)
3. (6, -6)
4. (4, 1)
5. (2, 2)
6. (4, 9)
7. (1, 5)
8. (6, 7)
9. (-5, -3)

Page 103

1. 7 and 8
2. 4 and 14
3. 3 and 4
4. 2 and 3
5. 3 and 4
6. 3 and 5
7. 2 and 5
8. 4 and 5
9. 4 and 7
10. 5 and 6

Page 104

1. (8, 1)
2. (8, 2)
3. (4, 3)
4. (10, 5)
5. (6, -4)
6. (12, 2)

Page 105

1. 2 and 4
2. 5 and 6
3. 3 and 40
4. 5 and 6
5. 2 and 6
6. 3 and 4

Page 106

1. (-2, 4) and (2, 4)
2. no real solution
3. (2, 4)
4. (-0.5, 11) and (1.2, 4.2)
5. (-0.2, 5.5) and (4.2, 14.5)
6. (-1.6, -6.2) and (0.6, -1.8)

Page 107

1. 2; (-6.25, 16) and (0.5, -11)
2. 1: (1,4)
3. (0, -2)
4. (1.7, 1.7) and (5.3, 5.3)
5. no solution
6. (1, 1) and (-1, 1)
7. (1.3, 1.9) and (-2.3, -8.9)
8. (0.5, 13.5)

Page 108

1. $y = -5x + 9$
2. $y = 4x - 8$
3. $y = -2x - 8$
4. (7, 5)
5. (9, 1)
6. (3, 2)
7. (6, 5)

8. (16, 4)
9. (-1, 3)
10. 8 and 9
11. 2 and 6
12. (2, 32) and (6, 0)

Page 109

1. no; 3(36) = 108
2. yes; 5(12) + 4 = 64
3. yes; 60 − 10(5) = 10
4a. ×; ≥
4b. *b*; number of books
4c. $11.95b \geq 200$
4d. $11.95(16) \overset{?}{\geq} 200$, $191.20 \overset{?}{\geq} 200$, no; $11.95(17) \overset{?}{\geq} 200$, $203.15 \overset{?}{\geq} 200$, yes; $11.95(18) \overset{?}{\geq} 200$, $215.10 \overset{?}{\geq} 200$, yes
5a. Let *m* be the daily minutes used; $1 + 0.10m \leq 5$
5b. 40 minutes
5c. Any amount of time between 0 and 40 min is in the solution set.

Page 110

1. $x > 22$
2. $x \leq 15$
3. $x < 20$
4. $x \leq 1$
5. $x > 15$
6. $x \geq -4$
7. $x \geq 6$
8. $x > -24$
9. $x > -8$
10. $x < -4$
11. $x < 31$
12. $x \leq -16$
13. $x < -4$
14. $x > 2$
15. $x \leq -4$
16. $x \leq 1$
17. $x > -6$
18. $x \leq -34$

Page 111

1. $x > 10$
2. $x \leq -12$
3. $x \leq -12$
4. $x < 2$
5. $x \leq -5$
6. $x \geq 3$
7. $x > 2$
8. $x > 4$
9. $x < -3$
10. $x > 3$
11. $x > -1$
12. $x \geq 10$
13. $x < \frac{4}{5}$
14. $x \geq -\frac{1}{2}$
15. $x > -\frac{1}{2}$

Page 112

1. $115\frac{5}{9}$ pounds
2. $6,600
3. 60
4. 11

Page 113

1.
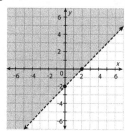

2.
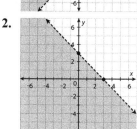

3.
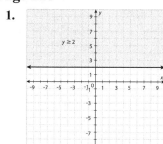

4. Possible answer: (-2, 6)
5. no
6. Possible answer: (1, 6)
7. 5 boxes
8. (0, 5), (3, 3), (6, 1)

Page 114

1.
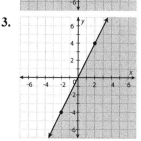

2.
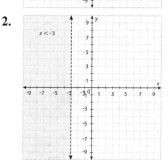

213

3.

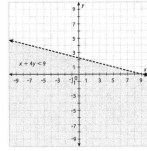

4.

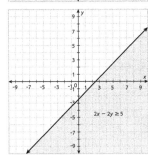

Page 115

1. $\{x \mid x \geq 1\}$
2. $\{x \mid x > 6\}$
3. $\{x \mid x > 2\}$

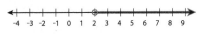

4. $\{x \mid x \geq 2\}$

5. $\{x \mid x < -\frac{3}{4}\}$

6. $\{x \mid x \leq -\frac{1}{2}\}$

Page 116

1.

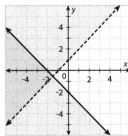

2.

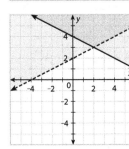

3.

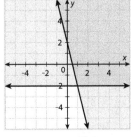

4.

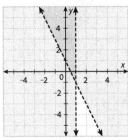

5.

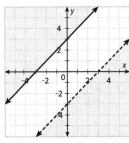

6.

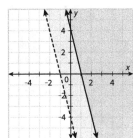

Page 117

1. 11	16. ab
2. 7	17. x^2y^2
3. 12	18. xy
4. 5	19. abc
5. 13	20. x^2bc^2
6. 15	21. $3a$
7. 9	22. $4b^2$
8. 4	23. $6ab$
9. 18	24. $8xy^2$
10. 14	25. $9ab^2c^4$
11. a	26. $13x^5y^2$
12. a^2	27. $17x^6$
13. x^3	28. $18b^2c^3$
14. y^4	29. $20ab^3$
15. b^2	30. $10x^2yz^3$

Page 118

1. ±10	9. ±3
2. ±5	10. ±5
3. ±7	11. ±5
4. ±4	12. ±2
5. ±5	13. ±2
6. ±6	14. ±3
7. ±8	15. ±4
8. ±10	

Page 119

1. Length = 24 centimeters, width = 12 centimeters
2. Length = 32 inches, width = 4 inches
3. Length = 20 meters, width = 5 meters
4. Length = 114 inches, width = 19 inches
5. Length = 25 centimeters, width = 5 centimeters
6. Length = 12 feet, width = 4 feet

Page 120

1. 3	14. $20a$
2. 4	15. $16b^4$
3. 12	16. $7ab$
4. 1	17. $9x^2y^5$
5. 16	18. $2c^4d^3$
6. y	19. $6xy^2$
7. y^2	20. $15z^9$
8. b^3	21. $8abc^2$
9. c^4	22. $10xy^2z^3$
10. z^5	23. $13r^3s^3$
11. $2y$	24. $18t^{10}$
12. $14x^2$	25. $5x^5y^5$
13. $11z^3$	

Page 121

1. $d^{\frac{1}{3}}$	10. $\sqrt[6]{x}$
2. $b^{\frac{2}{3}}$	11. $\frac{2x^2}{y^3}$
3. $m^{\frac{3}{4}}$	12. $\frac{\sqrt[4]{x}}{y^2}$
4. $y^3\sqrt{z}$	13. $4x^2$
5. $x^2\sqrt{y}$	14. x^9y^3
6. $7xy^2$	15. $\frac{2x}{y^3}$
7. $\sqrt[12]{x}$	16. $6a^3$
8. $6x^2$	17. $\frac{b^6}{a^3}$
9. x^2y^3	18. $\frac{b}{4}$ or $\frac{1}{4}b$

19. In radical form, $x^{\frac{1}{2}} = \sqrt{x}$ and the square root of a negative number is undefined in the real number system.

20. In rational exponent form, $\sqrt[n]{\frac{a}{b}} = (\frac{a}{b})^{\frac{1}{n}}$. Use the power of a quotient property to write $(\frac{a}{b})^{\frac{1}{n}}$ as $\frac{a^{\frac{1}{n}}}{b^{\frac{1}{n}}}$. Convert back to radical form to get $\frac{\sqrt[n]{a}}{\sqrt[n]{b}}$.

21. $\sqrt[n]{a^m} = a^{\frac{m}{n}} = a^{\frac{1}{n} \cdot m} = (a^{\frac{1}{n}})^m = (\sqrt[n]{a})^m$

22. $\sqrt[3]{x^2} = x^{\frac{2}{3}}$, not $x^{\frac{3}{2}}$; $\sqrt[3]{x^2} \cdot \sqrt{x} = x^{\frac{2}{3}} \cdot x^{\frac{1}{2}} = x^{\frac{2}{3}+\frac{1}{2}} = x^{\frac{7}{6}} = x^{1+\frac{1}{6}} = x^1 \cdot x^{\frac{1}{6}} = x\sqrt[6]{x}$

23. $\sqrt[n]{a^m} = \sqrt[n]{a^{kn}} = a^{\frac{kn}{n}} = a^k$; rational because raising a nonzero rational number a to the kth power is equivalent to the product consisting of k factors of a (if $k > 0$) or k factors of $\frac{1}{a}$ (if $k < 0$), and the set of rational numbers is closed under multiplication.

Page 122

1. 2	**6.** 16
2. 4	**7.** 14
3. 3	**8.** 15
4. 16	**9.** $114.00
5. 12	**10.** 30 miles

Page 123

1. $\frac{6}{5}$	**9.** $\frac{7}{2}$
2. $\frac{4}{3}$	**10.** $\frac{35}{8}$
3. $\frac{15}{4}$	**11.** 6
4. 3	**12.** 20
5. 2	**13.** $\frac{28}{27}$
6. 2	**14.** 4
7. $\frac{21}{20}$	**15.** 5
8. $\frac{15}{16}$	**16.** 20

Page 124

1. no; $3(24) = 72$
2. yes; $4(16) + 5 = 69$
3. yes; $37 - 3(20) = -23$
4.

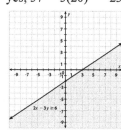

5.

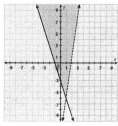

6. $\{x \mid x > 3\}$

7. 7
8. $8x^4y^2z$
9. xy^2
10. $16b^2c^5$
11. x^2y^2
12. $\sqrt[6]{x}$
13. $\sqrt[4]{x}$
14. ±8
15. ±5
16. no solution
17. 8 erasers
18. 58
19. Length $= 32$, width $= 8$

Page 125

1. 106
2. $81xy$
3. $\frac{-2m^2}{n}$
4. ab
5. $-3y$
6. $\frac{4r^2s}{3}$
7. $(0, 2)$ $(\frac{-2}{3}, 0)$
8. $(0, 6)$ $(-3, 0)$
9. $(0, 5)$ $(\frac{5}{2}, 0)$
10. 8
11. $k \geq 6$
12. $x \geq -3$
13. $(5, 1)$
14. $(10, -1)$
15. $(3, 8)$
16.

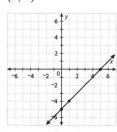

17.

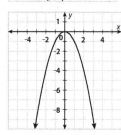

18.

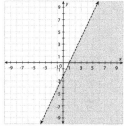

Page 126

1. m; mx_1, mx_3; b, b; $(mx_4 + b) - (mx_3 + b)$; $f(x_4) - f(x_3)$

2. b^{x_3}; ab^{x_3}; $\frac{f(x_4)}{f(x_3)}$

Page 127

1. constant rate
2. neither
3. constant percent rate
4. yes; in 65 months
5. no; Centerville's population decreases by 80 each year, while Easton's population decreases by 75 the first year and by smaller amounts each year thereafter. So, Easton will always have the greater population.
6. $g(x)$
7. $f(x)$
8. $g(x) = 100 + 4x$
9. $f(x) = 50(1.08)^x$

Page 128

1. $\frac{1}{8}, \frac{1}{4}, \frac{1}{2}, 1, 2, 4, 8$

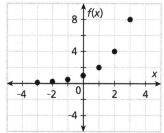

2. $\frac{128}{27}, \frac{32}{9}, \frac{8}{3}, 2, \frac{3}{2}, \frac{9}{8}, \frac{27}{32}$

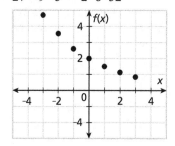

3. 4.17, 2.5, 1.5, 0.9, 0.54, 0.324, 0.1944

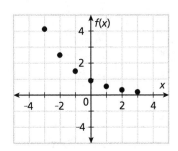

4. 1; increases
5. 1; decreases
6. horizontal line

Page 129

1. $f(x) = \left(\frac{1}{2}\right)^x$
2. $f(x) = 10(0.8)^x$
3. $f(x) = 3\left(\frac{2}{3}\right)^x$
4. $f(x) = \frac{1}{4}(2)^x$
5. $f(x) = \frac{1}{3}\left(\frac{1}{2}\right)^x$
6. $f(x) = 3(2)^x$

Page 130

1a. $A(n) = 93.5(0.5)^n$; the area decreases by a constant factor with each fold.
1b. $a = 93.5$ square inches; a is the area of the original piece of paper.
1c. 5.8 square inches
1d. $A(n) = 187(0.5)^n$; a is doubled but b stays the same where A is the area of the unfolded sheet and b is the number of times it is folded in half.
2a. 27, 81, 243
2b. $f(n) = 3^n$
2c. The domain is the set of positive integers: $\{1, 2, 3, 4, \ldots\}$. The range is the set of positive integral powers of three: $\{3, 9, 27, \ldots\}$.
2d. 59,049
2e. Sample answer. The number of favors done on Day 10 is 243 times, or 3^5 times, the number done on Day 5.
2f. $f(n) = 4^n$

Page 131

1. 1,250; 0.02; 1.02
2. 40; 0.50; 1.50
3. 50; 0.06; 1.06
4. $y = 1,500(1.04)^t$
5. $y = 255,000(1.06)^t$
6. $y = 2,000(1.16)^t$

7a. $y = 1,600(1.08)^t$
7b. $4,699.51
7c. 40th birthday

Page 132

1. $y = 2.50(1 + 0.20)^t$
2. 1.45; 1.74; 2.08; 2.50; 3.00; 3.60; 4.32; 5.18
3.

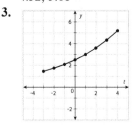

4. Domain: all real numbers from –3 to 4; Range: all real numbers from about $1.45 to about $5.18
5. $2.50; it represents the amount Sue paid for the coin.
6. $1.74; $5.18; $1.74 is the value of the function at $t = -2$, which corresponds to the end of 2003; $5.18 is the value of the function at $t = 4$, which corresponds to the end of 2009 when Sue sold the coin.

Page 133

1. 2.50, 0.4, 0.6
2. $y = 18,500(0.91)^t$
3a. $y = 2,500(0.9)^t$
3b. 2,500; 2,250; 2,025; 1,823; 1,640; 1,476
3c.

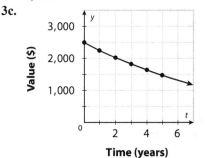

3d. $1,329
4. Sample answer: Parcel A's value is decreasing exponentially by a decay rate of about 14%. Parcel B's value is increasing exponentially at a growth rate of about 14%. Parcel A is worth more than Parcel B initially ($70,000 vs. $35,000), but after about 2.5 years, Parcel B is worth more than Parcel A.

Page 134

1. The y-intercept is a rather than 1. When $a > 1$, the graph of $f(x) = ab^x$ is a vertical stretch of the graph of $f(x) = b^x$. When $0 < a < 1$, the graph of $f(x) = ab^x$ is a vertical shrink of the graph of $f(x) = b^x$.
2. The y-intercept equals a for all values of $b > 1$, because $ab^0 = a$. As the value of b increases, the graph rises more quickly as x increases to the right of 0, and it falls more quickly as x decreases to the left of 0.
3. The y-intercept equals a for all values of b between 0 and 1. As the value of b decreases, the graph rises more quickly as x decreases to the left of 0, and the graph falls more quickly as x increases to the right of 0.
4. Y_2; Y_2 has the greater growth rate (3% rather than 2%) so you would expect Y_2 to increase more quickly as x increases to the right of 0.
5. Y_1; Y_1 has the greater decay rate (6% rather than 2%) so you would expect Y_1 to decrease more quickly as x increases to the right of 0.

Page 135

1. $\frac{2}{5}, \frac{2}{5}$; x, 5; 5
2. $\frac{1}{4}, \frac{1}{4}$; 3; 3
3. 4
4. 2
5. 3
6. 3
7. 4
8. 2
9. 2.80
10. 1.86
11. 4.03

Page 136

1a. $972 = 12(3)^x$
1b. Day 4
2a. $300 = 175(1.12)^x$
2b. 4.7560465 years or about 4.76 years
2c. This park's population will reach 300 sooner; solve $300 = 200(1.1)^x$. This park's population reaches 300 in about 4.25 years as opposed to 4.76 years.

216

3. November 2023; solve $642,000(0.98)^x = 500,000$ to find $x \approx 12.373599$ years; 0.373599 x 12 months ≈ 4.48 months. Add 12 years 4.48 months to July 1, 2011.

Page 137

1.
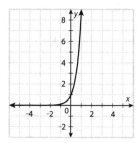

2.
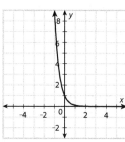

3.
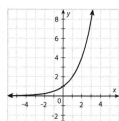

4.
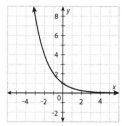

5–6.
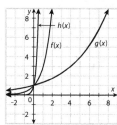

5. $g(x) = 3^{\frac{1}{4}x}$

6. $h(x) = 3^{4x}$

7. $g(x) = \left(\frac{1}{2}\right)^{2x} + 4$

8. $h(x) = 3\left(\frac{1}{2}\right)^{\frac{5}{6}x} - 8$

Page 138

1. $f(x) = 8^x$ and $f(x) = 2^{3x}$

2. Account B: \$683.41

3. no; a change in c results in a horizontal stretch or shrink of the graph of $f(x)$ and, if c changes from positive to negative (or vice versa), a reflection in the y-axis, but the range remains the set of all positive real numbers.

4. yes; a change in c from positive to negative (or vice versa) results in a reflection in the y-axis, which changes the end behavior.

5a. $0.08 = \left(1 + \frac{r}{12}\right)^{12} - 1$; $1.08 = \left(1 + \frac{r}{12}\right)^{12}$; $1.08^{\frac{1}{12}} = 1 + \frac{r}{12}$; $\frac{r}{12} = 1.08^{\frac{1}{12}} - 1 \approx 0.0064$, so $\frac{r}{12} \approx 0.64\%$

5b. Raise the base to the power of $\frac{1}{12}$; $A(t) = P(1.08)^t = P(1.08^{\frac{1}{12}})^{12t} \approx P(1.0064)^{12t}$, so the equivalent monthly interest rate is about 0.64%.

Page 139

1. $x = 3$

2. $x = 4$

3. $x = 5$

4. $f(x) = 20 + 5$

5. $g(x) = 73(1.5)^x$

6.
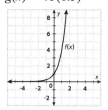

7.
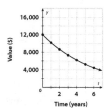

8. 12,000; 10,200; 8,670; 7,370; 6,264; 5,324; 4,526
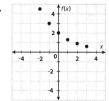

9. \$962.21

Page 140

1.
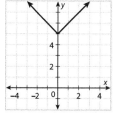

2.
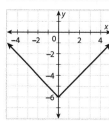

3.
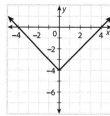

4.
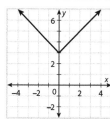

5.
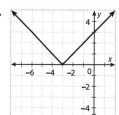

6.
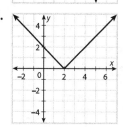

7.
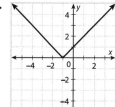

8.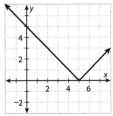

9.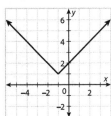

10.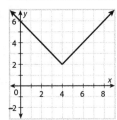

11.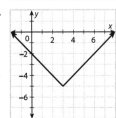

12.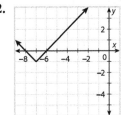

Page 141

1. $g(x) = |x - 5| + 1$
2. $g(x) = |x + 3| - 3$
3. $g(x) = |x + 2| + 3$
4. $g(x) = |x - 4| - 5$
5. D = {real numbers};
   R = $\{y \mid y \geq -7\}$
6. D = {real numbers};
   R = $\{y \mid y \geq 0\}$
7. D = {real numbers};
   R = $\{y \mid y \geq -1\}$
8. D = {real numbers};
   R = $\{y \mid y \geq 2\}$
9. D = {real numbers};
   R = $\{y \mid y \geq 1\}$
10. D = {real numbers};
    R = $\{y \mid y \geq 6\}$

11. When written in the form
$g(x) = |x - h| + k$, the function is
$g(x) = |x - (-3)| + (-1)$, so the
parent graph is translated 3 units
to the left and 1 unit down.

12. Add 4 inside the absolute value
and subtract 3 outside the absolute
value to get $h(x) = |x - 2 + 4| +
1 - 3$, or $h(x) = |x + 2| - 2$.

Page 142

1.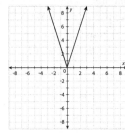

2.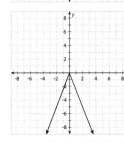

3.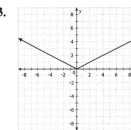

4.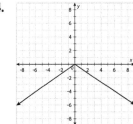

5a. 2, 1, 0, 1, 2; 2, 1, 0, 1, 2; -2, -1, 0,
-1, -2; 2, 1, 0, 1, 2

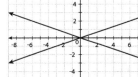

5b. For $a > 0$, they are the same;
for $a < 0$, they are reflections
across the x-axis.

Page 143

1. $f(x) = 4|x|$
2. $f(x) = -|x|$
3. $g(x) = \frac{2}{5}|x|$
4. $g(x) = -\frac{3}{2}|x|$
5a. $g(x) = \frac{7}{4}|x|$
5b. $g(-8) = \frac{7}{4}|-8| = 14$, so P is on the
path that the light takes.

Page 144

1.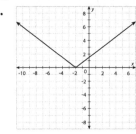

2.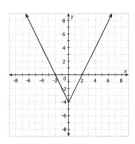

3.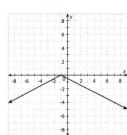

4.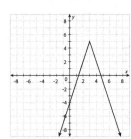

5.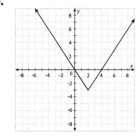

218

Answer Key
Core Skills Algebra

6.

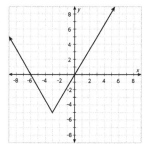

Page 145

1. $g(x) = 2|x - 1| - 5$
2. $g(x) = -3|x + 2| + 6$
3. $g(x) = \frac{3}{4}|x + 1| - 1$
4. $g(x) = -\frac{1}{2}|x - 1|$
5. {real numbers}, $\{y \geq 0\}$;
   {real numbers}, $\{y \geq -4\}$;
   {real numbers}, $\{y \leq 0\}$;
   {real numbers}, $\{y \leq 5\}$;
   {real numbers}, $\{y \geq -3\}$;
   {real numbers}, $\{y \geq -5\}$

Page 146

1. Domain = {real numbers};
   if $a > 0$, range = {real numbers greater than or equal to k};
   if $a < 0$, range = {real numbers less than or equal to k}
2. If $a > 0$ and $b < 0$, then $|ab| = a(-b) = |a||b|$; if $a < 0$ and $b < 0$, then $|ab| = (-a)(-b) = |a||b|$; in all cases, $|ab| = |a||b|$.
3. $g(x) = 2|x + 4| - 1$

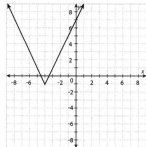

4. $g(x) = \frac{1}{2}|x - 4| + 3$

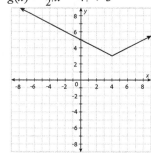

5. No; although the factor a produces a vertical stretch or shrink and a possible reflection in the x-axis, the vertex is still (0, 0) before the translation of h units horizontally and k units vertically.
6. You have obtained the graph of the parent function, $f(x) = |x|$.

Page 147

1. $x = -5$ or $x = 3$
2. $x = -1$ or $x = 7$
3. $x = -2$
4. $x = 0$ or $x = -6$
5. $x = -9$ or $x = 1$
6. no solution
7a. 200 and 376
7b. 1:20 P.M. and 4:16 P.M.
7c. 144
7d. 2:48 P.M.

Page 148

1.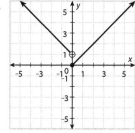

2.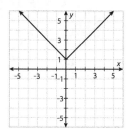

3.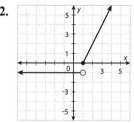

4. $f(x) = \begin{cases} x + 1 & \text{if } x < 0 \\ 2 & \text{if } x \geq 0 \end{cases}$

5. $f(x) = \begin{cases} -x - 1 & \text{if } x < 0 \\ 1 & \text{if } 0 \leq x < 2 \\ \frac{1}{2}x + 1 & \text{if } x \geq 2 \end{cases}$

6. $f(x) = \begin{cases} -2 & \text{if } x \leq -3 \\ x + 3 & \text{if } -3 < x \leq 0 \\ -x + 5 & \text{if } x > 0 \end{cases}$

7. Answers will vary.

Page 149

1a. $c(w) = \begin{cases} 4t & \text{if } 0 \leq t \leq 2 \\ 2t + 4 & \text{if } 2 < t \leq 6 \\ 16 & \text{if } 6 < t \leq 8 \end{cases}$

1b.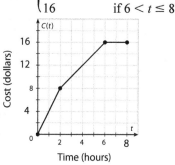

2a. $c(w) = 8 + 4 \llbracket w \rrbracket$
2b. 8, 12, 12, 16, 16

2c.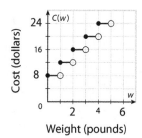

Page 150

1. $f(x) = |x|$
2. $f(x) = |x - 4|$
3. Domain = {real numbers}; range = $\{y \mid y \geq 0\}$
4. Domain = {real numbers}; range = $\{y \mid y \geq 2\}$
5. Domain = {real numbers}; range = $\{y \mid y \geq 0\}$
6.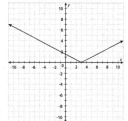

7.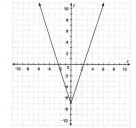

8.

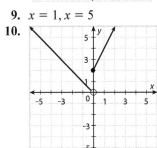

9. $x = 1, x = 5$

10.

Page 151

1. $a^2 + 2ab + b^2$
2. $b^2 + 2ab + a^2$
3. $m^2 + 2mn + n^2$
4. $r^2 + 2rs + s^2$
5. $b^2 + 2bc + c^2$
6. $c^2 + 2cd + d^2$
7. $4a^2 + 4ab + b^2$
8. $x^2 + 4xy + 4y^2$
9. $4a^2 + 8ab + 4b^2$
10. $4y^2 + 4yz + z^2$
11. $x^2 + 6xy + 9y^2$
12. $9x^2 + 6xy + y^2$
13. $4x^2 + 12xy + 9y^2$
14. $9x^2 + 12xy + 4y^2$
15. $9x^2 + 30x + 25$
16. $4x^2 + 28x + 49$
17. $m^2 + 8m + 16$
18. $36 + 12g + g^2$
19. $4x^2 + 12x + 9$
20. $16a^2 + 24a + 9$

Page 152

1. $x^2 - 8x + 16$
2. $x^2 - 6x + 9$
3. $x^2 - 10x + 25$
4. $x^2 - 16x + 64$
5. $9 - 6y + y^2$
6. $49 - 14x + x^2$
7. $a^2 - 24a + 144$
8. $a^2 - 20a + 100$
9. $c^2 - 4cd + 4d^2$
10. $x^2 - 6xy + 9y^2$
11. $x^2 - 12xy + 36y^2$
12. $x^2 - 20xy + 100y^2$
13. $9x^2 - 42xy + 49y^2$
14. $4x^2 - 36xy + 81y^2$
15. $9a^2 - 12ab + 4b^2$
16. $64c^2 - 64cd + 16d^2$
17. $49x^2 - 84xy + 36y^2$
18. $100m^2 - 60mn + 9n^2$
19. $36x^2 - 24xy + 4y^2$
20. $25x^2 - 40xy + 16y^2$

Page 153

1. $(a + y)^2$
2. $(m + n)^2$
3. $(c + d)^2$
4. $(r + s)^2$
5. $(x + 2y)^2$
6. $(2x + y)^2$
7. $(m + 3n)^2$
8. $(r + 7t)^2$
9. $(x + 4y)^2$
10. $(3x + 4)^2$
11. $(7y + 4)^2$
12. $(x + 5y)^2$
13. $(3 + y)^2$
14. $(2z + 3)^2$
15. $(2 + x)^2$
16. $(4x + 7y)^2$
17. $(8 + x)^2$
18. $(7 + x)^2$
19. $(3x + 2y)^2$
20. $(2x + 4y)^2$
21. $(9 + 2x)^2$
22. $(8x + 1)^2$
23. $(10 + x)^2$
24. $(6x + 2)^2$

Page 154

1. $(x - y)^2$
2. $(c - d)^2$
3. $(b - d)^2$
4. $(m - n)^2$
5. $(r - s)^2$
6. $(y - z)^2$
7. $(x - 2)^2$
8. $(2a - 3)^2$
9. $(a - 4)^2$
10. $(x - 6)^2$
11. $(3x - 6)^2$
12. $(x - 7)^2$
13. $(x - 3y)^2$
14. $(4x - 2y)^2$
15. $(x - 6y)^2$
16. $(x - 8y)^2$
17. $(5a - 3b)^2$
18. $(x - 7y)^2$
19. $(2m - 5n)^2$
20. $(x - 11y)^2$
21. $(3x - 2)^2$
22. $(4x - 2)^2$
23. $(6x - 3)^2$
24. $(7x - 3)^2$

Page 155

1. $a^2 - b^2$
2. $y^2 - z^2$
3. $x^2 - 36$
4. $x^2 - 49$
5. $x^2 - 9$
6. $x^2 - 64$
7. $25d^2 - g^2$
8. $36 - b^2$

9. $4x^2 - 9$
10. $9m^2 - 25$
11. $64x^2 - 4$
12. $36x^2 - z^2$
13. $25 - 9x^2$
14. $49 - 36x^2$
15. $9k^2 - 49m^2$
16. $81a^2 - 25b^2$
17. $9x^2 - 16y^2$
18. $16m^2 - 36n^2$

Page 156

1. $(x + y)(x - y)$
2. $(x + 6)(x - 6)$
3. $(x + 10)(x - 10)$
4. $(a + 9)(a - 9)$
5. $(5 + a)(5 - a)$
6. $(m + 3)(m - 3)$
7. $(15 + x)(15 - x)$
8. $(x + 11)(x - 11)$
9. $(2x - 7)(2x + 7)$
10. $(8 + a)(8 - a)$
11. $(5a - 4)(5a + 4)$
12. $(30 + z)(30 - z)$
13. $(10x + 3)(10x - 3)$
14. $(6x + 8)(6x - 8)$
15. $(12x + 10)(12x - 10)$
16. $(7a - 7)(7a + 7)$
17. $(3a + 4b)(3a - 4b)$
18. $(6m + 7n)(6m - 7n)$
19. $(5x + 5y)(5x - 5y)$
20. $(4x + 9y)(4x - 9y)$

Page 157

1. $x^2 + 9x + 20$
2. $x^2 + 8x + 12$
3. $x^2 + 4x + 3$
4. $x^2 + 7x + 12$
5. $x^2 + 9x + 14$
6. $x^2 + 10x + 24$
7. $x^2 + 11x + 10$
8. $x^2 + 13x + 42$
9. $x^2 + 3x - 4$
10. $x^2 - x - 6$
11. $x^2 + 6x - 16$
12. $x^2 + 5x - 14$
13. $x^2 - 5x - 14$
14. $x^2 - 9x - 10$
15. $x^2 - 6x + 5$
16. $x^2 - 10x + 21$
17. $x^2 - 9x + 20$
18. $x^2 - 8x + 15$

Page 158

1. $(x + 5)(x + 3)$
2. $(x + 3)(x + 2)$
3. $(x + 2)(x + 1)$
4. $(x + 6)(x + 2)$
5. $(x + 5)(x + 2)$
6. $(x + 8)(x + 1)$
7. $(x + 6)(x - 2)$
8. $(x - 6)(x - 3)$
9. $(x + 4)(x - 2)$

10. $(x + 8)(x - 3)$
11. $(x + 2)(x - 6)$
12. $(x + 2)(x - 10)$
13. $(x + 1)(x - 10)$
14. $(x + 2)(x - 12)$
15. $(x - 3)(x - 4)$
16. $(x - 5)(x - 4)$

Page 159

1. $2x^2 + 7x + 6$
2. $2x^2 + 5x + 2$
3. $2x^2 + 5xy + 2y^2$
4. $2x^2 + 5xy + 3y^2$
5. $2x^2 + 11xy + 5y^2$
6. $2x^2 + 7xy + 3y^2$
7. $2x^2 + 5x - 3$
8. $2x^2 + x - 3$
9. $2x^2 + 3xy - 2y^2$
10. $2x^2 - 3xy - 2y^2$
11. $3x^2 - 5x - 2$
12. $2x^2 + 2xy - 12y^2$
13. $2x^2 - 7x + 3$
14. $2x^2 - 9x + 4$
15. $2x^2 - 7xy + 3y^2$
16. $2x^2 - 5x + 3$
17. $2x^2 - 5xy + 2y^2$
18. $6x^2 - 9xy + 3y^2$

Page 160

1. $(2x + 1)(x + 2)$
2. $(3x + 2)(x + 1)$
3. $(7x - 1)(x - 2)$
4. $(5x + 1)(x + 2)$
5. $(2x - 1)(x - 3)$
6. $(3x - 2)(x - 2)$
7. $(5y - 1)(y - 5)$
8. $(7x - 2)(x - 2)$
9. $(2x - 1)(x + 2)$
10. $(3x - 2)(x + 1)$
11. $(5y + 3)(y - 2)$
12. $(7x + 4)(x - 2)$

Page 161

1. $x^2 - y^2$
2. $16 - 48t + 36t^2$
3. $2x^2 + 7xy - 4y^2$
4. $9 + 12x + 4x^2$
5. $10x^2 - 41x + 21$
6. $x^2 + 4x - 21$
7. $3x^2 - 5xy + 2y^2$
8. $36x^2 + 60x + 25$
9. $81x^2 - 54x + 9$
10. $(x + y)^2$
11. $(5x - 4)^2$
12. $(8 - 4x)(8 + 4x)$
13. $(x + 2)(x - 4)$
14. $(x + 1)(x - 4)$
15. $(3x - 2)(x + 1)$
16. $(3x + 2)^2$
17. $(3x - 5)(x + 2)$

Answer Key
Core Skills Algebra

18. $(4a - 6)^2$
19. $(2x - 7)(x + 4)$
20. $(x - 5)(x + 8)$
21. $(2a - b)^2$

Page 162

1. $x = -4$ and $x = 0$; exact
2. $x \approx 1.6$ and $x \approx 4.4$; approximate
3. $x \approx -3.5$ and $x \approx 3.5$; approximate
4. $x = 1$ and $x = 5$; exact
5a. $-16t^2 + 18 = 8$; $t \approx 0.8$ second
5b. $-16t^2 + 18 = 0$; $t \approx 1.1$ seconds
5c. For the first 10 feet, the average rate of fall was $\frac{10 \text{ feet}}{0.8 \text{ second}} = 12.5$ feet per second. For the remainder of the fall, the average rate of fall was $\frac{18 \text{ feet} - 10 \text{ feet}}{1.1 \text{ seconds} - 0.8 \text{ second}}$ $= \frac{8 \text{ feet}}{0.3 \text{ second}} = 26.7$ feet per second. So, the rate of fall was not constant; in fact, it was increasing.

Page 163

1. ± 8
2. $\pm 4\sqrt{2}$
3. $\pm \frac{2\sqrt{2}}{3}$
4. 37 has no factors that are perfect squares.
5. $\pm 3\sqrt{2}$
6. $\pm \sqrt{5}$
7. $\pm \sqrt{6}$
8. ± 10
9. 0 or 10
10. -5 or 3
11. 0 or 14
12. -7 or 1
13. -8 or 4
14. $1 \pm \sqrt{6}$
15a. $-16t^2 + 8 = 0$; $t \approx 0.7$ second
15b. No; if you double the height to 16 and solve $-16t^2 + 16 = 0$, you get $t = 1$ second, which is not double the elapsed time found in part a.
15c. About $1 + 0.7 + 0.7 = 2.4$ seconds

Page 164

1. -2
2. -3
3. -4
4. -7
5. $\frac{-2}{3}$
6. $\frac{-3}{4}$
7. $\frac{-3}{2}$
8. -1
9. -2

Page 165

1. 8
2. 5
3. 4
4. 6
5. 2
6. $\frac{1}{4}$
7. $\frac{2}{3}$
8. $\frac{1}{3}$
9. $\frac{2}{5}$

Page 166

1. ± 7
2. ± 8
3. ± 9
4. ± 12
5. ± 20
6. ± 4
7. $\pm 2\frac{1}{2}$
8. ± 2
9. $\pm \frac{2}{3}$
10. ± 3
11. ± 2
12. ± 2

Page 167

1. -4, -3
2. -6, -1
3. -5, -4
4. -2, 4
5. -1, 6
6. -1, 10
7. -3, 11
8. -4, 11
9. -3, 13
10. 1, 6
11. 1, 4
12. 2, 10

Page 168

1. 1
2. -, 11
3. 8, 3
4. 2, x^2
5. $(y + 4)(y - 1)$
6. $(x - 1)^2$
7. $(p - 6)(p + 4)$
8. $(g - 10)(g + 10)$
9. $(z - 3)(z - 4)$
10. $(q + 20)(q + 5)$
11. -4
12. -2, 12
13. -25, 0
14. -2, 15
15. -3, 3
16. -9, 6
17. -14, 3
18. -3, 17
19. ± 9
20. 0, 25
21. -6, -5
22. -4, 5
23. -7, 1
24. -1

Page 169

1. $-2, -\frac{1}{2}$
2. $-5, -\frac{1}{2}$
3. $-\frac{1}{5}, 3$
4. $-2, \frac{1}{7}$
5. $-\frac{1}{3}, 5$
6. $1, \frac{3}{2}$
7. $-2, \frac{1}{5}$
8. $-\frac{1}{2}, 2$
9. $-\frac{3}{2}, 1$
10. $-1, \frac{5}{3}$
11. $-\frac{2}{5}, 1$
12. $-5, \frac{1}{3}$

Page 170

1. $(2x + 1)(x + 7)$
2. $(z - 3)(7z - 9)$
3. $(4x + 1)(2x - 3)$
4. $(6d + 5)(5d - 3)$
5. $-\frac{3}{2}, -\frac{4}{5}$
6. $-1, \frac{7}{5}$
7. $\frac{5}{2}, 3$
8. $-2, \frac{5}{6}$
9. $-\frac{5}{4}, \frac{4}{3}$
10. $\pm \frac{5}{3}$
11. $\frac{1}{6}$
12. $\frac{2}{3}, 6$
13. $-\frac{2}{3}$
14. $-\frac{9}{4}, 2$
15a. 6, 1
15b. 0.2, 1
15c. The ball will reach the platform in 0.2 second. If the trainer misses, the ball goes up, and comes back down, reaching the platform again 1 second after the dolphin bounces it.

Page 171

1. ± 7
2. 2
3. 1, -5
4. -5
5. ± 8
6. 5, 10
7. 1
8. -3, 10
9. $-1\frac{1}{2}, -1$
10. $-\frac{1}{2}, -2$
11. $-\frac{5}{3}, 1$
12. 8
13. 5, 15
14. -3
15. -1, 3

Page 172

1. -6 or 5
2. -9 and -10, or 9 and 10
3. -5 or 4
4. -7 or 8
5. -10 and -8, or 8 and 10
6. -11 and -9, or 9 and 11
7. -6 or 4
8. Width = 15 meters, length = 20 meters

221

Answer Key
Core Skills Algebra

9. Width = 5 centimeters, length = 25 centimeters
10. Width = 10 meters, length = 20 meters

Page 173

1. -1, 3
2. -4, 2
3. -4, 8
4. -1, 5
5. $\pm\sqrt{7}$
6. $-3 \pm \sqrt{2}$

Page 174

1. $x^2 + 4x + 4; (x + 2)^2$
2. $25; (m + 5)^2$
3. $100; (g - 10)^2$
4. $1; (y + 1)^2$
5. $\frac{121}{4}; \left(w - \frac{11}{2}\right)^2$
6. -8, -7
7. -11, 15
8. -13, -6
9. 7, 12
10. -16, 14
11. -25, 7
12. no real solution
13. 6, -3
14. $3 \pm \sqrt{7}$
15. 5

Page 175

1. $-6, \frac{2}{3}$
2. $-\frac{10}{7}, \frac{6}{7}$
3. $-\frac{1}{11}, \frac{5}{11}$
4. $-\frac{11}{2}, \frac{1}{2}$
5. $\frac{3}{2}, 3$
6. $-\frac{10}{3}, 2$

7a. $(3x + 2)(x + 1) = 24$
7b. $-\frac{11}{3}, 2; 2;$ only the positive solution produces positive side lengths.
7c. 8 ft by 3 ft

Page 176

Step 1: $-c$
Step 2: $4ab$
Step 3: $b^2, 2ax + b$
Step 4: $2ax + b, b^2 - 4ac;$
$b, b^2 - 4ac;$
$\frac{-b \pm \sqrt{b^2 - 4ac}}{2a}$
Derivations will vary.

Page 177

1. -3, -2
2. $-2, -\frac{1}{2}$
3. $\frac{1}{4}, 2$
4. $\frac{1}{2}, 3$
5. $\frac{1}{2}, 6$
6. $-\frac{4}{5}, 1$
7. $-1, \frac{1}{2}$
8. $-4, \frac{5}{3}$
9. -5, 3

Page 178

1. 0
2. 2
3. 1
4. 0
5. 4
6. -2.61, 1.28
7. ± 7
8. 0, 2.5
9. -8.59, 3.26
10. -1, 0.44
11. -2.67, -1.5
12. -14.33, 0.04
13. Factor. $4x^2 - 20x + 25$ is a perfect square trinomial.
14. Apply the definition of a square root after dividing by 2.
15. Quadratic formula. $4x^2 - 18x + 25$ cannot be factored.
16. Factor. $g^2 - 3g - 4$ is easily factored.
17. 3 seconds

Page 179

1. $1 \pm \sqrt{3}$
2. $\frac{4 \pm \sqrt{10}}{2}$
3. $\frac{-3 \pm \sqrt{17}}{4}$
4. $\frac{2 \pm \sqrt{10}}{3}$
5. $\frac{5 \pm \sqrt{97}}{12}$
6. $\frac{1 \pm \sqrt{10}}{3}$
7. $\frac{5 \pm \sqrt{13}}{6}$
8. $\frac{3 \pm \sqrt{69}}{10}$
9. $\frac{-5 \pm \sqrt{33}}{4}$

Page 180

1. -4 or 8
2. -13 and -11, or 11 and 13
3. -17 and -19, or 17 and 19
4. -8 or 9
5. Length = 42 inches, width = 16 inches
6. Length = 50 centimeters, width = 14 centimeters

Page 181

1. -5
2. -8
3. -4
4. $\frac{1}{2}$
5. ± 4
6. -4, -1
7. $2 \pm \sqrt{3}$
8. $1 \pm \sqrt{2}$
9. -1, 5
10. $-2, \frac{-3}{2}$
11. $3 \pm \sqrt{11}$
12. $4 \pm \sqrt{13}$
13. $\pm 2\sqrt{2}$
14. 4, 8
15. $x \approx 2.3, x \approx 5.7$
16. Length = 15 inches, width = 5 inches
17. 3 or -4
18. $-16x^2 + 20 = 5;$ The performer lands in the net in approximately 1 second.

Page 182

1. 177 millimeters
2. 10 feet
3. 40.23 kilograms
4. minimum: 14.175 square meters; maximum: 17.496 square meters
5. 4
6. 1
7. 5
8. perimeter: 239 centimeters; area: 3,100 square centimeters
9. He should have used 3 significant digits and given the area as 1.69 square meters.
10. perimeter: 15.8 centimeters; area 14 square centimeters

Page 183

1. about 15 seconds
2. about $\frac{4}{5}$ or 0.8 mile
3. Sound travels 2 miles in 10 seconds.
4. $\frac{1}{5}$
5. 0
6. $y = \frac{1}{5}x$
7. 50 seconds

Page 184

1a.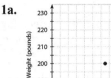

1b. Weak positive correlation; 0.5
2. Walking speed is positively correlated to life span; causation is not likely; there is probably a lurking variable such as general health that causes people to walk faster and live longer.

Page 185

1–2.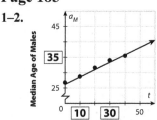

3–4. Answers will vary.
5. Median ages will vary. The 1995 age is an interpolation; The 2015 age is an extrapolation. The 1995 interpolation is a better approximation to the Census Bureau data than the 2015 extrapolation.

Page 186

1. $l = 0, 10, 20, 30, 40, 50; w_m = 3.4, 5.9, 8.4, 10.8, 13.0, 15.5;$
$w_f = 3.4, 5.8, 8.3, 10.6, 12.8, 15.2$

Answer Key
Core Skills Algebra

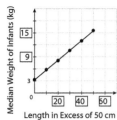

2.

3. $w_m = 0.2406x + 3.4857$, the weight changes 0.2406 kg per cm; $w_f = 0.2351x + 3.4714$, the weight changes 0.2351 kg per cm

4. $l = 0, 10, 20, 30, 40, 50$; actual $w_m = 3.4, 5.9, 8.4, 10.8, 13.0, 15.5$; actual $w_f = 3.4, 5.8, 8.3, 10.6, 12.8, 15.2$; predicted $w_m = 3.5, 5.9, 8.3, 10.7, 13.1, 15.5$; predicted $w_f = 3.5, 5.8, 8.2, 10.5, 12.9, 15.2$; residual for males = $-0.1, 0, 0.1, 0.1, -0.1, 0$; residual for females = $-0.1, 0, 0.1, 0.1, -0.1, 0$

5. The graph is a good fit because the residuals are all within 0.1 of the actual values.

Page 187

1a. $y = 0.46125x + 39.64$ where x = years since 1928

1b. $r \approx 0.89$

1c. Residual plot is random, so a linear fit is suitable, but the correlation isn't particularly strong, so the fit is acceptable but not great.

2a. x = age; y = median height

2b. Girls: $y = 6.61x + 73.9$; boys: $y = 6.51x + 75.5$

2c. Girls: $r \approx 0.9975$; boys: $r \approx 0.9975$

2d. Residual plot shows a pattern, which suggests that some non-linear model is more appropriate; linear fit is still good, however.

Page 188

1. $y = 135.9(1.037)^x$

2. $a = 135.9$ is the population in 1900; $b = 1.037$ is the growth factor; the yearly growth rate is about 3.7%.

3. 136; 196; 283; 407; 587; 847; 1,120; 1,760; 2,540; 3,660; 5,280

4. -13, 8, 51, 29, -88, -97, 182, 11, 178, 5, -149

5. 1975: about 2,073 thousand; 2030: about 15,292 thousand; the prediction for 1975; it falls within the given time period, not 30 years later, when the pattern might have changed.

6. Yes; the points look randomly distributed. About half are positive and about half are negative. A few residuals are between 10% and 20% of the data values, but the rest are 10% of the data values or less.

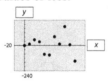

Page 189

1. 29
2. 29.5
3. 5
4. 28
5. 30
6. 2
7. -1, 1; 1, 1; 0, 0; -3, 9; 2, 4; 1, 1; $2.\overline{6}$; 1.8
8. The mean and the median do not change; of the measures of spread, the range decreases from 5 to 3 and the standard deviation decreases from 1.6 to 1.3 while the IQR remains unchanged.

Page 190

1a. 191.25, 192, 12, 7.00; 175.5, 175, 6, 3.35

1b. For male swimmers and for female swimmers, the measures of center are approximately equal, so they are consistent. On average, a male swimmer is $191 - 175 = 16$ cm taller than a female swimmer.

1c. There is about twice as much variation in the heights of the male swimmers as there is in the heights of the female swimmers.

Page 191

1a.

1b. The mean, range, IQR, and standard deviation

1c. yes: Q3 = 350 and IQR = 100, so any value greater than $350 + 1.5(100) = 500$ is an outlier.

2. Without: mean and median = 300; with: mean ≈ 332, median = 300; mean suggests realtor sells homes for higher values

3. Sample answer: 10, 23, 23, 25, 25, 25, 26, 26, 40

4. Remove the outlier from the data set before calculating the statistics.

Page 192

1.

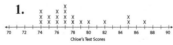

2. 78.1, 77, 13, 4, 3.75

3. 87

4. 77.6, 77, 11, 4, 3.32

5. The mean, range, and standard deviation changed.

6. Skewed to the right

7. Median and IQR because they are not affected by the outlier.

Page 193

1a. 46–50, 8; 51–55, 16; 56–60, 9; 61–65, 7; 66–70, 2

1b.

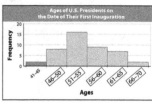

1c. Skewed to the right; the median and IQR because they are not as affected by the data values in the right tail as the mean and standard deviation are.

1d. Median ≈ $51 + \frac{12.5}{16} \cdot 5 \approx 55$; $Q_1 \approx 51 + \frac{1.5}{16} \cdot 5 \approx 51$ and $Q_3 \approx 56 + \frac{7.5}{9} \cdot 5 \approx 60$; IQR ≈ $60 - 51 = 9$

2. Estimate the mean, square the deviation of the midpoint of each interval from the mean, multiply each squared deviation by its frequency, add the products and divide by the sum of the frequencies, then take the square root.

Page 194

1. 1.7, 1.3; 2.1, 2.2; 3.3, 3.0; 4.3, 3.7; 8.3, 5.4

2.

3. The center for the AL is slightly greater than the center for the NL. The spread of the middle 50% for the AL is also greater than the spread of the middle 50% for the NL. For both distributions, the spread of the upper and lower halves (ignoring the AL outlier) are approximately equal, so the two distributions are approximately symmetric.

Page 195

1. 45, 15; 15, 18, 21, 6; 60

2. $\frac{12}{60} = 0.2, \frac{13}{60} \approx 0.217, \frac{16}{60} \approx 0.267, \frac{4}{60} \approx 0.067, \frac{45}{60} = 0.75; \frac{3}{60} = 0.05, \frac{5}{60} \approx 0.083, \frac{5}{60} \approx 0.083, \frac{2}{60} \approx 0.033, \frac{15}{60} = 0.25; \frac{15}{60} = 0.25; \frac{18}{60} = 0.3; \frac{21}{60} = 0.35; \frac{6}{60} = 0.1, \frac{60}{60} = 1$

3a. 20%
3b. 25%
3c. About 36%

4. There does not appear to be any influence; within each category of school activity, the percent of students who have a part-time job is fairly close to 75%, the percent for the whole group.

Page 196

1. minimum $w = 15.5$ cm, $l = 23.55$ cm; maximum $w = 16.4$ cm, $l = 23.64$ cm

2. minimum $A = 365.025$ cm^2; maximum $A = 387.696$ cm^2

3. 5
4. 2
5. 2
6.

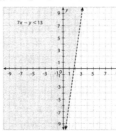

7. Correlation: strong negative; coefficient: close to -1

8. $a_F = 0.25t + 29$
9. 86
10. 86
11. 16
12. 11
13. standard deviation ≈ 5.5
14. The distribution is centered on one value (91) with the data values to the left of the center balanced with the data values to the right, so the distribution is symmetric.

Page 197

1. 26
2. 26
3. 0
4. 23
5. $3b + 10$
6. $-2m + 3$
7. $6c - 12$
8. $r - 10$
9. 6
10. 6
11. 3
12. $-49x^3y^3$
13. r^6s^{10}
14. $\frac{-2n^2}{m}$
15. $3a^2$
16. $8xy^4z^2$
17. $6b^2c^3d^6$
18. $12z^{10}x^5w^4$
19. $9rst$
20. $3x^2 - 11xy + 6y^2$
21. $6ac + 3ab - 2bc - b^2$
22. $2x^3y - 2x^2y - xy^3 + y^3 - 3xy + 3y$
23. $4x^2 - 4xy + y^2$
24. $x - y$
25. $a - 3b$
26. (5, 2)
27. (-26, 22)
28. (8, -2)
29. $(\frac{1}{2}, \frac{5}{3})$
30. (-2, 5)
31. (5, 0)
32. Carlos is 42, Marie is 14
33. 30, 60, 90

Page 198

34. Small pitcher is 2 cups, large pitcher is 4 cups
35. $(2x - 7)(2x + 7)$
36. $(5 - 7x)^2$
37. $(x + 9)(x + 11)$
38. -7
39. $\frac{3}{4}$
40. $1, -\frac{3}{2}$
41. -2, 5
42. $\frac{1}{2}, 4$
43. -3
44. -2
45. 3
46. 3

47. Sample answers: x: -2, 0, 1; y: -7, -3, -1

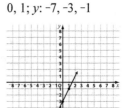

48. $b \leq -6$
49. $x \leq -1$
50.

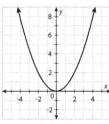

51. The dashed line will become solid.
52. The line will be solid and everything to the right of the line will be shaded.

Page 199

53.

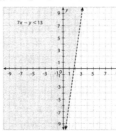

54.

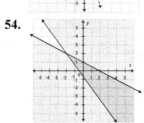

55. decay, 16, 0.75
56. growth, 5, 6, 5, 1.2
57. The point (3, 2) falls on the intersection of the two lines. The correct solution for the inequality represented by the dashed line cannot fall on the line.
58. $g(x) = -\frac{1}{3}|x + 3| - 1$
59. $f(x) = |x - 2| - 1$
60. Domain: {real numbers}; Range: $\{y \mid y \geq -1\}$
61. (0, 1) and (4, 1)

Page 200

62.

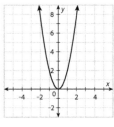

63.

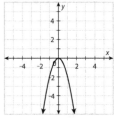

64.

65. There is no solution within the set of real numbers.

66.

67. $f(y) = 110(1.29)^x$; $r = 0.998$
68. The model is a good fit, because the correlation coefficient is close to 1.
69. 2010 = 1,090,000,000 hosts, 2020 = 13,900,000,000 hosts
70. The trend may or may not continue over time, but 2010 is closer to the actual data, so that prediction may be more accurate.
71. $3,955
72. 289
73.

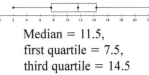

Median = 11.5, first quartile = 7.5, third quartile = 14.5

9 780544 261822